Contents

One-pot chicken & chickpea pilau...

One-pot cabbage & beans with white fish 15

One-pot lentil chicken 16

Sausage & bean one-pot..17

Pancakes for one..18

Chinese pork one-pot 19

One-pot roast pork chops with fennel & potatoes 19

Chicken, kale & mushroom pot pie 20

Meatball black bean chilli 21

Spring chicken pot pie...22

One-pot roast guinea fowl 23

Creamy chicken stew 24

Spinach, sweet potato & lentil dhal 25

Peach & orange yogurt pots with ginger oats 26

Curried cod...27

Pot-roast Bombay chicken 28

One-pan Thai green salmon 29

Herby spring chicken pot pie 30

One-pot fish with black olives & tomatoes....................................31

Baked tomato & mozzarella orzo..32

Quick beef & broccoli one-pot..32

Spicy vegetable & quinoa one-pot 33

Honey & mustard chicken thighs with spring veg.........................34

Spiced coconut chicken with coriander & lime 34

Turkey & mushroom pot pies 35

Squid & pinto bean stew with garlic toasts....................................36

Sweet potato, chickpea & chorizo hash 37

Sausage & prawn jambalaya 38

Lingonberry & ginger cheesecake pots 39

Sweet spiced lamb shanks with quince 40

One-pan simple summer chicken 41

Classic potted shrimps 41

Slow-cooked lamb with onions & thyme 42

Easy banoffee pie 43

Bean & pasta stew with meatballs 44

One-pan Spanish fish stew 45

Mexican chicken burger 46

One pan spicy rice 46

Harissa-crumbed fish with lentils & peppers 47

Easter nest cake 48

Halloumi, carrot & orange salad 49

Irish stew 50

Microwave biryani 51

Leftover turkey casserole 52

Spanish bean stew 52

Fragrant courgette & prawn curry 53

Melty cheese fondue pot 54

Curried chicken & new potato traybake 55

Pot-roast loin of pork in cider with celeriac 55

Chicken & chickpea rice 56

Special lamb biryani 57

Sharing potted shrimp 59

Snowman biscuits 60

Basque-style salmon stew 61

Malabar prawns 62

Greek lamb with potatoes & olives 63

Spicy teriyaki prawns & sesame fried rice 63

Spicy chicken couscous...64

Lemony prawn & chorizo rice pot 65

Double cheese & spring vegetable tart 66

Hearty lamb stew..67

Thai prawn fried rice 67

All-in-one fish supper 68

Sweet & sour tofu...69

Leek & freekeh pilaf with feta & toasted pine nuts ...70

Amatriciana chicken traybake 71

Easy chicken pie..71

Sausage & mushroom pot pies 72

Easy chicken tagine 73

One-pan jerk roast chicken..74

Cumin roast veg with tahini dressing.........................75

Braised pork belly with borlotti beans 76

Green burgers 77

Breakfast naans 78

Crispy chicken with pancetta & butter beans 79

Sticky ginger skillet parkin 80

Honeyed nut & pomegranate pots 81

Mushroom & spinach risotto...81

Jacket potato with whipped feta & sumac 82

Easy ratatouille with poached eggs 83

Burrito bowl with chipotle black beans 84

Golden amaretti Christmas cake 84

Healthy veg patch hummus 87

Bulgur & quinoa lunch bowls 88

Goan-style vegetable curry with kitchari 89

All-in-one spring roast chicken 91

All-in-one chunky winter broth 92

Ginger chicken & green bean noodles 92

Potted salmon rillette 93

Chicken & sweet potato curry 94

Smoked salmon, quinoa & dill lunch pot 94

Spanish chicken 95

Chicken bhuna 96

Sea trout with samphire, potted shrimp & lemon 97

Slow cooker vegetable curry 98

Salted caramel choc pots 99

Mushroom brunch 100

Egyptian courgettes with dukkah sprinkle 100

Three-hour shoulder of lamb 101

Prawn jambalaya 102

Sticky Chinese chicken traybake 103

Double chocolate cardamom pots 104

Veggie noodle pot 104

One-pan glazed rack of lamb with spiced red onions & potatoes 105

Spicy Spanish rice 106

Creamy prawn & spring vegetable pot 107

Charred cauliflower, lemon & caper orzo 108

Christmas dinner Wellington 109

How to make oat milk 111

All-in-one roast chicken & veg 112

Thai fried prawn & pineapple rice 113

Chocolate & raspberry pots 113

Chocolate & berry mousse pots 114

Oat & chia porridge 115

Chocolate hazelnut ice cream cheesecake 116

Pot-roast pheasant with cider & bacon 117

Lentil & cauliflower curry 118

Beetroot & apple salad pots 119

Spicy baby aubergine stew with coriander & mint 119

Chia & oat breakfast scones with yogurt and berries 120

Kleftiko-style lamb shanks 121

Spiced cauliflower hummus 122

Pot-roast veal with new-season carrots & orange 122

Ploughman's pork & cheese picnic pie 123

Quick & spicy nasi goreng 124

Steak & chips pie 125

Halloween cheeseboard with creepy crackers 127

Coconut & tamarind chicken curry 128

Super speedy chilli 129

One-pan prawn & tomato curry 130

20-minute beef in red wine 131

Baked fennel pork with lemony potatoes & onions 132

Chicken fajitas 133

Super-easy birthday cake 134

All-in-one chicken traybake 135

Cherry chocolate meringue pots 136

Easy pulled beef ragu 136

Meal prep: pasta 137

Italian aubergine traybake 138

Beetroot hummus party platter 139

Coconut chai traybake 140

Chorizo hummus bowl 141

Sweet potato jackets with guacamole & kidney beans 142

Peach Melba pots 143

All-in-one gammon, egg & chips 143

Roast cod with curried cauliflower purée & onion bhaji 144

Quick prawn, coconut & tomato curry 146

Easy risotto with bacon & peas 147

5-a-day chicken with kale & pistachio pesto 147

Mini nut roasts with candied carrots 148

Baked ginger & spinach sweet potato 150

Mix & match seafood tacos 151

Roast potato, turkey, sausage & stuffing pie 152

Spaghetti & meatballs 153

One-pan baked chicken with squash, sage & walnuts 154

Rhubarb & strawberry meringue pots 155

Chicken & vegetable stew with wholemeal couscous 156

Potato & leek gratin 157

Healthy egg & chips 157

Asian prawn noodles 158

Sausage & squash risotto 159

Summer courgette risotto 160

Beetroot & butternut stew 161

Lamb masala meatball curry 162

Pot-roast pheasant with fino & porcini 163

Caponata pasta 164

Meatball & tomato soup 165

Raspberry coconut porridge 166

Roasted summer vegetable casserole 166

All-in-one posh lamb balti 167

One-pan prawn pilau 168

Paprika pork 169

French-style chicken with peas & bacon 170

Ham & tarragon pot pie 171

Blackcurrant jam 171

Succulent honey & lemon chicken 172

Lemon-spiced chicken with chickpeas 173

Mediterranean vegetables with lamb 174

Spiced bulgur pilaf with fish 175

Milk chocolate pots with citrus shortbread 176

Tomato, runner bean & coconut curry 177

Wild mushroom, potato & pancetta gratin 178

Spring chicken paella 179

Squash & chorizo pot pies 180

Rhubarb & custard sandwich biscuits 181

Chocolate honeycomb 182

Chilli beef with black beans and avocado salad 183

One-pan salmon with roast asparagus 184

Turkey tortilla pie 185

Chilli con carne recipe 186

Serve with soured cream and plain boiled long grain rice 188

Beef & bean hotpot 188

Pastrami & sweet potato hash 189

Creamy cod chowder stew 190

Lentil & sweet potato curry...191

Smoked haddock & bacon gratin...192

All-in-one-baked mushrooms..192

Sausage & white bean casserole 193

Next level steak & ale pie...194

Braised pork belly with borlotti beans 195

Egg fried rice with prawns & peas..196

Summer pork, fennel & beans..197

Spicy seafood stew with tomatoes & lime.................................198

Panzanella...199

One-pan roast dinner...200

Winter warmer hearty risotto...200

Family meals: Chicken & veg casserole.....................................202

Swede, lamb & feta bake 203

Pork & parsnip cobbler 204

Melon & crunchy bran pots..205

Spicy merguez & couscous pot...206

Orange & rhubarb amaretti pots..207

Lighter Lancashire hotpot...208

Turkish lamb pilau 209

Red braised ginger pork belly with pickled chillies..................210

Spinach & ricotta pancake bake...211

One-pan lamb & couscous...212

Curried mango & chickpea pot..213

Slow-cooker chicken curry 213

Vegetarian bean pot with herby breadcrumbs 214

Roast chicken traybake 215

Courgette & lemon risotto..216

Pot-roast chicken with stock 217

Vegan jambalaya 218

Chicken tagine with lemons, olives & pomegranate 218

Smoky bacon pot noodle for one 220

Potted cheddar with ale & mustard 220

Peanut butter & date oat pots 221

One-pan lamb with hasselback potatoes 222

One-pan seafood roast with smoky garlic butter 223

Christmas dinner for one 224

Potted crab 226

Ultimate apple pie 227

One-pan roast butter chicken 228

Smoky sausage casserole 229

Slow-cooker beef pot roast 230

Honey mustard chicken pot with parsnips 231

Home-style chicken curry 232

Spiced chicken, spinach & sweet potato stew 234

Spanish meatball & butter bean stew 235

Coconut fish curry 236

Chicken & chorizo rice pot 237

Spring chicken in a pot 238

Easter chocolate pots with pick 'n' mix toppings 239

Lamb shank Madras 239

All-in–one chicken with wilted spinach 241

Prawn laksa curry bowl 242

One-pan egg & veg brunch 242

Beer-braised brisket pot roast 243

Simple fish stew 244

Butter bean, mushroom & bacon pot pies 245

Sausage & bean casserole 246

Peri-peri chicken pilaf 247

Penang prawn & pineapple curry 248

One-pan spaghetti with nduja, fennel & olives 249

Fruity lamb tagine 250

Pea & ham pot pie 251

One-pan nachos with black beans 252

Layered rainbow salad pots 252

Slow-cooked Greek lamb 253

All-in-one leek & pork pot roast 254

Baked cauliflower pizzaiola 255

One-pan coriander-crusted duck, roasted plums & greens 256

Smoky BBQ pork buns with crushed avocado 257

Chicken & mushroom hot-pot 258

Easy chicken & chickpea tagine 259

Berry yogurt pots 260

Chicken, morel mushroom & asparagus one-pan pie 261

One-pan Easter lamb 262

Coconut fish curry traybake 263

Lemony chicken stew with giant couscous 264

Smoked chicken, pot barley & cranberry salad 265

Chicken & new potato traybake 266

Red berry granola yogurt pots 267

One-pan pigs-in-blanket beans 268

One-cup pancakes 269

Brazilian pork stew with corn dumplings 269

Indian chicken protein pots 271

Chicken biryani 272

One-pan tikka salmon with jewelled rice 273

Spicy chicken & bean stew 274

Chicken & chorizo jambalaya 275

Summer chicken stew 275

Moroccan vegetable stew 276

Bean & pepper chilli 277

Greek-style roast chicken 278

Spicy harissa chicken with lentils 279

Andalusian-style chicken 279

Spicy asparagus & chorizo baked egg 280

Winter berry & white chocolate pots 281

Jambalaya 282

Tuna Niçoise protein pot 284

Pesto chicken stew with cheesy dumplings 284

Pesto chicken stew with cheesy dumplings 286

Salted caramel popcorn pots 287

Sticky orange chicken with parsnips, maple & pecans 288

Chorizo & cabbage stew 289

Chicken casserole with herby dumplings 289

One-pan lentil dhal with curried fish & crispy skin 291

Muffin tin chilli pots 292

5-minute mocha pots 292

One-pan pigeon breast with spinach & bacon 293

Moroccan fish stew 294

Mexican beef chilli 295

Bean & barley soup 296

Beef in red wine with melting onions 297

Chilli Marrakech 298

Lamb & aubergine pastitsio 299

Keralan chicken coconut ishtu 300

Spiced lamb pilaf 301

Steak & broccoli protein pots 302

Lemon drizzle cake 303

Roast dinner for one 304

Spaghetti puttanesca 305

Slow-braised pork shoulder with cider & parsnips 306

Thai shellfish pot 307

Steak & broccoli protein pots 308

Roast dinner for one 309

Rosemary chicken with oven-roasted ratatouille 309

Honey, mustard & crème fraîche baked chicken 310

Pork & chorizo enchiladas 311

Chicken & egg-fried rice 312

Sausages with oregano, mushrooms & olives 313

Vegetarian casserole 314

Thai shellfish pot 315

Seafood paella 316

Oven-baked leek & bacon risotto 317

Chicken, ginger & green bean hotpot 318

Baked eggs with potatoes, mushrooms & cheese 319

One-pan summer eggs 319

Pot-roast beef with French onion gravy 320

Korean rice pot 321

Greek lamb with orzo 322

Poached salt beef & root veg 323

Turkish one-pan eggs & peppers (Menemen)..323

Chipotle bean chilli with baked eggs 324

Spinach & chickpea curry 325

Piri-piri chicken with smashed sweet potatoes & broccoli..........................326

Sausage, kale & gnocchi one-pot...326

Chicken cacciatore one-pot with orzo...327

One-pot paneer curry pie...328

Hearty lentil one pot..329

Lemony tuna, tomato & caper one-pot pasta 330

Tomato, pepper & bean one pot..331

One-pot coconut fish curry...332

One-pot chicken & mushroom risotto...333

Sausage, roasted veg & Puy lentil one-pot 334

Moroccan chicken one-pot..335

One-pot Chinese chicken noodle soup...336

Spring one-pot roast chicken..337

Chicken nacho one-pot...338

Chicken & couscous one-pot 339

One-pot chicken chasseur 340

One-pot poached spring chicken...341

One-pot crystal chicken..343

One-pot chicken with chorizo & new potatoes..344

Easy one-pot chicken casserole..345

One-pot chicken with quinoa 346

Spicy sausage & bean one-pot 347

Spring chicken one-pot 347

One-pot mushroom & potato curry...348

Smoky pork & Boston beans one-pot 349

Chilli chicken one-pot 350

Chinese-style braised beef one-pot 351

Spanish rice & prawn one-pot 352

Sausage & lentil one-pot 353

Sausage & veg one-pot 353

One-pot Moroccan chicken 354

Fragrant pork & rice one-pot 355

One-pot partridge with drunken potatoes 356

Chorizo, new potato & haddock one-pot 357

Summer chicken one-pot 358

One-pot chicken pilaf 358

One-pot chicken & bacon stew 359

Squash, chicken & couscous one-pot 360

Mushroom & rice one-pot 361

One-pot pork with orange, olives & bay 361

Squash, lentil & bean one-pot with fig raita 363

One-pot beef brisket & braised celery 363

Speedy salmon and leek one-pot 364

One-pot chicken with braised vegetables 365

Sea bass & seafood Italian one-pot 366

Bean & bangers one-pot 367

One-pot chicken & chickpea pilau

Prep: 10 mins **Cook:** 30 mins

Serves 4

Ingredients

- 1 tbsp olive oil
- 4 chicken thighs , skin removed and trimmed of fat
- 2 large leeks , thinly sliced
- 2 garlic cloves , crushed

- 400g can chickpeas in water, drained and rinsed
- grated zest of 1 lemon
- 200g easy-cook brown rice
- 450ml chicken stock
- 1 head broccoli , broken into florets

Method

STEP 1

Heat a large, lidded frying pan or fl ameproof casserole and add the oil. Fry the chicken thighs for 2 mins, turning halfway through cooking, until lightly coloured, then lift onto a plate. Add the leeks to the pan and stir-fry for 3 mins, then add the garlic and tip in the chickpeas, most of the lemon zest and rice. Stir together until well mixed.

STEP 2

Nestle the chicken in the rice mix. Pour over the stock and season lightly. Cover and cook on a low heat for 20 mins until the chicken is nearly cooked through and the rice has absorbed nearly all the liquid. Sit the broccoli on top of the rice, cover and continue to cook until the rice and broccoli are tender and the chicken cooked. Sprinkle with the remaining lemon zest to serve.

One-pot cabbage & beans with white fish

Prep: 20 mins **Cook:** 30 mins

Serves 4

Ingredients

- small knob of butter

15

- 5 rashers smoked streaky bacon , chopped
- 1 onion , finely chopped
- 2 celery sticks, diced
- 2 carrots , diced
- small bunch thyme

For the fish

- 4 fillets sustainable white fish , such as hake, about 140g/5oz each, skin on

- 1 Savoy cabbage , shredded
- 4 tbsp white wine
- 300ml chicken stock
- 410g can flageolet bean in water, drained

- 2 tbsp plain flour
- 2 tbsp olive oil

Method

STEP 1

Heat the butter in a large sauté pan until starting to sizzle, add the bacon, then fry for a few mins. Add the onion, celery and carrots, then gently cook for 8-10 mins until softening, but not brown. Stir in the thyme and cabbage, then cook for a few mins until the cabbage starts to wilt. Pour in the wine, simmer until evaporated, then add the stock and beans. Season, cover the pan, then simmer gently for 10 mins until the cabbage is soft but still vibrant.

STEP 2

When the cabbage is done, cook the fish. Season each fillet, then dust the skin with flour. Heat the oil in a frying pan. Fry the fish, skin-side down, for 4 mins until crisp, then flip over and finish on the flesh side until cooked through. Serve each fish fillet on top of a pile of cabbage with a few small potatoes, if you like.

One-pot lentil chicken

Total time40 mins Ready in 40 minutes

Serves 2

Ingredients

- 1 tsp vegetable oil
- 2rasher lean dry-cure back bacon , trimmed and chopped
- 2large bone-in chicken thighs , skin removed

- 1medium onion , thinly sliced
- 1 garlic clove , thinly sliced
- 2 tsp plain flour
- 2 tsp tomato purée

- 150ml dry white wine
- 200ml chicken stock
- 50g green lentil
- ½ tsp dried thyme
- 85g chestnut mushroom , halved if large

Method

STEP 1

Heat the oil in a non-stick wide, shallow pan, add bacon and fry briskly until lightly coloured, then lift on to a plate. Add the chicken and fry on each side until lightly brown. Set aside with the bacon. Tip onion and garlic into the pan and cook for 5 minutes. Stir in the flour and tomato purée, then stir over a low heat for 2-3 minutes. Add the wine, stock, lentils and thyme. Bring to the boil, reduce the heat, cover and simmer for 5 minutes.

STEP 2

Stir in the mushrooms. Add the bacon and chicken, pushing them under the liquid. Cover and simmer for 20-25 minutes, or until lentils are tender and the chicken cooked. Season with salt and pepper.

Sausage & bean one-pot

Prep:15 mins **Cook:**30 mins

Serves 4

Ingredients

- 1 tbsp olive oil
- 8 good-quality pork sausages (Toulouse are great for this dish)
- 2 leeks , trimmed and thinly sliced
- 1 carrot , roughly chopped
- 2 slices day-old white or brown bread , whizzed into breadcrumbs
- 1 tbsp chopped sage , plus a little extra
- 1 garlic clove , crushed
- 200ml beef stock
- 400g can chopped tomatoes
- 2 x 400g cans cannellini beans , rinsed and drained

Method

STEP 1

Heat the oil in a large ovenproof pan, add the sausages and brown for few mins. Remove from the pan. Add the leeks and carrot and gently soften for 10 mins.

STEP 2

Mix the breadcrumbs with a little sage. Heat grill to medium. Add 1 tbsp sage and the garlic to the pan. Cook for 1 min, then add the stock and tomatoes. Tuck in the sausages. Simmer for 10 mins until the sauce has reduced a little and the sausages are cooked. Season, stir in the beans, then simmer for 2 mins more. To serve, scatter the sage crumbs over the top and grill for 5 mins until golden.

Pancakes for one

Prep: 10 mins **Cook:** 10 mins

Serves 1

Ingredients

- 1 large egg
- 40g plain flour
- ½ tsp baking powder
- 45ml milk (dairy, nut or oat based)

- 1 tsp butter
- ½ tbsp oil
- maple syrup or honey and berries, to serve (optional)

Method

STEP 1

Separate the egg, putting the white and yolk in seperate bowls. Mix the egg yolk with the flour, baking powder and milk to make a smooth paste.

STEP 2

Beat the egg white and a pinch of salt with an electric whisk (or by hand) until fluffy and holding its shape. Gently fold the egg white into the yolk mixture. Be extra careful not to knock any of the air out.

STEP 3

Heat the butter and oil in a non-stick frying pan. Dollop a third of the mixture into the pan and cook on each side for 1-2 mins or until golden brown. Repeat with the remaining mixture to make three pancakes. Drizzle over some maple syrup or honey and serve with berries, if you like.

Chinese pork one-pot

Total time 15 mins

Serves 4

Ingredients

- 400g pork tenderloin , cut into long thin strips
- 600ml chicken stock
- 1 tbsp soy sauce
- 2 tsp Chinese five-spice powder
- large knob of ginger , peeled and cut into matchsticks

- 200g pack baby leaf green quartered
- 1 red chilli , deseeded and finely chopped or 1 tsp chilli flakes
- bunch spring onions , whites and greens sliced

Method

STEP 1

Tip all the ingredients, except the spring onion greens, into a large saucepan, put the lid on and bring to a gentle simmer. Cook, without boiling, for about 8 mins, until the pork has changed colour and the greens are cooked, but still a bit crunchy. Ladle into bowls, scatter with the spring onion and serve with boiled rice or noodles on the side.

One-pot roast pork chops with fennel & potatoes

Prep: 10 mins **Cook:** 50 mins

Serves 4

Ingredients

- 2 potatoes , cut into 8 wedges
- 1 fennel bulb , cut into 8 wedges
- 1 red pepper , halved, deseeded and cut into 8 wedges
- 4 thyme sprigs

- 4 garlic cloves , unpeeled
- 1 tbsp sundried tomato paste
- 300ml hot chicken stock
- 4 bone-in pork loin chops

Method

STEP 1

Heat oven to 200C/180C fan/gas 6. Put the potatoes, fennel, pepper, thyme and garlic in a large roasting tin. Mix together the tomato paste and stock, then pour into the pan. Tightly cover with foil and cook for 30 mins. Take out of the oven and increase the temperature to 220C/200C fan/gas 7.

STEP 2

Remove the foil and place the pork in the roasting tin, nestling in between the veg. Season well and return to the oven for 15-20 mins more or until golden brown and cooked through. Serve with the pan juices drizzled over.

Chicken, kale & mushroom pot pie

Prep: 10 mins **Cook:** 40 mins

Serves 4

Ingredients

- 1 tbsp olive oil
- 1 large onion, finely chopped
- 3 thyme sprigs, leaves picked
- 2 garlic cloves, crushed
- 350g chicken breasts, cut into small chunks
- 250g chestnut mushrooms, sliced
- 300ml chicken stock
- 100g crème fraîche
- 1 tbsp wholegrain mustard
- 100g kale
- 2 tsp cornflour, mixed with 1 tbsp cold water
- 375g pack puff pastry, rolled into a circle slightly bigger than your dish
- 1 egg yolk, to glaze

Method

STEP 1

Heat 1/2 tbsp oil over a gentle heat in a flameproof casserole dish. Add the onion and cook for 5 mins until softening. Scatter over the thyme and garlic, and stir for 1 min. Turn up the heat and add the chicken, frying until golden but not fully cooked. Add the mushrooms and the remaining oil. Heat oven to 200C/180 fan/gas 6.

STEP 2

Add the stock, crème fraîche, mustard and kale, and season well. Add the cornflour mixture and stir until thickened a little.

STEP 3

Remove from the heat and cover with the puff pastry lid, pressing into the sides of the casserole dish. Slice a cross in the centre and glaze with the egg. Bake for 30 mins until the pastry is puffed up and golden.

Meatball black bean chilli

Prep: 10 mins **Cook:** 30 mins

Serves 4

Ingredients

- 2 tbsp olive oil
- 12 beef meatballs
- 1 onion, finely sliced
- 2 mixed peppers, sliced
- ½ large bunch coriander, leaves and stalks chopped
- 2 large garlic cloves, crushed
- cooked rice, to serve

- 1 tsp hot smoked paprika
- 2 tsp ground cumin
- 1 heaped tbsp light brown soft sugar
- 2 x 400g cans chopped tomatoes
- 2 x 400g cans black beans, drained and rinsed

Method

STEP 1

Heat the oil in a large flameproof casserole dish over a medium heat. Fry the meatballs for 5 mins until browned, then transfer to a plate with a slotted spoon.

STEP 2

Fry the onion and peppers with a pinch of salt for 7 mins. Add the coriander stalks, garlic, paprika and cumin and fry for 1 min more. Tip in the sugar, tomatoes and beans, and bring to a simmer. Season, return the meatballs to the pan and cook, covered, for 15 mins. *To freeze, leave to cool completely and transfer to large freezerproof bags.*

STEP 3

Serve the chilli with the rice and the coriander leaves scattered over.

Spring chicken pot pie

Prep: 15 mins **Cook:** 1 hr and 5 mins

Serves 6

Ingredients

- 4-6 skinless, boneless chicken thighs
- 1 tbsp olive oil
- 100g smoked bacon lardons
- 2 leeks , sliced
- 3 tbsp plain flour
- 100ml white wine (or extra stock)
- 200ml chicken stock

- 200g crème fraîche
- 100g frozen or fresh podded peas
- 1½ tbsp Dijon mustard
- small bunch of tarragon , chopped
- 1 egg , beaten
- 320g sheet puff pastry

Method

STEP 1

Season the chicken thighs with some salt and pepper. Heat the oil in a heavy-based saucepan and fry the chicken for 3-4 mins on each side until lightly golden, then transfer to a plate. Add the bacon to the pan and fry for 5 mins until golden. Tip in the leeks and fry for another 5 mins.

STEP 2

Sprinkle the flour over the leeks and bacon, and stir until combined. Add the wine, if using, and bubble for a few minutes, then add the stock and stir well. Slice the chicken and return it to the pan – don't worry if it's not fully cooked through at this point, it will finish cooking in the oven.

STEP 3

Stir in the crème fraîche, peas, 1 tbsp mustard and the tarragon, and bubble for a few minutes until thick and saucy. Add a splash more stock or water if it seems too thick Remove the pie filling from the heat. Whisk the remaining ½ tbsp mustard with the egg in a bowl.

STEP 4

Heat the oven to 200C/180C fan/gas 6. Spoon the filling into a pie dish with a lip and use some of the egg mix to brush the sides of the dish. Unroll the pastry over the top of the pie and crimp the edges against the sides of the dish, then cut away any excess with a knife. *Will keep frozen, well covered, for up to three months.*

STEP 5

Brush the remaining egg glaze over the pie and make a small steam hole in the middle. Bake for 40 mins until golden and puffed. Serve with buttered new potatoes and steamed greens or carrots, if you like.

One-pot roast guinea fowl

Prep: 20 mins **Cook:** 1 hr and 40 mins

Serves 2

Ingredients

- 1 onion , cut into wedges, through the root
- 2 carrots , quartered lengthways
- 1 large potato , cut into bite-size chunks
- 1 tbsp olive oil
- 1 small guinea fowl (around 1kg/2lb 4oz)
- 1 tbsp butter at room temperature, plus 2 tsp for the gravy

- 4 smoked streaky bacon rashers
- 6 garlic cloves , unpeeled
- few thyme sprigs
- 300ml chicken stock
- 100ml white wine
- 2 tsp plain flour
- 1 tbsp redcurrant jelly

Method

STEP 1

Heat oven to 180C/160C fan/gas 4. Toss the vegetables with the oil and some seasoning in a large flameproof roasting tin. Place the bird on top of the veg, smear with 1 tbsp butter and lay the rashers in a row over the breast. Season generously, then roast for 40 mins.

STEP 2

Remove from the oven and give the veg a stir while adding the garlic and thyme. Pour 200ml stock and the wine over the veg and return to oven to roast for another 40 mins until the bird is cooked through and the juices run clear.

STEP 3

Remove the bird, place on a serving plate, cover with foil to keep warm and leave to rest. Turn the oven up to 200C/180C fan/gas 6 and roast the veg for a further 15 mins until tender.

STEP 4

Remove the veg with a slotted spoon and transfer to the serving plate with the bird. Mix 2 tsp butter and flour in a small bowl to form a smooth paste. Place the roasting tin with all the cooking juices, plus any resting juices, on the hob. Whisk the paste and redcurrant jelly into the juices until dissolved, then add the remaining stock and extra seasoning, if you like. Bubble for a few mins until the sauce thickens. Slice and serve the guinea fowl, crisp bacon and the veg with the sauce on the side.

Creamy chicken stew

Prep:10 mins **Cook:**55 mins

Serves 4-6

Ingredients

- 3 leeks , halved and finely sliced
- 2 tbsp olive oil , plus extra if needed
- 1 tbsp butter
- 8 small chicken thighs
- 500ml chicken stock

- 1 tbsp Dijon mustard
- 75g crème fraîche
- 200g frozen peas
- 3 tbsp dried or fresh breadcrumbs
- small bunch of parsley , finely chopped

Method

STEP 1

Tip the leeks and oil into a flameproof casserole dish on a low heat, add the butter and cook everything very gently for 10 mins or until the leeks are soft.

STEP 2

Put the chicken, skin-side down, in a large non-stick frying pan on a medium heat, cook until the skin browns, then turn and brown the other side. You shouldn't need any oil but if the skin starts to stick, add a little. Add the chicken to the leeks, leaving behind any fat in the pan.

STEP 3

Add the stock to the dish and bring to a simmer, season well, cover and cook for 30 mins on low. Stir in the mustard, crème fraîche and peas and bring to a simmer. You should have quite a bit of sauce.

STEP 4

When you're ready to serve, put the grill on. Mix the breadcrumbs and parsley, sprinkle them over the chicken and grill until browned.

Spinach, sweet potato & lentil dhal

Prep: 10 mins **Cook:** 35 mins

Serves 4

Ingredients

- 1 tbsp sesame oil
- 1 red onion, finely chopped
- 1 garlic clove, crushed
- thumb-sized piece ginger, peeled and finely chopped
- 1 red chilli, finely chopped
- 1 ½ tsp ground turmeric
- 1 ½ tsp ground cumin
- 2 sweet potatoes (about 400g/14oz), cut into even chunks
- 250g red split lentils
- 600ml vegetable stock
- 80g bag of spinach
- 4 spring onions, sliced on the diagonal, to serve
- ½ small pack of Thai basil, leaves torn, to serve

Method

STEP 1

Heat 1 tbsp sesame oil in a wide-based pan with a tight-fitting lid.

STEP 2

Add 1 finely chopped red onion and cook over a low heat for 10 mins, stirring occasionally, until softened.

STEP 3

Add 1 crushed garlic clove, a finely chopped thumb-sized piece of ginger and 1 finely chopped red chilli, cook for 1 min, then add 1 ½ tsp ground turmeric and 1 ½ tsp ground cumin and cook for 1 min more.

STEP 4

Turn up the heat to medium, add 2 sweet potatoes, cut into even chunks, and stir everything together so the potato is coated in the spice mixture.

STEP 5

Tip in 250g red split lentils, 600ml vegetable stock and some seasoning.

STEP 6

Bring the liquid to the boil, then reduce the heat, cover and cook for 20 mins until the lentils are tender and the potato is just holding its shape.

STEP 7

Taste and adjust the seasoning, then gently stir in the 80g spinach. Once wilted, top with the 4 diagonally sliced spring onions and ½ small pack torn basil leaves to serve.

STEP 8

Alternatively, allow to cool completely, then divide between airtight containers and store in the fridge for a healthy lunchbox.

Peach & orange yogurt pots with ginger oats

Prep: 10 mins **Cook:** 7 mins

Makes 4

Ingredients

- 4 peaches or nectarines, stoned and diced
- 1 orange , juiced and zested
- 120g porridge oats

- 25g pine nuts
- ½ tsp ground ginger
- 1 tsp ground cinnamon

- 2 tbsp sultanas
- 4 x 150ml pots bio yogurt

Method

STEP 1

Put the peaches and orange juice in a small pan. Put the lid on and cook gently for 3-5 mins, depending on their ripeness, until softened. Set aside to cool.

STEP 2

Tip the oats and pine nuts into a pan and heat gently, stirring frequently until they're just starting to toast. Turn off the heat and add the spices, zest and sultanas.

STEP 3

Spoon the peaches and juices into four tumblers and top with the yogurt. Cover and chill until needed. Keep the oat mixture in an airtight container. When ready to serve, top the peaches and yogurt with the oat mixture.

Curried cod

Prep: 10 mins **Cook:** 25 mins

Serves 4

Ingredients

- 1 tbsp oil
- 1 onion, chopped
- 2 tbsp medium curry powder
- thumb-sized piece ginger, peeled and finely grated
- 3 garlic cloves, crushed

- 2 x 400g cans chopped tomatoes
- 400g can chickpeas
- 4 cod fillets (about 125-150g each)
- zest 1 lemon, then cut into wedges
- handful coriander, roughly chopped

Method

STEP 1

Heat the oil in a large, lidded frying pan. Cook the onion over a high heat for a few mins, then stir in the curry powder, ginger and garlic. Cook for another 1-2 mins until fragrant, then stir in the tomatoes, chickpeas and some seasoning.

STEP 2

Cook for 8-10 mins until thickened slightly, then top with the cod. Cover and cook for another 5-10 mins until the fish is cooked through. Scatter over the lemon zest and coriander, then serve with the lemon wedges to squeeze over.

Pot-roast Bombay chicken

Prep: 20 mins **Cook:** 1 hr and 30 mins

Serves 4 - 6

Ingredients

- 1 small whole chicken
- 5 tbsp tikka masala paste
- 1 tbsp sunflower oil
- 1 large red onion, halved and sliced
- 2 large tomatoes, halved and chopped
- 1 tbsp fenugreek seeds
- 1 thumb-sized piece ginger, grated

- 2 x 400g cans full-fat coconut milk
- 500g new potatoes, halved
- 100g baby spinach
- 25g pack coriander, torn, to serve
- poppadums and chutney, to serve (optional)

Method

STEP 1

Heat oven to 220C/200C fan/gas 6. Put the chicken on a chopping board and, using your hands, rub the skin generously with half the spice paste. Season well, tie the legs together and set aside.

STEP 2

Heat the oil in a large flameproof casserole dish over a medium heat. Add the onion and a good pinch of salt and cook for 5 mins or until beginning to soften. Add the tomatoes, fenugreek seeds, ginger and remaining spice paste, and cook for 3 mins more. Stir through the coconut milk and bring to a simmer. Add the chicken and the potatoes to the dish, and cook in the oven for 20 mins, uncovered.

STEP 3

Lower the heat to 180C/160C fan/ gas 4 and cook for 55 mins more. Check that the meat is cooked by cutting through one of its legs – the flesh shouldn't be pink.

STEP 4

Remove the chicken and place on a chopping board. Stir the spinach through the sauce and leave to rest for 5 mins. Put the chicken back in the dish, top with the coriander and carve at the table. Serve with poppadums and chutney, if you like.

One-pan Thai green salmon

Prep: 10 mins **Cook:** 50 mins

Serves 4

Ingredients

- 2 tbsp vegetable oil
- 2 shallots , thickly sliced
- 1 green chilli , deseeded if you like, and sliced, plus extra to serve
- 300g baby new potatoes , quartered
- 1 lemongrass stalk, bashed
- 4 tbsp Thai green curry paste
- 400g can coconut milk
- 200-300ml vegetable stock
- 1-2 tbsp fish sauce
- ½-1 tbsp brown or palm sugar

- 1 courgette , trimmed and peeled into ribbons
- 100g baby spinach
- 4 skinless salmon fillets
- 3 limes , 2 juiced plus 1 cut into wedges to serve
- 3 spring onions , finely sliced (optional)
- handful of coriander or Thai basil, roughly chopped, to serve
- cooked jasmine rice or rice noodles, to serve (optional)

Method

STEP 1

Heat the oven to 200C/180C fan/ gas 6. Put the oil in a deep roasting tin or dish about 30 x 25cm and toss through the shallots, chilli, potatoes and lemongrass. Roast for 10 mins until fragrant, keeping an eye on the shallots to ensure they don't burn. Remove from the oven and stir in the curry paste to coat everything. Return to the oven for 2 mins until its aroma is released before mixing in the coconut milk and 200ml stock. Put back in the oven again for 15-20 mins until the sauce is slightly thickened and the potatoes are turning tender.

STEP 2

Season to taste with the fish sauce and sugar, then stir through the courgette ribbons and spinach. Add another 50ml-100ml stock now if the sauce is too thick, but be aware that the courgette and spinach will release some water as well. Nestle the salmon fillets in the sauce and bake for a further 10-15 mins until the salmon is cooked to your liking.

STEP 3

Add the lime juice and taste the sauce for a balance of sweet and sour, adding more lime juice and fish sauce, if you like. Scatter over the spring onions, if using, along with the herbs and chilli. For a more filling meal, serve with rice or noodles and the lime wedges on the side.

˒ Herby spring chicken pot pie

Prep:10 mins **Cook:**30 mins

Serves 4

Ingredients

- 2 tbsp olive oil , plus a little extra for brushing over the pastry
- bunch spring onions , sliced into 3cm pieces
- 250g frozen spinach
- 6 ready-cooked chicken thighs (or see tip, below)
- 350ml hot chicken stock

- ½ tbsp wholegrain mustard
- 200g frozen peas
- 200ml half-fat crème fraîche
- ½ small bunch tarragon , leaves finely chopped
- small bunch parsley , finely chopped
- 270g pack filo pastry

Method

STEP 1

Heat oven to 200C/180C fan/gas 6. Heat the oil in a large, shallow casserole dish on a medium heat. Add the spring onions and fry for 3 mins, then stir through the frozen spinach and cook for 2 mins or until it's starting to wilt. Remove the skin from the chicken and discard. Shred the chicken off the bone and into the pan, and discard the bones. Stir through the stock and mustard. Bring to a simmer and cook, uncovered, for 5-10 mins.

STEP 2

Stir in the peas, crème fraîche and herbs, then remove from the heat. Scrunch the filo pastry sheets over the mixture, brush with a little oil and bake for 15-20 mins or until golden brown.

One-pot fish with black olives & tomatoes

Prep: 10 mins **Cook:** 15 mins - 20 mins

Serves 4

Ingredients

- 175g black olive in oil, stones removed
- 1 large onion , roughly chopped
- 400g can chopped tomato

To serve

- chopped parsley

- 4 boneless white fish fillets such as Icelandic cod or hoki, each weighing about 175g/6oz

- lemon wedges

Method

STEP 1

Preheat the oven to fan 180C/conventional 200C/gas 6. Heat 1 tbsp of the oil from the olives in an ovenproof pan. Tip in the onion and stir well, leave to cook for a minute or two and then give it another good stir. Add the tomatoes and some salt and pepper. Bring to the boil, then add the olives.

STEP 2

Put the fish, skin side down, onto the sauce and drizzle over a splash more oil from the olive jar. Bake, uncovered, for 15 minutes until the fish is cooked. Sprinkle with chopped parsley and serve straight from the pan, with lemon wedges for squeezing over.

Baked tomato & mozzarella orzo

Prep: 10 mins **Cook:** 30 mins

Serves 2

Ingredients

- 150g orzo
- ½ tbsp olive oil
- 2 roasted red peppers from a jar, roughly chopped
- handful olives , roughly chopped
- big pinch chilli flakes

- ½ tsp dried oregano
- 400g can chopped tomatoes with garlic (if you can't find ready mixed, crush 1 garlic clove into a can of tomatoes)
- 125g ball mozzarella

Method

STEP 1

Heat oven to 200C/180C fan/gas 6. Tip the orzo into a medium casserole dish, then stir in the oil, red peppers, olives, chilli flakes and dried oregano. Tip in the chopped tomatoes, then refill the can halfway with water and pour that in too. Give everything a good mix, season, then cover and bake for 20 mins until the pasta is almost cooked. Take it out of the oven and give the orzo a stir. Remove the foil and return to the oven for a further 5 mins.

STEP 2

Heat the grill to high. Take the orzo out of the oven and tear the mozzarella over the top, then grill until melted and bubbling. Serve with salad on the side, if you like.

Quick beef & broccoli one-pot

Prep: 10 mins **Cook:** 10 mins

Serves 4

Ingredients

- 1 tbsp olive oil
- 50g unsalted cashew nuts
- 400g frying beef steak, cut into strips

- 1 large head broccoli , broken into florets
- 4 sticks celery , sliced

- 150ml beef stock (from a cube is fine)
- 2 tbsp horseradish sauce
- 2 tbsp low-fat fromage frais

Method

STEP 1

Heat the oil in a frying pan, add the nuts and toss for a few secs until lightly toasted. Set aside.

STEP 2

Season the steak strips with plenty of pepper and stir-fry over a high heat for 1-2 mins to brown. Set aside with the nuts. Tip the broccoli and celery into the pan and stir-fry for 2 mins. Pour the stock over, cover and simmer for 2 mins. Meanwhile, mix the horseradish and fromage frais together.

STEP 3

Return the steak to the pan and toss with the veg, then sprinkle over the nuts and serve with the creamy horseradish. Great with mashed potatoes.

Spicy vegetable & quinoa one-pot

Prep: 5 mins **Cook:** 15 mins

Serves 4

Ingredients

- 1 onion , sliced
- 4 tbsp vegetarian korma or Madras curry paste
- 1l milk
- 750g frozen mixed vegetable
- 175g quinoa , rinsed

Method

STEP 1

Simmer the onion and the curry paste with a splash of water for 5 mins in a large saucepan, stirring from time to time. Heat the milk in a jug in the microwave.

STEP 2

Add the vegetables and quinoa, then stir in the milk. Bring to the boil, simmer gently for 10 mins until the quinoa is cooked. Check seasoning. Serve with warm naan bread.

Honey & mustard chicken thighs with spring veg

Prep: 10 mins **Cook:** 40 mins

Serves 2

Ingredients

- 1 tbsp honey
- 1 tbsp wholegrain mustard
- 2 garlic cloves, crushed
- zest and juice 1 lemon
- 4 chicken thighs, skin on
- 300g new potatoes, unpeeled, smaller left whole, bigger halved
- 1 tbsp olive oil
- 100g spinach
- 100g frozen peas

Method

STEP 1

Heat oven to 200C/180C fan/gas 6. In a small bowl, mix together the honey, mustard, garlic and the lemon zest and juice. Pour the marinade over the chicken thighs and season.

STEP 2

Put the chicken, skin-side up, on a large baking tray, then dot the new potatoes in between them. Drizzle the oil over the potatoes and sprinkle with sea salt. Roast in the oven for 35 mins until the chicken skin caramelises and is charred in places.

STEP 3

Add the spinach and peas to the roasting tray. Return to the oven for 2-3 mins until the spinach has begun to wilt and the peas are hot and covered in the mustardy sauce.

Spiced coconut chicken with coriander & lime

Prep: 20 mins **Cook:** 1 hr

Serves 4-6

Ingredients

- 1 tbsp oil
- 8 skin-on and bone-in chicken thighs
- 1 large onion , roughly chopped
- 4 garlic cloves , grated to a purée
- 3cm piece ginger , peeled and grated
- ½ tsp turmeric
- 2 tsp ground cumin
- 2 green chillies , halved, deseeded and finely chopped
- 200g butternut squash , peeled, deseeded and cut into slices (prepared weight)
- 100g cauliflower florets
- 225g basmati rice
- 10g bunch coriander , chopped
- 2 limes , zested and juiced
- 2 lime leaves
- 300ml coconut milk
- 400ml chicken stock

Method

STEP 1

Heat oven to 200C/180C fan/gas 6. Heat the oil in a 30cm shallow casserole dish or high-sided frying pan. Fry the chicken thighs, skin-side down, just to get some colour on them (they will take on a deeper colour in the oven). Transfer them to another dish. Fry the onion in the pan until soft and pale gold. Add the garlic, spices and chillies. Cook for 2 mins more, then stir in the squash, cauliflower, rice, half the coriander, the lime zest, half the lime juice, the lime leaves and some seasoning. Put the chicken back in the pan, this time skin-side up, and season that as well.

STEP 2

Heat the coconut milk and the chicken stock together until just below boiling point. Pour this around the chicken and put the pan in the oven, uncovered. Cook for 40 mins, or until the chicken is cooked through and the liquid has been absorbed by the rice. Squeeze over the remaining lime and scatter with the rest of the coriander. You could gently push the coriander into the rice, so it's not all on top. Serve immediately.

Turkey & mushroom pot pies

Prep:25 mins **Cook:**40 mins - 45 mins

Serves 2

Ingredients

- 1 tbsp butter
- 1 large onion , finely chopped

- 4 rashers streaky bacon , chopped
- 140g chestnut mushrooms , sliced
- 250g turkey mince (thigh is best)
- 25g plain flour
- 200ml chicken stock
- a few thyme sprigs , leaves picked
- ½ x 375g sheet ready-rolled puff pastry
- 1 egg yolk , beaten
- wilted spring greens , to serve

Method

STEP 1

Heat the butter in a large pan. Add the onion and cook for 8-10 mins until softened. Add the bacon and mushrooms, and cook until both are browned. Add the turkey mince, breaking up with a wooden spoon, and cook for another 5 mins until browned.

STEP 2

Add the flour, stir for 1 min or so, then pour in the chicken stock and add the thyme. Mix well and cook over a medium heat for 1-2 mins until it boils and thickens slightly. Season to taste and set aside to cool for 10-15 mins.

STEP 3

Heat oven to 220C/200C fan/gas 7. Once cooled, divide the turkey mixture between 2 ramekins or mini pie dishes. Unroll the pastry and cut out 2 squares to sit on top. Press the edges down the side of the dishes and glaze with the egg yolk. Bake in the oven for 30 mins until golden and cooked through. Serve with wilted spring greens.

Squid & pinto bean stew with garlic toasts

Prep: 15 mins **Cook:** 1 hr and 40 mins

Serves 4

Ingredients

- 175g dried pinto bean , soaked overnight
- 2 large onions , 1 halved, 1 finely chopped
- 4 carrots , peeled, 1 left whole, 3 cut into rounds
- 4 sticks of celery , 2 halved, 2 diced
- 1 bay leaf
- 2 tbsp olive oil , plus 2 tsp
- 4 garlic cloves , 3 finely chopped, 1 left whole
- 800g prepared squid and tentacles, cleaned and the body cut into thick

rings, the wings halved, tentacles left whole
- 1 tbsp tomato purée
- 1 thyme sprig
- 680g jar passata

- 500g pot fresh chicken stock
- 2 thick slices of brown bread , cut into quarters diagonally
- ¼ tsp smoked sweet paprika
- wilted greens , to serve (optional)

Method

STEP 1

Drain the pinto beans, rinse in water and put in a large saucepan. Add the halved onion, whole carrot and halved celery sticks, then cover with water and add the bay leaf. Bring to the boil, skim off any scum, turn down the heat and simmer until totally tender, for around 1 hr. When done, drain, discarding the bay leaf and cooked veg. Put the beans to one side until ready to use.

STEP 2

Meanwhile, heat a flameproof casserole dish with 2 tbsp oil. Toss in the remaining onion, carrot, celery and the chopped garlic. Fry gently for 15 mins until the vegetables are tender. Stir through the squid, tomato purée and thyme sprig. Cook for a min or two, then pour over the passata and chicken stock. Bring to the boil, turn down the heat, pop on the lid and simmer for 45 mins, stirring occasionally. Take off the lid and cook down for 30 mins.

STEP 3

Heat oven to 220C/200C fan/gas 7. Stir the beans into the squid and cook until the squid is totally tender and the sauce has thickened. Meanwhile, put the bread on a baking sheet. Mix the remaining oil with paprika and seasoning, then drizzle over the bread and put it in the oven, cooking for a few mins each side until golden and crisp. Rub the oil side with the whole garlic clove. Scatter parsley over the stew and serve with the garlic toasts and some wilted greens, if you like.

Sweet potato, chickpea & chorizo hash

Prep:10 mins **Cook:**20 mins

Serves 4

Ingredients

- 600g sweet potatoes , diced

- 1 tbsp sunflower oil

- 1 large red onion , thinly sliced
- 400g cooking chorizo sausages , skinned and crumbled
- 400g can chickpeas , rinsed and drained
- 4 large eggs
- 1 green chilli , thinly sliced into rings

Method

STEP 1

Boil the sweet potatoes for 8 mins until tender, then drain. Meanwhile, heat the oil in a large ovenproof pan and cook the onion and chorizo for 5 mins until softened. Add the sweet potatoes and chickpeas and cook for 5 mins more. Roughly break the mixture up with a fork, then flatten it down lightly to form a cake. Cook for a further 8 mins, without stirring, until cooked through, crispy and golden on the bottom.

STEP 2

Heat grill to high. Break the eggs onto the hash, season, then place the pan under the grill and cook for 2-3 mins until the whites are set. Sprinkle with chilli to serve.

Sausage & prawn jambalaya

Prep: 10 mins **Cook:** 35 mins

Serves 4

Ingredients

- 6 good-quality pork sausages (we used pork & chilli)
- sunflower oil , for frying
- 1 onion , chopped
- 1 red pepper , chopped
- 2 garlic cloves , crushed
- 1 tbsp sweet smoked paprika
- 250g easy-cook long grain rice
- 400g can chopped tomato with garlic & herbs
- 400-500ml chicken stock
- 260g pack cooked and peeled king prawn

Method

STEP 1

Fry the sausages in a large, deep, lidded frying pan until golden all over, then remove and set aside. Heat a little oil (unless there is enough fat from the sausages already in the pan) and gently cook the onion for 5 mins until soft.

STEP 2

Add the pepper, garlic and paprika, and cook for a few mins more, then stir in the rice, mixing to coat all the grains well. Tip in the tomatoes and enough stock to just cover the rice. Simmer with the lid on for about 10-12 mins until the rice is tender. Add more stock if you need to during cooking.

STEP 3

About 5 mins before the end of the cooking time, slice the sausages and return them to the pan. Cover and continue to cook until the rice is tender. Stir through the prawns, put the lid on and leave to heat through. Season and serve immediately.

Lingonberry & ginger cheesecake pots

Prep:15 mins **Cook:**1 min

Serves 2

Ingredients

- 50g full-fat cream cheese
- 75ml double cream
- grated zest 0.5 orange
- 4 tbsp lingonberry jam (we used Felix wild lingonberry jam) or cranberry jelly, plus a little extra to serve

- 8 Swedish pepparkakor ginger snaps or 4 ginger nuts , crushed, plus 1 extra to serve
- knob of butter , melted

Method

STEP 1

Whip the cream cheese, double cream and orange zest in a medium bowl until thick and holding its shape. Be careful not to overwhip or the cream cheese will become watery. Gently ripple through the lingonberry jam.

STEP 2

Mix together the crushed biscuits and butter, and spoon into 2 glasses. Divide the lingonberry mixture between the glasses and chill until needed – at least 30 mins. The cheesecakes can be made up to this point the day before.

STEP 3

To serve, mix a little of the jam with 1 tsp water and drizzle over the cheesecakes. Crumble the remaining biscuit and sprinkle on top.

Sweet spiced lamb shanks with quince

Prep: 10 mins **Cook:** 3 hrs

Serves 4

Ingredients

- 1 tbsp olive oil
- 4 lamb shanks
- large knob of butter
- 2 large onions , halved then cut into wedges
- 4 garlic cloves , crushed
- 4 strips zest from 1 unwaxed lemon , plus the juice
- 2 tsp ground cinnamon

- 2 tsp ground coriander
- 1 tsp ground ginger
- 1 tsp ground cumin
- good pinch of saffron strands (optional)
- 1 heaped tbsp tomato purée
- 1 tbsp clear honey
- 400ml good lamb or beef stock
- 2 quinces , peeled, quartered and cored

Method

STEP 1

Heat the oil in a large frying pan. Season the shanks, then brown in the oil for 10 mins, or until dark golden all over.

STEP 2

Meanwhile, in a casserole dish or large pan, melt the butter. Soften the onions for 10 mins on a medium heat until they're turning golden, then add the garlic. Heat oven to 160C/140C fan/gas 3.

STEP 3

Add the strips of lemon zest and spices to the onion pan. Cook for 1 min, then stir in the tomato purée, honey, stock and half the lemon juice. Sit the shanks in the pan, then poke the quince quarters in and around the meat. (It might be quite a tight fit, but the meat will shrink as it cooks.) Bring to a simmer, then cover with a lid and braise in the oven for 2 hrs.

STEP 4

Remove the lid and cook for 30 mins more. Spoon away any excess fat. The sauce will be fairly thin, so if you prefer a thicker stew, remove the lamb and quinces to a serving plate, then boil the cooking juices until thickened. Season, add the lemon juice and serve with the lamb.

One-pan simple summer chicken

Prep: 10 mins **Cook:** 50 mins

Serves 4

Ingredients

- 8 chicken thighs , skin on
- 800g potato , cut into chunks
- 1 garlic bulb, broken into cloves, skin left on
- 2 tbsp olive oil

- 200ml chicken stock
- 1 lemon , halved
- 2 courgettes , cut into thick batons
- 1 red chilli , deseeded and sliced
- large handful basil leaves , torn

Method

STEP 1

Heat oven to 220C/200C fan/gas 7. Pop the chicken, skin-side up, in a large roasting tin with the potatoes. Lightly crush the garlic cloves and nestle among the chicken pieces. Drizzle over the olive oil and chicken stock, then season. Squeeze over the juice from the lemon and pop the empty halves in the tin.

STEP 2

Bake for 45-50 mins, adding the courgettes and chilli 15 mins before the cooking time is up. Remove from the oven when the chicken is cooked through and golden, and the veg is tender. Stir through the basil leaves and serve.

Classic potted shrimps

Prep: 10 mins **Cook:** 15 mins

Serves 6

Ingredients

- 100g unsalted butter
- 2 pinches of cayenne pepper
- a generous grating of nutmeg
- 350g cooked and peeled North Atlantic prawns or shrimps

- 1 ciabatta loaf
- 1 tbsp olive oil
- 1 lemon , cut into wedges, to serve

Method

STEP 1

The day before, melt the butter in a small saucepan over a low heat and add the cayenne pepper and nutmeg. Add the prawns or shrimps to the pan, stir to warm through, and season.

STEP 2

Using a large slotted spoon, remove the prawns and press them into your ramekins (or serving dish). Allow to cool, then chill for 10-15 mins or until set. Once set, pour the leftover butter in the saucepan over the prawns to cover (you may need to reheat to melt). Return to the fridge to set overnight.

STEP 3

Before serving, heat oven to 200C/180C fan/gas 6. Cut the ciabatta into thin slices, drizzle with olive oil and toast on a tray in the oven. Once golden, arrange on a serving board with the potted prawns and lemon wedges alongside.

Slow-cooked lamb with onions & thyme

Total time3 hrs and 30 mins

Serves 4

Ingredients

- half a leg of lamb (about 1.25kg/2lb 12oz)
- 1kg onion (about 4 large ones)

- handful of thyme sprigs
- 300ml red wine
- large handful parsley

Method

STEP 1

Firstly, prepare the lamb. Heat oven to 160C/fan140C/gas 3. Wipe the meat all over and season well. Heat 3 tbsp of olive oil in a large heavy flameproof casserole, add the meat and fry all over on a fairly high heat for about 8 mins, turning until it is evenly well browned. Remove to a plate.

STEP 2

Thinly slice the onions. Add to the pan and fry for about 10 mins, until softened and tinged with brown. Add a few of the thyme sprigs and cook for a further minute or so. Season with salt and pepper.

STEP 3

Sit the lamb on top of the onions, then add the wine. Cover tightly. Bake for 3 hrs. You can make to this stage up to 2 days in advance, then reheat for 45 mins.

STEP 4

To finish off, strip the leaves from 2 thyme sprigs and chop them with the parsley. Scatter over before serving.

Easy banoffee pie

Prep:25 mins **Serves 8-10**

Ingredients

- 225g digestive biscuits
- 150g butter , melted
- 397g can caramel or 400g dulce de leche

- 3 small bananas , sliced
- 300ml double cream
- 1 tbsp icing sugar
- 1 square dark chocolate (optional)

Method

STEP 1

Crush the digestive biscuits, either by hand using a wooden spoon, or in a food processor, until you get fine crumbs, tip into a bowl. Mix the crushed biscuits with the melted butter until fully combined. Tip the mixture into a 23cm loose bottomed fluted tart tin and cover the tin, including the sides, with the biscuit in an even layer. Push down with the back of a spoon to smooth the surface and chill for 1 hr, or overnight.

STEP 2

Beat the caramel to loosen and spoon it over the bottom of the biscuit base. Spread it out evenly using the back of a spoon or palette knife. Gently push the chopped banana into the top of the caramel until the base is covered. Put in the fridge.

STEP 3

Whip the cream with the icing sugar until billowy and thick. Take the pie out of the fridge and spoon the whipped cream on top of the bananas. Grate the dark chocolate over the cream, if you like, and serve.

Bean & pasta stew with meatballs

Prep:15 mins **Cook:**40 mins

Serves 4

Ingredients

- 6-8 pack pork sausages
- 1 tbsp olive oil
- 2 onions , finely chopped
- 3 celery sticks, diced
- 2 carrots , diced
- 3 garlic cloves , finely chopped

- 400g can chopped tomatoes
- 1l chicken stock
- 175g macaroni
- 410g can cannellini beans , rinsed and drained
- handful flat-leaf parsley , chopped

Method

STEP 1

Snip the ends off the sausages and squeeze out the meat. Roll into rough walnut-sized meatballs. Heat half the oil in a large, wide pan and fry until browned, around 10 mins. Remove from pan and set aside.

STEP 2

Add the rest of the oil to the pan. Tip in the onions, celery and carrots and fry for 10 mins until soft. Add garlic and cook for 1 min more. Tip in the tomatoes and stock. Bring to the boil and simmer for 10 mins.

STEP 3

Stir in the macaroni and return the meatballs. Simmer for about 10 mins until pasta is cooked and meatballs are cooked though. Stir in beans and heat until piping hot. Season, mix in parsley and serve.

One-pan Spanish fish stew

Prep: 10 mins **Cook:** 40 mins

Serves 4

Ingredients

- handful flat-leaf parsley leaves, chopped
- 2 garlic cloves , finely chopped
- zest and juice 1 lemon
- 3 tbsp olive oil , plus extra to serve
- 1 medium onion , finely sliced
- 500g floury potato , cut into small chunks, no larger than 2cm cubes
- 1 tsp paprika
- pinch cayenne pepper
- 400g can chopped tomato
- 1 fish stock cube
- 200g raw peeled king prawn
- ½ a 410g/14oz can chickpeas , rinsed and drained
- 500g skinless fish fillets, cut into very large chunks

Method

STEP 1

In a small bowl, mix the parsley with ½ the garlic and lemon zest, then set aside. Heat 2 tbsp oil in a large sauté pan. Throw in the onion and potatoes, cover the pan, then sweat everything for about 5 mins until the onion has softened. Add the remaining oil, garlic and spices, then cook for 2 mins more.

STEP 2

Pour over the lemon juice and sizzle for a moment. Add the tomatoes, ½ a can of water and crumble in the stock. Season with a little salt, then cover the pan. Simmer everything for 15-20 mins until the potatoes are just cooked.

STEP 3

Stir through the prawns and chickpeas, then nestle the fish chunks into the top of the stew. Reduce the heat and recover the pan, then cook for about 8 mins, stirring very gently once or twice. When the fish is just cooked through, remove from the heat, scatter with the parsley mix, then bring the dish to the table with the bottle of olive oil for drizzling over and some crusty bread, if you want.

Mexican chicken burger

Prep: 10 mins **Cook:** 8 mins

Serves 1

Ingredients

- 1 chicken breast
- 1 tsp chipotle paste
- 1 lime , juiced
- 1-2 slices cheese
- 1 brioche bun , split

- ½ avocado
- 2 cherry tomatoes , chopped
- 3-4 pickled jalapeño slices, chopped
- ½ small garlic clove , finely grated

Method

STEP 1

Put the chicken breast between two pieces of cling film and bash with a rolling pin or pan to about 1cm thick. Mix the chipotle paste with half the lime juice and spread over the chicken.

STEP 2

Heat a griddle pan over a high heat. Once hot, cook the chicken for 3 mins each side until cooked through, adding the cheese for the final 2 mins of cooking. Add the bun, cut-side down, to the griddle pan to toast lightly. Season the chicken.

STEP 3

Meanwhile, mash the avocado with the remaining lime juice. Stir in the cherry tomatoes, jalapeño and garlic, and season with a little salt. Spread over the base of the bun, then add the chicken followed by the top of the bun.

One pan spicy rice

Total time 20 mins Ready in 20 minutes

Serves 4

Ingredients

- 1 tbsp sunflower oil
- 2 garlic cloves , crushed
- 2 tbsp medium curry paste (Madras is a good one to use)
- 250g basmati rice , rinsed
- 450ml vegetable stock
- 400g can chickpeas , drained and rinsed
- handful of raisins
- 175g frozen leaf spinach , thawed
- handful of cashew nuts
- natural yogurt to serve, optional

Method

STEP 1

Heat the oil in a large nonstick pan that has a lid, then fry the garlic and curry paste over a medium heat for 1 minute, until it smells toasty.

STEP 2

Tip the rice into the pan with the stock, chickpeas and raisins and stir with a fork to stop the rice from clumping. Season with salt and pepper, then cover and bring to the boil. Reduce to a medium heat and cook for 12-15 minutes or until all the liquid has been absorbed and the rice is tender.

STEP 3

Squeeze the excess water from the spinach with your hands. Tip it into the pan along with 2 tbsp of hot water and fluff up the rice with a fork, making sure the spinach is mixed in well. Toss in the cashews. Serve drizzled with natural yogurt if you like.

Harissa-crumbed fish with lentils & peppers

Prep: 15 mins **Cook:** 15 mins

Serves 4

Ingredients

- 2 x 200g pouches cooked puy lentils
- 200g jar roasted red peppers , drained and torn into chunks
- 50g black olives , from a jar, roughly chopped
- 1 lemon , zested and cut into wedges
- 3 tbsp olive or rapeseed oil
- 4 x 140g cod fillets (or another white fish)
- 100g fresh breadcrumbs
- 1 tbsp harissa
- ½ small pack flat-leaf parsley , chopped

Method

STEP 1

Heat oven to 200C/180C fan/gas 6. Mix the lentils, peppers, olives, lemon zest, 2 tbsp oil and some seasoning in a roasting tin. Top with the fish fillets. Mix the breadcrumbs, harissa and the remaining oil and put a few spoonfuls on top of each piece of fish. Bake for 12-15 mins until the fish is cooked, the topping is crispy and the lentils are hot. Scatter with the parsley and squeeze over the lemon wedges.

Easter nest cake

Prep:45 mins **Cook:**30 mins

Serves 12 - 15

Ingredients

For the chocolate sponges

- 200ml vegetable oil , plus extra for the tin
- 250g plain flour
- 6 tbsp cocoa powder
- 2 tsp baking powder
- 1 tsp bicarbonate of soda
- 280g soft light brown sugar
- 250ml buttermilk
- 2 tsp vanilla extract
- 3 large eggs

For the nest

- 200g marshmallows
- 100g butter , chopped into chunks
- 2 tbsp cocoa powder
- 75g salted pretzels , crushed
- 4 shredded wheat biscuits , crushed
- chocolate eggs, to decorate

For the icing

- 150g slightly salted butter , softened
- 2 tbsp cocoa powder
- 300g icing sugar
- 4 tbsp milk

Method

STEP 1

Heat oven to 180C/160C fan/gas 4. Oil and line two 20cm round cake tins. Add the flour, cocoa powder, baking powder, bicarb, sugar and a large pinch of salt to a bowl. Mix with a whisk, squeezing any large lumps of sugar through your fingers, until you have a fine, sandy mix.

STEP 2

Whisk the oil with the buttermilk in a jug. Stir in the vanilla and eggs, then pour the wet ingredients into the dry and mix until there are no more streaks of flour. Divide the mixture between the tins and bake for 25 mins. Test the cakes by inserting a skewer into the centre – if there is any wet mixture on the skewer, return the cakes to the oven for 5 mins more, then check again. Leave the cakes to cool in the tins for 15 mins, then transfer to wire racks to cool fully.

STEP 3

Next, make the nest. Clean one tin and line it with some oiled baking parchment. Put the marshmallows and butter in a heatproof bowl and microwave on high for 1 min, stirring halfway through (or heat gently in a pan on the hob). Continue microwaving in 20-second blasts until you get a runny mixture. Stir in the cocoa, pretzels and shredded wheat until well combined. Tip the mixture into your lined tin and use the back of your spoon to create a nest shape. Leave to cool at room temperature for a few hrs, or chill in the fridge if you need it to set faster.

STEP 4

To make the icing, beat the butter, cocoa, icing sugar and milk together until smooth, adding a splash more milk if the mixture is too stiff. Assemble the cake by stacking the sponges with icing in between, topping with more icing and the nest. Fill your nest with as many chocolate eggs as it will hold, then serve. It may be easier to cut the cake if you remove the nest – you can then chop the nest into chunks and serve alongside the cake.

Halloumi, carrot & orange salad

Prep: 5 mins **Cook:** 15 mins

Serves 4

Ingredients

- 2 large oranges
- 1½ tbsp wholegrain mustard
- 1½ tsp honey

- 1 tbsp white wine vinegar
- 3 tbsp rapeseed or olive oil, plus extra for frying

- 2 large carrots, peeled
- 225g block halloumi, sliced
- 100g bag watercress or baby spinach

Method

STEP 1

Cut the peel and pith away from the oranges. Use a small serrated knife to segment the orange, catching any juices in a bowl, then squeeze any excess juice from the off-cut pith into the bowl as well. Add the mustard, honey, vinegar, oil and some seasoning to the bowl and mix well.

STEP 2

Using a vegetable peeler, peel carrot ribbons into the dressing bowl and toss gently. Heat a drizzle of oil in a frying pan and cook the halloumi for a few mins until golden on both sides. Toss the watercress through the dressed carrots. Arrange the watercress mixture on plates and top with the halloumi and oranges.

Irish stew

Prep:30 mins **Cook:**2 hrs

Serves 6

Ingredients

- 1 tbsp sunflower oil
- 200g smoked streaky bacon, preferably in one piece, skinned and cut into chunks
- 900g stewing lamb, cut into large chunks
- 5 medium onions, sliced
- 5 carrots, sliced into chunks
- 3 bay leaves
- small bunch thyme
- 100g pearl barley
- 850ml lamb stock
- 6 medium potatoes, cut into chunks
- small knob of butter
- 3 spring onions, finely sliced

Method

STEP 1

Heat oven to 160C/fan 140C/gas 3. Heat the oil in a flameproof casserole. Sizzle the bacon for 4 mins until crisp. Turn up the heat, then cook the lamb for 6 mins until brown. Remove the meats with a slotted spoon. Add the onions, carrots and herbs to the pan, then cook for about 5 mins until softened. Return the meat to the pan, stir in the pearl barley, pour over the stock, then bring to a simmer.

STEP 2

Sit the chunks of potato on top of the stew, cover, then braise in the oven, undisturbed, for about 1½ hrs until the potatoes are soft and the meat is tender. The stew can now be chilled and kept in the fridge for 2 days, then reheated in a low oven or on top of the stove. Remove from the oven, dot the potatoes with butter, scatter with the spring onions and serve scooped straight from the dish.

Microwave biryani

Prep:15 mins **Cook:**7 mins - 10 mins

Serves 2

Ingredients

- 2 spring onions , finely sliced
- 1 fat garlic clove , crushed
- knob of butter
- seeds from 1 cardamom pod
- ¼ tsp chilli flakes
- 140g rice
- 400ml vegetable or chicken stock
- ¼ tsp turmeric
- ¼ tsp ground cumin

- pinch of cinnamon
- 1 tbsp raisins or sultanas
- 200g vegetables of your choice, finely chopped or grated (try a combination of grated carrot, frozen peas, peppers in 1cm chunks or finely sliced mushrooms)
- small handful of coriander or mint leaves, to serve

Method

STEP 1

Add the onions, garlic, butter, cardamom seeds and the chilli flakes to a large microwaveable bowl and cook in the microwave on High for 30 secs. Tip in the rice and stock, along with the turmeric, cumin, cinnamon and raisins. Stir well and then cover with cling film.

STEP 2

Place a few sheets of kitchen paper on your microwave turning plate to absorb any spills, then place the bowl on top and cook on High for 2 mins. Remove and stir, then leave to stand for 1 min; it will continue to cook even after it has been removed, so allowing it to stand is really important.

STEP 3

Repeat 2-3 more times until the rice is just cooked, the last time adding your finely chopped veg to the bowl and stirring through. Garnish with fresh coriander or mint, to serve.

Leftover turkey casserole

Prep:15 mins **Cook:**25 mins

Serves 4

Ingredients

- 2 onions, finely chopped
- 1 eating apple, cored and chopped
- 2 tbsp olive oil
- 1 tsp dried sage, or 5 sage leaves, chopped
- 2 tbsp plain flour
- 300ml vegetable or chicken stock

- 2 tbsp wholegrain mustard
- 2 tbsp runny honey
- 400g-500g leftover turkey, shredded
- about 350g leftover roasted vegetables like roast potatoes, parsnips, celeriacs and carrots, chunkily diced

Method

STEP 1

Fry the onion and apple in the oil until softened in a casserole or deep pan. Stir in the sage for 1 min, then stir in the flour. Gradually stir in the stock followed by the mustard and honey.

STEP 2

Bring up to a simmer and stir in the turkey and roast veg. Cover and gently simmer for 15 mins until turkey is piping hot. Season and eat with mash or jacket potatoes.

Spanish bean stew

Prep:10 mins **Cook:**30 mins

Serves 4

Ingredients

- 1 tbsp olive oil
- 200g chorizo sausage, thickly sliced
- 1 onion , chopped
- 400g/14oz chicken thigh fillets, cubed
- 1 tomato , roughly chopped

- 410g can cannellini bean , drained
- 1 large potato , cut into small cubes
- 500ml hot chicken stock
- 4 tbsp chopped parsley

Method

STEP 1

Heat the oil in a large pan. Cook the chorizo, onion and chicken over a high heat for 5 mins. Add the tomato and cook for a further 2-3 mins until pulpy.

STEP 2

Stir in the beans, potato and stock. Bring to the boil, then cover and gently simmer for 20 mins until the potato is soft and the chicken cooked through. Stir through the parsley and serve. You can cool and freeze the stew for up to 2 months. To serve, defrost and heat through thoroughly.

Fragrant courgette & prawn curry

Prep: 15 mins **Cook:** 20 mins

Serves 2

Ingredients

- 2 tbsp sunflower oil
- 500g courgettes , thickly sliced
- ½ tsp cumin seeds
- 2 tbsp ginger , finely chopped
- 6 garlic cloves , crushed
- 1 red chilli , deseeded and finely chopped
- 1 tsp ground coriander

- ¼ tsp ground turmeric
- 500g tomato , chopped
- 150ml hot vegetable stock
- 225g pack raw peeled frozen jumbo prawn , thawed
- ½ small bunch coriander , roughly chopped

Method

STEP 1

Heat the oil in a large wok and stir-fry the courgettes for 5-6 mins until softened. Lift from the pan with a slotted spoon, leaving the oil behind.

STEP 2

Add the cumin seeds to the pan and toast for a few secs, then add the ginger, garlic, chilli and spices. Cook, stirring for 1-2 mins, then tip in the tomatoes and cook for a few mins more.

STEP 3

Pour in the stock and simmer to make a pulpy sauce, then add the courgettes and prawns. Cook gently until the prawns change from grey to pink and the courgettes are tender, but not too soft. Stir in most of the coriander, saving some to sprinkle over the top. Serve with basmati rice and mango chutney, if you like.

Melty cheese fondue pot

Prep:10 mins **Cook:**28 mins

Serves 4 - 6

Ingredients

- 200g brie , rind removed, roughly chopped
- 100g cream cheese (not light versions)
- 100g gruyère , rind removed, grated
- 2 tbsp grated parmesan (or vegetarian alternative)

- 2 tbsp milk
- 2 tsp cornflour
- few thyme sprigs , leaves picked and roughly chopped
- 100g caramelised onion chutney
- crusty bread , to serve

Method

STEP 1

Put the brie, cream cheese, gruyère, half the parmesan, the milk and cornflour into a food processor, and blitz until smooth. Stir through the thyme and a little black pepper. Spoon the chutney into an ovenproof baking dish (ours was 15cm round) and spread it over the base. Top with the cheese mixture, spread to cover the chutney, then scatter over the remaining parmesan. It can now be covered with cling film and chilled for up to 3 days.

STEP 2

Heat oven to 160C/140C fan/gas 3. Put the baking dish on a baking tray and cook for 25 mins until bubbling. Turn the grill to a medium-high setting and grill for 2-3 mins or until golden brown and crispy on top. Remove from the oven and leave to cool for 5 mins before serving with crusty bread for dunking.

Curried chicken & new potato traybake

Prep: 15 mins **Cook:** 45 mins

Serves 4

Ingredients

- 8 chicken drumsticks
- 3 tbsp olive oil
- 1 tsp garlic paste
- 1 tsp ginger paste
- 1 tsp garam masala
- 1 tsp turmeric

- 150ml pot natural yogurt
- 500g new potatoes, halved
- 4 large tomatoes, roughly chopped
- 1 red onion, finely chopped
- small pack coriander, roughly chopped

Method

STEP 1

Put the drumsticks in a large bowl with 1 tbsp oil, the garlic, ginger, garam masala, turmeric and 2 tbsp yogurt. Toss together with your hands until coated. Leave to marinate for at least 30 mins (can be left in the fridge overnight). Heat oven to 180C/160C fan/gas 4.

STEP 2

Put the potatoes in a large roasting tin with the remaining oil and plenty of seasoning. Add the chicken drumsticks and bake for 40-45 mins until cooked and golden.

STEP 3

Scatter the tomatoes, onion, coriander and some seasoning over the chicken and potatoes, with the remaining yogurt served on the side.

Pot-roast loin of pork in cider with celeriac

Prep: 20 mins **Cook:** 1 hr and 45 mins

Serves 4 - 6

Ingredients

- 2 ½kg pork loin , bone in
- 1 tbsp olive oil
- 100g smoked bacon lardons
- 300g banana shallots , halved horizontally
- 500-600g celeriac , peeled and cut into 3cm chunks
- 6 thyme sprigs
- 1 garlic bulb , halved
- 600ml dry cider
- 140g frozen peas
- mash , to serve

Method

STEP 1

Heat oven to 180C/160C fan/gas 4. Season the pork and put in a large roasting tin.

STEP 2

Heat a large frying pan, add the oil and fry the lardons, shallots, celeriac and thyme until golden brown. Arrange around the pork with the garlic bulb.

STEP 3

Add the cider to the frying pan, bring to the boil, then pour around the pork. Cover with foil and roast for 1 hr. Remove the foil and cook, uncovered, for a further 45 mins.

STEP 4

Finally, add the peas and cook for 3 mins more. Leave the pork to stand, covered, for 15 mins before carving. Serve with buttery mash (add the soft roasted garlic cloves if you like) to soak up the delicious juices.

Chicken & chickpea rice

Prep:15 mins **Cook:**25 mins

Serves 2-3

Ingredients

- 25g butter
- 1 shallot , finely chopped

- 1 skinless chicken breast (about 180g), cut into strips
- 1 carrot (about 100g), cut into thin batons
- 1 cinnamon stick
- 1 strip lemon zest
- 125g basmati rice
- 2 heaped tbsp raisins or sultanas
- 250ml chicken stock
- 215g can chickpeas (drained weight 130g)

Method

STEP 1

Melt half the butter in a frying pan with a lid. Fry the shallot for a couple of minutes, then add the chicken and carrot. Fry the veg until starting to brown, then add the cinnamon and lemon, and season well. Stir in the rice and raisins, then add the stock and bring to a simmer.

STEP 2

Scatter the chickpeas on top, then cover with the lid. Cook for 15 mins over a low heat until the rice has absorbed all the stock – if the rice is still firm, add 50ml water. Stand for 5 mins, then fluff up the rice. Dot over the remaining butter, then serve.

Special lamb biryani

Prep:25 mins **Cook:**2 hrs

Serves 4-5

Ingredients

- 500g lamb neck or shoulder, chopped into small chunks
- 3 tbsp Indian spice mix , plus a pinch (see below)
- 100g yogurt , plus extra to serve
- ½ lemon , juiced
- 3 tbsp vegetable oil
- 2 large onions , halved and sliced
- 300g basmati rice
- 4 garlic cloves , crushed
- thumb-sized piece ginger , peeled and finely chopped
- 4 plum tomatoes , chopped or 200g can chopped tomatoes
- good pinch saffron
- 100g butter
- 2 cinnamon sticks
- 6 cardamom pods
- 4 bay or 6 curry leaves
- 2 star anise
- 320g sheet ready-rolled puff pastry

- 1 egg , beaten
- 2 tsp nigella seeds

For the Indian spice mix

- 2 tbsp coriander seeds
- 2 tbsp cumin seeds
- 1 tbsp sweet paprika
- 2 tsp mild chilli powder (kashmiri chilli powder if you can find it)
- 2 tsp fenugreek seeds

- handful chopped coriander or mint
- 1 red onion , halved and thinly sliced

- 3 whole cloves
- 1 tsp fennel seeds
- 1 tsp ground turmeric
- 10 cardamom pods , seeds removed and pods discarded

Method

STEP 1

Mix the lamb with the spice blend, yogurt, lemon juice and a pinch of salt. Leave at room temperature for at least 30 mins or chill overnight.

STEP 2

Heat 2 tbsp oil in a large frying pan and cook the onions over a low-medium heat for 15-20 mins until caramelised. Meanwhile, rinse the rice three times under cold water. Drain, then cover with fresh water and leave for 30 mins.

STEP 3

Transfer the onions to a bowl, add the remaining oil to the pan and brown the lamb in batches. If the marinade starts to catch, scrape it from the bottom of the pan and keep stirring – it'll add to the flavour. Tip the meat back into the pan with the garlic and ginger. Cook for another minute or 2, then add the tomatoes and 200ml water (swill the water around the dish the lamb was marinating in to pick up all the marinade before adding it to the pan). Season with salt and bring to a gentle simmer. Cover and cook for 45 mins, stirring now and then and topping up with a splash of water if the sauce is catching. You can now chill the lamb for up to two days.

STEP 4

Pour away the rice water, cover with fresh water and season. Bring to the boil, bubble for 2 mins, then drain and leave to cool. Put the saffron in a bowl, pour over 50ml boiling water and leave for 10 mins to steep.

STEP 5

Smear 50g butter inside a casserole dish. Sprinkle over a little of the Indian spice mix and some salt. To assemble the biryani, start with 1/3 of the lamb, top with 1/3 of the rice, 1/3 of the onions, a cinnamon stick, a couple of cardamom pods, a few bay or curry leaves and a star anise. Repeat until all of the ingredients have been used up. Spoon the saffron and its water over the final layer of rice, dot with the remaining butter and season with salt. You can now chill it for up to 24 hrs.

STEP 6

Heat oven to 200C/180C fan/gas 6. Unroll the pastry and cut into a circle a little larger than the dish. Brush a little egg around the outside lip of the dish, then lift the pastry on top, pressing it around the edge to seal. Brush with more egg and sprinkle with nigella seeds. Bake for 45-50 mins until golden brown. Mix the herbs and onion, and serve with the biryani and extra yogurt.

Sharing potted shrimp

Prep:5 mins **Serves 4**

Ingredients

- 250g pack unsalted butter
- 1 bay leaf
- 280g cooked and peeled small brown shrimp
- ¼ tsp ground mace
- 2 good pinches cayenne pepper
- juice ½ lemon

Method

STEP 1

Melt the butter with the bay leaf in a pan or in a bowl in the microwave for 1 min. Add the shrimps, mace, a good pinch of cayenne pepper, the lemon juice and some seasoning. Mix everything together well.

STEP 2

Tip the mixture into a shallow soufflé or gratin dish, or a jar, put the bay leaf on top and sprinkle with a pinch extra cayenne. Chill for at least 2 hrs, or up to 3 days before serving.

Snowman biscuits

Prep: 1 hr **Cook:** 14 mins

Makes 20

Ingredients

- 125g butter, softened
- 125g golden caster sugar
- 1 egg, beaten

For the decoration

- 400g white fondant icing
- icing sugar, for dusting
- 100g pack mixed red, yellow, black and blue ready-to-roll icing

- 1 tsp vanilla extract
- 250g plain flour, plus extra for dusting

- tube white icing, for sticking
- tube black icing

Method

STEP 1

Heat the oven to 190C/170C fan/gas 5. Cream the butter and sugar until pale and fluffy, then beat in the egg and vanilla. Stir in the flour and mix to a fairly soft dough. Tip onto a lightly floured surface and knead gently. Put the dough on a plate, cover and chill for at least 2 hrs.

STEP 2

On a lightly floured surface, roll out the dough to a thickness of around 0.5cm. Use a cookie cutter or water glass to stamp out 7cm rounds. Re-roll the trimmings and repeat.

STEP 3

Transfer the biscuits to two lined baking trays and bake for 8-14 mins until the edges turn lightly golden in colour. Leave to cool.

STEP 4

To decorate, roll out the white fondant icing on a surface lightly dusted with icing sugar. Stamp out 7cm circles using the same cookie cutter or glass as before, then use a dab of the white tube of icing to stick a fondant round on each biscuit.

STEP 5

Knead together some of the yellow and blue icing to make green icing, then do the same with the red and yellow icing to make orange (alternatively, buy separate packs of each colour). Roll out one icing colour at a time. Stamp out a 7cm circle of icing, cut in half and stick on for a hat. Cut a strip of another colour and make some markings to make it look like the elasticated band of a hat, then trim to fit and stick on. Repeat with all the biscuits, mixing and matching colours.

STEP 6

Decorate the hats with icing spots and stripes, if you like. Roll out balls of coloured icing, poke holes all over with a cocktail stick and stick on as pom poms. Mould lumpy balls of the orange icing for noses and roll out balls of the black icing for eyes. Press down to flatten, then stick on with white icing. Use the tube of black icing to pipe rows of dots for the smiles. Leave to set. Will keep for up to five days in an airtight container.

Basque-style salmon stew

Prep:10 mins **Cook:**25 mins

Serves 4

Ingredients

- 1 tbsp olive oil
- 3 mixed peppers , deseeded and sliced
- 1 large onion , thinly sliced
- 400g baby potatoes , unpeeled and halved
- 2 tsp smoked paprika

- 2 garlic cloves , sliced
- 2 tsp dried thyme
- 400g can chopped tomatoes
- 4 salmon fillets
- 1 tbsp chopped parsley , to serve (optional)

Method

STEP 1

Heat the oil in a large pan and add the peppers, onion and potatoes. Cook, stirring regularly for 5-8 mins until golden. Then add the paprika, garlic, thyme and tomatoes. Bring to the boil, stir and cover, then turn down heat and simmer for 12 mins. Add a splash of water if the sauce becomes too thick.

STEP 2

Season the stew and lay the salmon on top, skin side down. Place the lid back on and simmer for another 8 mins until the salmon is cooked through. Scatter with parsley, if you like, and serve.

Malabar prawns

Prep: 15 mins **Cook:** 12 mins

Serves 4

Ingredients

- 400g raw king prawns
- 2 tsp turmeric
- 3-4 tsp Kashmiri chilli powder
- 4 tsp lemon juice , plus a squeeze
- 40g ginger , half peeled and grated, half finely sliced into matchsticks
- 1 tbsp vegetable oil

- 4 curry leaves
- 2-4 green chillies , halved and deseeded
- 1 onion , finely sliced
- 1 tsp cracked black pepper
- 40g fresh coconut , grated
- ½ small bunch coriander , leaves only

Method

STEP 1

Rinse the prawns in cold water and pat dry. Toss them with the turmeric, chilli powder, lemon juice and grated ginger and set aside.

STEP 2

Heat the oil in a pan and add the curry leaves, chilli, sliced ginger and onion. Cook until translucent, about 10 mins, then add the black pepper.

STEP 3

Toss the prawns in with any marinade, and stir-fry until cooked, about 2 mins. Season if required and add a squeeze of lemon juice. Serve sprinkled with the coconut and coriander leaves.

Greek lamb with potatoes & olives

Prep: 20 mins **Cook:** 1 hr and 10 mins

Serves 4

Ingredients

- 800g medium-size potatoes , skin on, thinly sliced
- 4 large tomatoes , thinly sliced
- 1 aubergine , thinly sliced
- 4 garlic cloves , chopped
- 3 tbsp oregano leaves, plus extra for sprinkling
- 85g pitted Kalamata olives , halved
- 5 tbsp olive oil , plus a drizzle
- 100g feta cheese , crumbled
- 4 lamb steaks

Method

STEP 1

Heat oven to 200C/180C fan/gas 6. Layer up half the potato, tomato and aubergine in a baking dish, scattering with garlic, oregano and olives, and drizzling with oil and seasoning as you go.

STEP 2

Scatter over the feta, then repeat the layers until all the ingredients are used up. Finish with potatoes and a little oil.

STEP 3

Bake for 50 mins or until the veg are tender (cover with foil if they're getting too brown). Top with the lamb steaks, rubbing with a little more oil and seasoning. Bake for 15-20 mins more until the lamb is cooked. Allow to rest and cool a bit before scattering with oregano and serving with crusty bread.

Spicy teriyaki prawns & sesame fried rice

Prep: 5 mins **Cook:** 10 mins

Serves 1

Ingredients

- 125g microwave brown basmati rice
- oil , for frying
- 2 baby pak choi , halved
- 2 spring onions , cut into 3cm slices
- 1 medium egg , lightly beaten
- 1 tbsp toasted sesame seeds , plus more to serve
- 50g raw king prawns
- 3 tbsp teriyaki sauce
- 2 tsp chilli sauce (such as sriracha)

Method

STEP 1

Microwave the rice for 1 min. Heat a glug of oil in a frying pan over a high heat. Fry the pak choi and spring onions for 2 mins. Stir in the egg until scrambled, then add the rice and sesame seeds and cook for 2 mins or until piping hot. Set aside.

STEP 2

In another frying pan, heat a glug of oil and fry the prawns for 2 mins. Add the sauces and cook until sticky. Serve with the veg, rice and sesame seeds.

Spicy chicken couscous

Total time30 mins Ready in 25-30 minutes

Serves 4

Ingredients

- 250g couscous
- 3 tbsp olive oil
- 1 chopped onion
- 2 large sliced skinless boneless chicken breast fillets
- 85g blanched almonds
- 1 tbsp hot curry paste
- 100g halved ready-to-eat apricots
- 120g pack fresh coriander

Method

STEP 1

Prepare couscous with chicken stock, according to the packet instructions. Heat olive oil in a pan and cook the onion for 2-3 mins until softened.

STEP 2

Toss in chicken breast fillets and stir fry for 5-6 mins until tender. Add the blanched almonds and, when golden, stir in the hot curry paste and cook for 1 min more.

STEP 3

Add the couscous along with the apricots and the coriander. Toss until hot then serve with plain yogurt if you like.

Lemony prawn & chorizo rice pot

Prep:15 mins **Cook:**25 mins

Serves 4

Ingredients

- 1 tbsp olive oil
- 1 onion , sliced
- 2 small red peppers , deseeded and sliced
- 50g chorizo , thinly sliced
- 2 garlic cloves , crushed
- 1 red chilli (deseeded if you don't like it too hot)

- ½ tsp turmeric
- 250g long grain rice
- 200g raw peeled prawn , defrosted if frozen
- 100g frozen pea
- zest and juice 1 lemon , plus extra wedges to serve

Method

STEP 1

Boil the kettle. Heat the oil in a shallow pan with a lid, add the onion, peppers, chorizo, garlic and chilli, then fry over a high heat for 3 mins. Add the turmeric and rice, stirring to ensure the rice is coated. Pour in 500ml boiling water, cover, then cook for 12 mins.

STEP 2

Uncover, then stir – the rice should be almost tender. Stir in the prawns and peas, with a splash more water if the rice is looking dry, then cook for 1 min more until the prawns are just pink and the rice tender. Stir in the lemon zest and juice with seasoning and serve with extra lemon wedges on the side.

Double cheese & spring vegetable tart

Prep: 30 mins **Cook:** 1 hr

Serves 8

Ingredients

- 500g block shortcrust pastry
- plain flour , for dusting
- 25g mature cheddar , finely grated
- 200g asparagus spears , woody ends trimmed
- 100g fresh podded or frozen peas
- 2 eggs

- 100g crème fraîche
- 150g double cream
- whole nutmeg , for grating
- 100g watercress
- 300g or 2 logs of soft, rindless goat's cheese

Method

STEP 1

Roll the pastry out into a rectangle on a work surface lightly dusted with flour. Scatter over the cheese, fold the pastry in half and roll out again into a circle that fits a 25cm tart tin with an overhang. Chill for 20 mins. Meanwhile, cook the asparagus in boiling water for 3 mins, then drain and refresh under cold water. Cook the fresh peas the same way for a minute, or simply defrost the frozen peas.

STEP 2

Heat oven to 200C/180C fan/gas 6. Prick the base of the tart well with a fork, line with baking parchment and fill with baking beans. Bake the tart for 30 mins, remove the parchment and beans, prick again if it has puffed up, then bake for another 10-15 mins until biscuit brown.

STEP 3

Meanwhile, beat the eggs in a bowl, add the crème fraîche and cream, season and add a pinch of freshly grated nutmeg. Scatter the peas and most of the watercress over the tart and crumble over half the goat's cheese. Pour over the creamy egg mixture, then lay the asparagus spears on top. Finally, slice the remaining goat's cheese and arrange on top, then bake for 25-30 mins until the custard is just set and the cheese is golden brown. Leave to cool in the tin, trim the edges of the pastry, then remove from the tin, scatter with the remaining watercress and serve cut into slices. Can be made up to a day ahead, leave out the fridge to keep the pastry crisp.

Hearty lamb stew

Prep: 10 mins **Cook:** 1 hr and 40 mins

Serves 4

Ingredients

- 1 tbsp vegetable oil
- 500g cubed stewing lamb
- 1 onion, thickly sliced
- 2 carrots, thickly sliced
- 2 leeks, thickly sliced
- 400ml hot vegetable or chicken stock

- 1 tsp dried rosemary or 1 fresh sprig
- 400g cannellini bean, rinsed and drained
- crusty bread or boiled potatoes to serve (optional)

Method

STEP 1

Heat the oil in a large casserole. Tip in the lamb and cook for 5 mins until any liquid has disappeared, then add the onion, carrots and leeks. Cook for 5 mins more, stirring often, until the veg is starting to soften.

STEP 2

Pour over the stock, add the rosemary, cover with a lid and cook over a low heat for 1 hr. Stir in the beans and cook for 30 mins more, topping up with water if necessary, until the lamb is tender and cooked through. Serve with some crusty bread or potatoes, if you like.

Thai prawn fried rice

Prep: 10 mins **Cook:** 10 mins

Serves 2

Ingredients

- 1 tbsp sunflower oil

- 1 red pepper , deseeded, quartered and cut into diagonal strips

- 5 spring onions , whites roughly chopped, greens finely chopped
- 100g broccoli , cut into small florets
- 2 tbsp green curry paste
- about 200g pack raw king prawns , thawed if frozen
- 250g pack pre-steamed coconut basmati rice (we used Tilda)
- 100g frozen pea
- 100g beansprout
- handful chopped basil
- fish sauce , to taste

Method

STEP 1

Heat the oil in a wok and stir-fry the pepper, whites of the onions, and broccoli for a few mins to soften. Stir in the curry paste and prawns, and cook for 1 min more.

STEP 2

Add a splash of water, then crumble in the coconut rice, breaking it up with a spoon. Tip in the peas, beansprouts and greens of the onions, and stir-fry until everything has heated through, then add the basil and fish sauce to taste.

All-in-one fish supper

Prep: 15 mins **Cook:** 25 mins

Serves 2

Ingredients

- 2 slices prosciutto or similar
- 3 tbsp olive oil
- 2 red peppers , thinly sliced
- 2 red onions , thinly sliced
- 2 garlic cloves , thinly sliced
- 280g jar artichoke hearts , drained
- handful black olives
- ½ tsp chilli paste or powder
- splash of white wine
- 4 fish fillets, such as bass or bream

Method

STEP 1

Tear each slice of prosciutto in half. Heat a little oil in a large frying pan, add the prosciutto, cook quickly until crisp, then remove. Add the remaining oil to the pan and heat through. Add the peppers, onions and garlic and cook gently, stirring from time to time, for about 10 mins or until softened.

STEP 2

Add the artichoke hearts, olives, chilli and wine, then season and cook for a couple of mins. Season the fish and lay it on top of the vegetables. Cover the pan tightly with a lid or foil and cook for 5-6 mins until the fish is cooked through. Scatter with prosciutto and serve with crusty bread.

Sweet & sour tofu

Prep: 10 mins **Cook:** 15 mins

Serves 1

Ingredients

- 1 tbsp rapeseed or vegetable oil
- 75g extra-firm tofu , cut into 2cm chunks
- ½ onion , cut into thin wedges
- ½ red pepper , chopped into chunks
- 1 large garlic clove , finely sliced

- 80g fresh pineapple chunks
- 1 tbsp low-salt ketchup
- 1 tbsp rice wine vinegar
- ½ tbsp dark soy sauce
- cooked basmati rice , to serve
- sesame seeds , to serve

Method

STEP 1

Heat half the oil in a non-stick frying pan over a medium heat. Add the tofu and fry for 5 mins, turning regularly, until golden brown on all sides. Remove to a plate with a slotted spoon and set aside.

STEP 2

Heat the remaining oil in the pan over a high heat. Fry the onion, pepper and garlic for 5-6 mins, or until the veg begins to soften. Add the pineapple, ketchup, vinegar, soy sauce and 50ml water, and simmer for 1 min, or until slightly reduced. Stir the tofu back into the pan.

STEP 3

Cook the basmati rice following pack instructions. Serve the tofu in bowls with the rice and a sprinkling of sesame seeds.

Leek & freekeh pilaf with feta & toasted pine nuts

Prep: 5 mins **Cook:** 40 mins

Serves 2

Ingredients

- 400g leeks
- 3 tbsp olive oil
- 200g freekeh
- 50ml white wine
- 400ml vegetable stock
- a few thyme sprigs

- 2 plump garlic cloves , sliced
- 3 tbsp pine nuts
- 100g feta
- 2 tbsp finely chopped mint
- juice and zest 1 lemon

Method

STEP 1

Finely slice the leeks, keeping all the dark green tops. Put in a colander and rinse well under running water, then set aside to drain.

STEP 2

Put a large heavy-based pan on the hob over a moderate heat, pour in 2 tbsp of the oil and tip in the leeks. Stir well and cover with a lid. Cook the leeks for 10–15 mins, stirring occasionally, until they are very soft.

STEP 3

While the leeks cook, soak the freekeh in a bowl for 5 mins in plenty of cold water. Tip it into a sieve and rinse under running cold water, then drain well.

STEP 4

Add the freekeh to the leeks along with the wine, stock and thyme and bring to a simmer. Cook the freekeh over a low heat, stirring from time to time, for 20-25 mins. Switch off the heat and let the contents of the pan stand while you prepare the feta and pine nuts.

STEP 5

Heat the remaining tbsp oil in a frying pan until hot, add the garlic and pine nuts, and cook until both the nuts and the garlic are lightly browned. Crumble the feta and toss this along with the garlic-nut mix, the mint and lemon juice and zest into the freekeh. Taste and correct the seasoning, then serve at room temperature.

Amatriciana chicken traybake

Prep: 15 mins **Cook:** 1 hr

Serves 4

Ingredients

- 1 long red chilli
- 3 tbsp tomato purée
- 3 tbsp olive oil
- 3 garlic cloves
- 8 skinless chicken thighs
- 500g new potato
- 4 thyme sprigs

- 140g cubetti di pancetta (or smoked bacon lardons)
- 400g tomato, half cherry or baby plum, the rest is up to you - any larger ones halved
- green salad and bread, to serve (optional)

Method

STEP 1

Heat oven to 200C/180C fan/gas 6. Find a large roasting tin that will hold the chicken thighs and potatoes in a single layer. Halve the chilli, scrape out and discard the seeds if you don't like it too hot, and remove the stalk. Put in a small food processor or mini chopper with the tomato purée, olive oil and garlic. Whizz to a paste, then spread over the chicken. Add the chicken and potatoes to the tin with a good grinding of black pepper and some salt, then mix everything together well with your hands. Add the thyme and roast for 30 mins.

STEP 2

Stir in the pancetta and roast for 15 mins more, then add the tomatoes and roast for another 15 mins until the tomatoes have softened and the chicken is cooked. Serve straight from the pan and eat with a green salad and some bread, if you like, for mopping up the juices.

Easy chicken pie

Prep: 10 mins **Cook:** 35 mins

Serves 4

Ingredients

- 1 onion, sliced
- 400g pack skinless chicken thighs, cut into chunks
- 1 tbsp vegetable oil
- 150ml chicken stock
- 325g can sweetcorn, drained
- 6 tbsp crème fraîche
- handful parsley or basil leaves, chopped
- 750g potatoes, cut into chunks

Method

STEP 1

Heat oven to 180C/160C fan/gas 4. Heat the oil in a large saucepan then add the onion and chicken. Fry for 5-10 mins until the onion is soft and the chicken is golden. Pour over the stock, bring to the boil, then simmer for 20 mins until the chicken is cooked. Stir in the corn, then 3 tbsp crème fraîche and the herbs.

STEP 2

Meanwhile, boil potatoes until soft. Drain and mash with remaining crème fraîche. Spoon the chicken mix into 4 pie dishes and top with mash. Place on a baking tray, then bake until potato is golden.

Sausage & mushroom pot pies

Prep:12 mins **Cook:**40 mins

Serves 2

Ingredients

- 2 tsp olive oil
- 1 small onion , chopped
- 6 pork sausages
- 250g chestnut mushroom , halved
- 1 tbsp wholegrain mustard
- 4 tbsp low-fat crème fraîche
- small bunch parsley , chopped
- 85g ciabatta , torn into small chunks

Method

STEP 1

Heat half the oil in a large frying pan. Add the onion and cook for 5 mins until softened, then push to one side. Squeeze the meat from the sausages and roll into balls. Add to the pan and fry for 5 mins until golden. Add the mushrooms and cook for 5 mins more until softened.

STEP 2

Season, then stir in the mustard, crème fraîche and 4 tbsp water. Bubble for 2 mins, then remove from the heat and scatter in the parsley.

STEP 3

Heat oven to 200C/180C fan/gas 6. Transfer sausage mixture to 2 small pie dishes or 1 large baking dish. Toss the ciabatta in the remaining oil, scatter over the top of the pies and bake for 20 mins until golden and bubbling.

Easy chicken tagine

Prep:10 mins **Cook:**40 mins

Serves 4

Ingredients

- 2 tbsp olive oil
- 8 skinless boneless chicken thighs, halved if large
- 1 onion, chopped
- 2 tsp grated fresh root ginger
- pinch saffron or tumeric
- 1 tbsp honey
- 400g carrot, cut into sticks
- small bunch parsley, roughly chopped
- lemon wedges, to serve

Method

STEP 1

Heat the oil in a large, wide pan with a lid, add the chicken, then fry quickly until lightly coloured. Add the onion and ginger, then fry for a further 2 mins.

STEP 2

Add 150ml water, the saffron, honey and carrots, season, then stir well. Bring to the boil, cover tightly, then simmer for 30 mins until the chicken is tender. Uncover and increase the heat for about 5 mins to reduce the sauce a little. Sprinkle with parsley and serve with lemon wedges for squeezing over.

One-pan jerk roast chicken

Prep:30 mins **Cook:**2 hrs and 10 mins

Serves 4 - 6

Ingredients

- 1 ½kg whole chicken
- 2 red onions , halved, then cut into wedges, leaving the root intact
- 2 red peppers , deseeded and chopped into chunks
- 4 sweet potatoes , peeled and cut into chunks
- 400g can black beans , drained and rinsed
- 400ml coconut milk
- cooked rice , to serve
- flatbreads , to serve
- For the jerk paste
- 1 red onion , chopped into large chunks

- 5 garlic cloves , peeled
- 1 scotch bonnet chilli, deseeded
- 3 fat green chillies , deseeded
- bunch coriander , stalks roughly chopped, and leaves reserved, to serve
- large bunch thyme , leaves picked
- zest and juice 2 limes (save the juiced halves for the chicken)
- 1 tbsp honey
- 2 tbsp olive or rapeseed oil , plus a drizzle
- ½ nutmeg , grated
- 1 tsp ground allspice

Method

STEP 1

First make the jerk paste. Put all the ingredients in a food processor, add a good pinch of salt and blend to a fine purée, adding a splash of water if the mixture is struggling to break down. Tie the legs together if you like, and put in a large flameproof roasting tin. Pour over the jerk paste and rub all over and inside the chicken. Stuff the cavity with the juiced lime halves and cover the tray with foil. Chill for up to 48 hrs or a minimum of 2 hrs.

STEP 2

Heat oven to 200C/180C fan/gas 6. Cook the chicken for 45 mins.

STEP 3

Take the chicken out the oven, remove the foil and carefully lift it onto a plate, pouring any juice from the cavity into the tin. Tip the onions, peppers and sweet potatoes into the tin, and season well, then toss in the tray to coat in any residual jerk paste. Put the chicken on top of the veggies and drizzle it with a little oil. Lower the oven to 180C/160C fan/gas 4 and return the roasting tin to the middle shelf, uncovered. Roast for a further 45 mins or until the vegetables are soft and the chicken is cooked through – if you have a meat thermometer, check that the temperature has reached 75C. Carefully remove the chicken from the tin, place on a plate and wrap in foil, then leave to rest.

STEP 4

Place the roasting tin on the hob over a medium heat. Stir in the beans and coconut milk, scraping the bottom of the tin to lift off any tasty bits. Simmer until the sauce has thickened a little, then season to taste. If the sauce looks oily, skim the fat off the surface with a spoon. Put the chicken back in the pan and scatter over the coriander leaves before taking to the table. Serve with rice and flatbreads for mopping up the sauce.

Cumin roast veg with tahini dressing

Prep: 10 mins **Cook:** 45 mins - 50 mins

Serves 4

Ingredients

- 3 large carrots , roughly chopped
- 3 peeled raw beetroots , roughly chopped
- 1 sweet potato , sliced
- 3 red onions , cut into wedges
- 250g cauliflower florets
- 1 tsp cumin seeds
- 2 tbsp rapeseed oil
- 1 tbsp balsamic vinegar
- 2-3 tbsp chopped mint
- 2-3 tbsp chopped coriander
- 400g can chickpeas
- 2 hard-boiled eggs , halved
- 100g young spinach leaves

For the dressing

- 3 tbsp tahini
- 1 tbsp crunchy peanut butter
- 1 lemon , zested and juiced
- 1 tsp ground coriander
- 1 garlic clove , finely grated

Method

STEP 1

Heat oven to 200C/180C fan/gas 6. Tip all of the vegetables into a large roasting tin. Add the cumin seeds, oil and balsamic vinegar, then toss together. Roast for 45-50 mins until the veg is tender and starting to char.

STEP 2

Meanwhile, mix the tahini and peanut butter with the lemon juice, coriander, garlic and about 4-5 tbsp water to make a dressing.

STEP 3

When the veg is ready, leave to cool a little. Add the mint, coriander, lemon zest and chickpeas, then toss well.

STEP 4

If you're following our Healthy Diet Plan, serve two portions now with the eggs, some dressing and half the spinach, then serve the remainder on another day without the eggs.

Braised pork belly with borlotti beans

Prep:20 mins **Cook:**1 hr and 40 mins

Serves 4

Ingredients

- 800g skinless, boneless pork belly, cut into large chunks, or 800g pork belly slices
- 1 tbsp plain flour
- 2 tbsp olive oil
- 1 large onion, finely chopped
- 2 carrots, finely chopped
- 2 celery sticks, finely chopped, any leaves reserved and chopped, to serve
- 1 rosemary sprig
- 2 bay leaves
- 2 garlic cloves, roughly chopped
- 1 tbsp tomato purée
- 200ml white wine

- 500ml chicken stock
- 2 x 400g cans borlotti beans, drained
- large handful of parsley, leaves picked and finely chopped, to serve
- 1 lemon, zested, to serve

Method

STEP 1

Heat the oven to 160C/140C fan/gas 3. Toss the pork in the flour with some seasoning. Heat the oil in an ovenproof casserole dish and fry the pork for 10 mins until golden, then transfer to a plate. Tip all the veg into the pan with the rosemary, bay leaves and garlic, and cook on a low heat for 10 mins until softened. Stir in the tomato purée and cook for a minute, then add the wine. Pour over the stock, then bring to a simmer and stir in the fried pork.

STEP 2

Cover, then cook in the oven for 1 hr. Remove from the oven, stir through the beans, cover again and return to the oven for 30 mins, or until the pork is very tender. Leave to cool a little, then scatter over the parsley, lemon zest and reserved celery leaves.

Green burgers

Prep:30 mins **Cook:**20 mins

makes 8 (4 for now, 4 for the freezer)

Ingredients

- 2 tbsp olive oil
- 2 onions , finely chopped
- 250g bag spinach
- 5 slices white bread , blitzed into breadcrumbs (or 150g dried breadcrumbs)
- good grating of fresh nutmeg
- 100g mature cheddar , grated
- 40g parmesan , finely grated
- 1-2 large eggs , beaten
- 3 tbsp plain flour

To serve

- 6 crusty bread rolls
- 4 ripe, juicy tomatoes , thickly sliced
- good-quality ketchup or other relish
- sweet potato fries (optional)

Method

STEP 1

Heat half the oil in a frying pan and gently fry the onions for about 10 mins until pale and soft, then leave to cool a little.

STEP 2

Finely chop the spinach in a food processor and tip into a bowl. Add the cooled onion, breadcrumbs, nutmeg, cheddar and Parmesan, and mash together. Add the beaten egg, a little at a time (you may not need all of it), until the mixture holds together. Divide into eight (see tip below) and shape into fat burgers.

STEP 3

Put the flour in a shallow bowl, season well and dip the burgers into the flour to coat. Store in a plastic container between layers of baking parchment. Either chill until ready to cook, or freeze.

STEP 4

Heat the remaining oil in the frying pan and fry for about 5 mins each side until browned all over. Serve in the crusty rolls, with a couple of slices of tomato, ketchup and sweet potato fries on the side, if you like.

Breakfast naans

Prep:5 mins **Cook:**5 mins

Serves 2

Ingredients

- 1 tbsp vegetable or sunflower oil
- 2 eggs
- 2 small naan breads
- 4 tbsp low-fat cream cheese
- 2 tbsp mango chutney

- 1 avocado , halved and sliced
- ½ lime , juiced
- 1 green chilli
- small handful coriander , leaves picked

Method

STEP 1

Heat oven to 200C/180C fan/gas 6. Heat the oil in a pan, then fry the eggs. Warm the naan breads in the oven while the eggs are cooking.

STEP 2

Spread the warm naans with the cream cheese, then drizzle with the chutney. Add a fried egg to each naan and top with the avocado, lime juice, chilli and coriander. Season and tuck in.

Crispy chicken with pancetta & butter beans

Prep: 5 mins **Cook:** 1 hr

Serves 6

Ingredients

- 1 tbsp olive oil
- 6 chicken legs
- 200g pack cubetti di pancetta
- 4 red onions , cut into wedges
- 2 garlic cloves , crushed
- 2 rosemary sprigs, leaves finely chopped, plus one extra whole sprig
- 250g red wine
- 250g chicken stock
- 2 x 400g/14oz cans cherry tomatoes
- 3 x 400g/14oz cans butter bean
- 2 tbsp sugar
- 1 bay leaf

Method

STEP 1

Heat oven to 190C/fan 170C/gas 5. Heat the oil in a large roasting tin, then brown the chicken legs in batches until golden and crisp. Remove from the tin and set aside.

STEP 2

Sizzle the pancetta cubes in the same tin. When they're just beginning to brown, add the onion, garlic and rosemary. Fry for a few mins, stirring, then pour in the wine and stock. Bring to the boil, then simmer for 10 mins until the onion wedges are starting to soften and the liquid has reduced. Tip in the cherry tomatoes, beans, sugar, bay leaf, remaining rosemary sprig and seasoning. Give everything a good stir, then bring back to a simmer.

STEP 3

Sit the chicken legs on top of the bean mixture and pour over any extra juices from the chicken. Bake for 40-45 mins until the chicken is cooked and crisp, the sauce is bubbling and the onions are soft.

Sticky ginger skillet parkin

Prep: 10 mins **Cook:** 50 mins

Serves 10-12

Ingredients

- 200g salted butter , chopped
- 85g light brown soft sugar
- 85g treacle
- 185g golden syrup
- 250g self-raising flour
- 2 tsp ground ginger
- 1 tsp mixed spice

- 100g porridge oats
- 2 large eggs
- 2 tbsp milk
- 2 balls stem ginger from a jar, chopped, plus 2 tbsp syrup from the jar, and extra to serve
- custard or ice cream, to serve (optional)

Method

STEP 1

Heat the oven to 150C/130C fan/gas 2. Put a heavy-bottomed 25cm ovenproof frying pan or skillet over a low heat and gently melt the butter, sugar, treacle and golden syrup together, stirring with a wooden spoon, until the butter is just melted and everything is combined. Remove from the heat and leave to cool slightly for 5-10 mins.

STEP 2

Sieve the flour and spices together, then mix in the oats. Whisk the eggs, milk, stem ginger and ginger syrup together in a bowl or jug. Stir the dry ingredients into the cooled butter mixture until well combined. Stir in the ginger, milk and egg mixture until you have a thick cake batter. Transfer to the oven and bake for 45-50 mins until firm and risen. Serve scooped from the pan with extra ginger syrup and custard or ice cream, if you like, or leave to cool and eat cold. *Will keep, wrapped in baking parchment, for up to seven days.*

Honeyed nut & pomegranate pots

Prep: 20 mins

Ingredients

- 85g shredded wheat , crushed
- 200g pistachio , chopped
- 100g honey
- juice ½ orange

- 300ml pot double cream
- ½ x 250g pot Greek yogurt
- 2 tsp rosewater
- 110g pot pomegranate seeds

Method

STEP 1

In a bowl, mix the crushed shredded wheat with the nuts, 50ml of the honey and the orange juice, then divide between 8 small glasses or teacups.

STEP 2

Whip the cream until very softly whipped, then fold in the yogurt, remaining honey and rose water. Divide this between the pots, too. Chill for at least 2 hrs, or up to 24 hrs. Before serving, top the pots with pomegranate seeds.

Mushroom & spinach risotto

Prep: 50 mins - 55 mins **Serves 2**

Ingredients

- 1 tbsp olive oil
- 25g butter
- 1 onion, chopped
- 140g chestnut mushrooms, sliced
- 1 fat garlic clove, crushed
- 140g arborio rice
- 150ml dry white wine
- 4 sundried tomatoes, chopped

- 500ml hot vegetable stock
- 2 tbsp chopped fresh parsley
- 25g parmesan or vegetarian alternative, freshly grated
- 100g fresh young leaf spinach, washed if necessary
- warm ciabatta and green salad, to serve

Method

STEP 1

Heat the oil and butter in a large deep frying pan. Add the onion and cook gently for 5 minutes until softened. Stir in the mushrooms and garlic and cook gently for 2-3 minutes.

STEP 2

Stir in the rice to coat with the onion and mushroom mixture. Pour in the wine and cook over a moderate heat for about 3 minutes, stirring from time to time, until the wine is absorbed.

STEP 3

Reduce to a gentle heat. Add the tomatoes and 125ml/ 4fl oz of the stock and cook for about 5 minutes until the liquid is absorbed. Pour in a further 125ml/4fl oz stock and continue cooking until absorbed. Repeat with the remaining stock, until it is all absorbed and the rice is creamy and tender.

STEP 4

Stir in the parsley and half the parmesan. Season to taste. Scatter the spinach over the risotto. Cover and cook gently for 4-5 minutes until the spinach has just wilted. Serve immediately sprinkled with the remaining parmesan.

Jacket potato with whipped feta & sumac

Prep:10 mins **Cook:**1 hr and 15 mins

Serves 1

Ingredients

- 1 baking potato
- 2 tsp olive oil
- ½ tsp garlic salt
- 50g feta
- 50g Greek yogurt

- 1 roasted red peppers from a jar (about 25g), finely chopped
- ½ tsp sumac
- few basil leaves , to serve (optional)

Method

STEP 1

Heat oven to 220C/200C fan/ gas 6. Prick the potato all over with a fork and bake for 1 hr until it is golden outside and soft inside. Mix 1 tsp olive oil with the garlic salt. Cut a deep cross into the top of the jacket, drizzle the garlic oil into the cross and rub it all over the outside. Return to the oven and bake for 15 mins more until the edges are golden and crispy.

STEP 2

Meanwhile, crumble the feta into a bowl, add the yogurt and whisk together until creamy. Stir in the red pepper with a good grind of black pepper and spoon the whipped feta into the jacket. Sprinkle with the sumac, drizzle over the remaining 1 tsp olive oil and scatter a few torn basil leaves on top, if you like.

Easy ratatouille with poached eggs

Prep: 15 mins **Cook:** 50 mins

Serves 4

Ingredients

- 1 tbsp olive oil
- 1 large onion , chopped
- 1 red or orange pepper , deseeded and thinly sliced
- 2 garlic cloves , finely chopped
- 1 tbsp chopped rosemary

- 1 aubergine , diced
- 2 courgettes , diced
- 400g can chopped tomatoes
- 1 tsp balsamic vinegar
- 4 large eggs
- handful basil leaves

Method

STEP 1

Heat the oil in a large frying pan. Add the onion, pepper, garlic and rosemary, then cook for 5 mins, stirring frequently, until the onion has softened. Add the aubergine and courgettes, then cook for 2 mins more.

STEP 2

Add the tomatoes, then fill the can with water, swirl it around and tip into the pan. Bring to the boil, cover, then simmer for 40 mins, uncovering after 20 mins, until reduced and pulpy.

STEP 3

Stir the vinegar into the ratatouille, then make 4 spaces for the eggs. Crack an egg into each hole and season with black pepper. Cover, then cook for 2-5 mins until set as softly or firmly as you like. Scatter over the basil and serve with some crusty bread to mop up the juices.

Burrito bowl with chipotle black beans

Prep: 15 mins **Cook:** 15 mins

Serves 2

Ingredients

- 125g basmati rice
- 1 tbsp olive oil
- 2 garlic cloves, chopped
- 400g can black beans, drained and rinsed
- 1 tbsp cider vinegar

- 1 tsp honey
- 1 tbsp chipotle paste
- 100g chopped curly kale
- 1 avocado, halved and sliced
- 1 medium tomato, chopped
- 1 small red onion, chopped

To serve (optional)

- chipotle hot sauce
- coriander leaves

- lime wedges

Method

STEP 1

Cook the rice following pack instructions, then drain and return to the pan to keep warm. In a frying pan, heat the oil, add the garlic and fry for 2 mins or until golden. Add the beans, vinegar, honey and chipotle. Season and warm through for 2 mins.

STEP 2

Boil the kale for 1 min, then drain, squeezing out any excess water. Divide the rice between big shallow bowls and top with the beans, kale, avocado, tomato and onion. Serve with hot sauce, coriander and lime wedges, if you like.

Golden amaretti Christmas cake

Prep: 30 mins **Cook:** 3 hrs

Serves 15 - 20

Ingredients

- To make the cake

- 1 large orange

84

- 175g dried apricot
- 700g mixed dried fruit
- 120ml sweet marsala (or sweet cream sherry), plus extra for feeding the cake
- 250g unsalted butter , softened
- 250g bag crisp amaretti biscuits

- 150g light soft brown sugar
- 4 large eggs , at room temperature
- 125g plain flour
- ½ tsp baking powder
- 1 tsp mixed spice
- 50g toasted flaked almonds

To decorate

- 1 tbsp apricot cake glaze
- 125g royal icing sugar , plus extra for dusting
- 750g natural marzipan
- gold cake spray

- handful whole blanched almonds
- 50g crisp amaretti biscuits
- sugar balls, snowflakes or Christmassy sprinkles

Method

STEP 1

Grate the zest from the orange and squeeze the juice (about 120ml/1 cup) into a large bowl. Snip the apricots into small pieces with scissors, then add the dried fruit and the marsala. Cover with cling film and leave to soak overnight.

STEP 2

The next day, rub a little of the butter around the inside of a 20cm round, deep cake tin, then line the base and sides with a double layer of parchment. Heat oven to 160C/140C fan/gas 3.

STEP 3

Put 200g of the biscuits in a large food bag, squish out the air, then bash the biscuits to fine crumbs. It doesn't matter if there are a few nuggets left.

STEP 4

Put the remaining butter and the sugar into a large bowl and beat with an electric mixer for 2 mins or until paler and creamy.

STEP 5

Mix in the eggs, one by one. Sift in the flour, baking powder, mixed spice and 1 /4 tsp salt. Tip in the crumbs and beat together for a few seconds until evenly mixed.

STEP 6

Fold in the soaked fruit and almonds with a spatula.

STEP 7

Scrape the cake mixture into the prepared tin. Level the top and make a saucer-sized dimple in the middle of the batter. This will help your cake to rise evenly.

STEP 8

Bake for 2 hrs, then turn the oven down to 140C/fan 120C/ gas 1. Cover the cake with foil and bake for another 1 hr 30 mins or until risen and dark golden brown.

STEP 9

Check the cake is cooked by inserting a cocktail stick into the middle. It will come out dry when the cake is ready. Set on a cooling rack and leave for a few hours.

STEP 10

Using the cocktail stick, poke deep holes all over the cake. Slowly drizzle 2 tbsp marsala or sherry over the cake.

STEP 11

When completely cold, wrap the cake in clean baking parchment and store in a tin in a cool, dark place. Feed it every seven to 10 days until you are ready to decorate it.

STEP 12

Unwrap the cake and put it on a flat plate or board (25cm or bigger). Brush a thin layer of apricot glaze over the cake.

STEP 13

Sift a little of the royal icing sugar onto your work surface. Unwrap the marzipan and knead it with your hands until it feels softer.

STEP 14

Sprinkle the marzipan with more sugar and roll it to an even circle about 35cm across.

STEP 15

Lift the marzipan over the cake, smooth it down to the board, then trim with a knife. Don't cut too close to the cake at first. You can smooth the icing with a jam jar or tumbler, then trim again if you need to

STEP 16

Spray the marzipan lightly with the gold spray. Spread the almonds out onto some baking parchment and spray these heavily.

STEP 17

Break four of the remaining 50g biscuits into nuggets using your fingers.

STEP 18

Mix the royal icing sugar with 4 tsp cold water. It should be thick but run very slowly when you drop it from the spoon. Spoon it over the cake and spread it to the edges, letting it drip here and there. Use a palette knife to help.

STEP 19

Put the whole biscuits on the cake first, then add the broken biscuits and the almonds in-between.

STEP 20

Put 1 tsp icing sugar in a fine sieve and shake a snowy dusting over the cake. Scatter the cake with the sugar balls, snowflakes or sprinkles, then leave the icing to set.

Healthy veg patch hummus

Prep:20 mins **Serves 6**

Ingredients

- 1 x 400g can chickpeas , drained and rinsed
- ½ lemon , juiced
- 1 garlic clove , crushed
- 2 tbsp olive oil
- 2 tbsp tahini
- 250g baby carrots
- 1 pot of parsley

Method

STEP 1

Put the chickpeas, lemon juice, garlic, olive oil and tahini into a food processor and blitz to a smooth consistency. Loosen with 1–2 tbsp water if it seems a little thick.

STEP 2

Make a hole in the top of each carrot with a skewer or by cutting a small hole with the tip of a sharp knife. Dab a small amount of hummus into the hole and push in a small sprig of parsley.

STEP 3

Spoon the hummus into thoroughly cleaned small, plant pots or bowls and push in the carrots. Let the children dunk into the hummus with the carrots.

Bulgur & quinoa lunch bowls

Prep:5 mins **Cook:**15 mins

Serves 4 (makes 2 of each flavour)

Ingredients

For the bulgur base

- 1 large onion , very finely chopped
- 150g bulgur and quinoa (this comes ready mixed)
- 2sprigs of thyme
- 2 tsp vegetable bouillon powder

For the avocado topping

- 1 avocado , halved, destoned and chopped
- 2 tomatoes , cut into wedges
- 4 tbsp chopped basil
- 6 Kalamata olives , halved
- 2 tsp extra virgin olive oil
- 2 tsp cider vinegar
- 2 big handfuls of rocket

For the beetroot topping

- 210g can chickpeas , drained
- 160g cooked beetroot , diced
- 2 tomatoes , cut into wedges
- 2 tbsp chopped mint
- 1 tsp cumin seeds
- several pinches of ground cinnamon
- 2 tsp extra virgin olive oil
- 2 tsp cider vinegar

- 1 orange , cut into segments
- 2 tbsp toasted pine nuts

Method

STEP 1

Tip the onion and bulgur mix into a pan, pour over 600ml water and stir in the thyme and bouillon. Cook, covered, over a low heat for 15 mins, then leave to stand for 10 mins. All the liquid should now be absorbed. When cool, remove the thyme and divide the bulgur between four bowls or plastic containers.

STEP 2

For the avocado topping, toss all the ingredients together except for the rocket. Pile onto two portions of the bulgur and top with the rocket.

STEP 3

For the beetroot topping, first pile the chickpeas on top, then toss the beetroot with the tomato, mint, cumin, a good pinch of cinnamon, the oil and vinegar. Toss well, add the orange, then pile onto the remaining portions of bulghur, scatter with the pine nuts and sprinkle with extra cinnamon. Chill in the fridge until needed.

Goan-style vegetable curry with kitchari

Prep: 10 mins **Cook:** 40 mins

Serves 4

Ingredients

For the kitchari

- 225g brown basmati rice
- 1 tsp rapeseed oil
- 1 tsp ground coriander
- 390g can green lentils , drained

For the curry

- 1 tbsp rapeseed oil
- 2 large onions (330g), 1 finely chopped, 1 sliced
- 2 red chillies , deseeded and sliced
- 25g ginger , finely chopped
- 1 tsp ground turmeric
- 1 tsp smoked paprika
- 1 tsp ground cumin
- 3 tsp ground coriander
- 3 garlic cloves , chopped

- 1 tbsp vegetable bouillon powder (check it's vegan if you need it to be), made up with 500ml boiling water
- 360g cauliflower florets (about 1/4 cauliflower)
- 1 ½ tsp tamarind

- 320g fine beans , trimmed and halved if large
- 4 large tomatoes , cut into wedges
- 2 large courgettes (320g), halved lengthways and thickly sliced
- 100g coconut yogurt
- ½ x 30g pack fresh coriander , chopped, to serve

Method

STEP 1

Boil the rice in a pan of water for 25 mins until tender, then drain.

STEP 2

Meanwhile, make the curry. Heat the oil in a large pan and fry the onions, chillies and ginger for 8-10 mins until softened. Add the spices and garlic, stir briefly, then pour in the bouillon and stir in the cauliflower. Cover and simmer for 5 mins.

STEP 3

Stir in the tamarind with the beans, tomatoes and courgettes, then cover the pan and cook for 10-15 mins more until the veg are tender, but still retain a little bite. Remove the lid for the last 5 mins to reduce the sauce a little. Remove from the heat and stir in the yogurt and half the fresh coriander.

STEP 4

Meanwhile, for the kitchari, heat the oil in a non-stick pan and add the ground coriander. Warm briefly, then tip in the rice and drained lentils. Warm through for 1 min, then stir through the remaining fresh coriander.

STEP 5

If you're following our Healthy Diet Plan, serve half the curry and rice now, then chill the rest to eat another night (cool the rice quickly on a wide tray, then chill immediately). Reheat the rice and curry in the microwave or on the hob. You may need to add a drop of water to the rice to stop it sticking.

All-in-one spring roast chicken

Prep:15 mins **Cook:**1 hr and 25 mins

Serves 4 - 5

Ingredients

- 1 free-range chicken , about 1.6kg/3lb 8oz
- 50g/ 2oz butter , softened
- 500g bag new potato
- 1 tbsp olive oil
- 150g pack baby carrot , scrubbed or peeled

- 140g/ 5oz podded broad bean , podded again if you like
- 100g/ 4oz frozen pea , defrosted
- good handful roughly-chopped mixed herbs (mint, tarragon, parsley, chervil and chives are all nice)

Method

STEP 1

Heat oven to 200C/180C fan/gas 6. Sit the chicken in a good-sized roasting dish or tin. Push your fingers between the breast and skin to separate, push in some of the softened butter and gently spread over the breasts without tearing the skin. Rub the rest of the butter all over the outside of the chicken. Season well and roast for 30 mins.

STEP 2

Toss the new potatoes with the olive oil and plenty of seasoning. When the chicken comes out, scatter the spuds around it and toss with the juices in the dish, too. Put back in the oven for another 30 mins.

STEP 3

Stir the carrots into the potatoes and put back into the oven for another 20 mins.

STEP 4

Check the chicken is cooked by piercing the thigh and making sure the juices run clear. Stir the broad beans and peas into the other veg with a splash of water and put back in the oven for 5 mins. Remove from the oven, cover loosely with foil and rest for 10 mins. Scatter over and stir in the herbs before serving.

All-in-one chunky winter broth

Cook:20 mins **Serves 4**

Ingredients

- 2 x 400g/14oz cans chopped tomatoes
- 2litres/3½ pints vegetable stock
- 4 carrots , peeled and sliced
- 2 x 420g/15oz cans mixed beans , drained and rinsed
- 175g spinach
- 1 tbsp roasted red pepper pesto

Method

STEP 1

Tip the canned tomatoes into a saucepan along with the stock, bring to the boil, then turn down the heat and throw in the carrots. Gently simmer the soup until the carrots are cooked, about 15 minutes.

STEP 2

Stir in the pulses and spinach and heat until the spinach has wilted. Spoon in the pesto and gently mix into the soup. Serve with some crusty bread.

Ginger chicken & green bean noodles

Prep:10 mins **Cook:**15 mins

Serves 2

Ingredients

- ½ tbsp vegetable oil
- 2 skinless chicken breasts, sliced
- 200g green beans , trimmed and halved crosswise
- thumb-sized piece of ginger , peeled and cut into matchsticks
- 2 garlic cloves , sliced
- 1 ball stem ginger , finely sliced, plus 1 tsp syrup from the jar
- 1 tsp cornflour , mixed with 1 tbsp water
- 1 tsp dark soy sauce , plus extra to serve (optional)
- 2 tsp rice vinegar
- 200g cooked egg noodles

Method

STEP 1

Heat the oil in a wok over a high heat and stir-fry the chicken for 5 mins. Add the green beans and stir-fry for 4-5 mins more until the green beans are just tender, and the chicken is just cooked through.

STEP 2

Stir in the fresh ginger and garlic, and stir-fry for 2 mins, then add the stem ginger and syrup, the cornflour mix, soy sauce and vinegar. Stir-fry for 1 min, then toss in the noodles. Cook until everything is hot and the sauce coats the noodles. Drizzle with more soy, if you like, and serve.

Potted salmon rillette

Prep: 10 mins plus 2 hrs chilling, no cook

Serves 4

Ingredients

- 100g cream cheese
- 100g crème fraîche , soured cream, double or whipping cream – or a mixture of all your leftovers
- 100g smoked salmon trimmings, half diced, plus extra to decorate (optional)

- 2-3 tsp creamed horseradish
- lemon wedge
- few dill sprigs, to decorate (optional)
- melba toast , crackers or toasted rye bread, and a few leaves, to serve

Method

STEP 1

Put the cream cheese, the leftover creams, 50g salmon, 2 tsp horseradish and a small squeeze of lemon juice in a food processor or blender. Whizz until smooth, then scrape into a mixing bowl. Fold in the remaining salmon, then taste – add another tsp horseradish if you like, plus seasoning if needed. Divide the mixture between 4 small ramekins and chill for at least 2 hrs.

Before serving, decorate the rillettes with a spiral of salmon or a few dill sprigs, if you like. Add a pot to a plate with a few leaves and some crunchy Melba toast, or similar, and serve.

Chicken & sweet potato curry

Prep: 10 mins **Cook:** 45 mins

Serves 4

Ingredients

- 1 tbsp sunflower oil
- 1 onion, chopped
- 450g boneless, skinless chicken thigh, cut into bite-sized pieces
- 165g jar korma paste
- 2 garlic cloves, crushed

- 500g sweet potato, cut into small chunks
- 400g can chopped tomato
- 100g baby spinach
- basmati rice, to serve

Method

STEP 1

Heat the oil in a pan, add the onion and cook over a low heat for about 5 mins until softened. Increase the heat slightly, add the chicken pieces and brown.

STEP 2

Stir in the curry paste and garlic, cooking for 2 mins before adding 100ml water, the sweet potatoes and chopped tomatoes. Simmer for 20-30 mins until the chicken is cooked through and the sweet potato is tender – add a splash more water if it starts to look dry. Season to taste and add the spinach, removing the pan from the heat and stirring until the spinach has wilted. Serve with basmati rice.

Smoked salmon, quinoa & dill lunch pot

Prep: 15 mins No cook

Serves 2

Ingredients

- 2 tbsp half-fat soured cream
- 2 tbsp lemon juice
- ½ pack dill , finely chopped
- 250g pouch ready-to-eat quinoa (we used Merchant Gourmet)
- ½ cucumber , halved and sliced
- 4 radishes , finely sliced
- 100g smoked salmon , torn into strips

Method

STEP 1

First, make the dressing. Mix the soured cream and lemon juice together in a bowl, then add most of the dill, reserving a quarter for serving.

STEP 2

In another bowl, combine the quinoa with the cucumber and radishes, and stir through half the dressing. Season and top with the salmon and the rest of the dill.

STEP 3

Put the other half of the dressing in a small pot and drizzle over the quinoa just before serving.

Spanish chicken

Prep: 15 mins **Cook:** 45 mins

Serves 4

Ingredients

- 8 chicken thighs , skin on and bone in
- 3 onions , thinly sliced
- 2 tsp paprika
- zest and juice 1 lemon
- good handful parsley , roughly chopped
- 150ml stock
- 1 tbsp olive oil

Method

STEP 1

Heat oven to 190C/170C fan/gas 5. Put all the ingredients into a large, wide ovenproof dish. Mix everything together with your hands and season.

STEP 2

Bake for 45 mins, stirring the onions after 20 mins, until the chicken is golden and the onions tender. Serve with rice.

Chicken bhuna

Prep: 15 mins **Cook:** 50 mins

Serves 6

Ingredients

- 3 medium onions, 2 finely chopped, 1 roughly chopped
- 100ml vegetable oil
- 1 tbsp ginger and garlic purée
- 1 tbsp mild curry powder
- 1 tsp turmeric
- 1 tsp chilli powder
- 800g chicken thighs, diced
- 100ml natural yogurt
- 4 tbsp tomato purée
- 2 tsp garam masala

Method

STEP 1

To make the onion purée, bring a small pan of water to the boil and add half the roughly chopped onion. Boil until soft (about 10 mins), drain and puree with a hand blender or mini food processor.

STEP 2

Heat a large saucepan on a high heat. Once it's hot add the oil and finely chopped onions and reduce to a low heat. Cook the onions slowly and gently until golden brown in colour, and season.

STEP 3

Add the ginger and garlic purée, curry powder, turmeric, chilli powder and a splash of water to the pan of onions and stir in well. Fry for a couple of mins. Add the diced chicken thighs and stir in well.

STEP 4

Mix the yogurt, tomato purée and onion purée together in a jug with 300ml water. Pour into the saucepan and mix well. Turn up the heat until the sauce begins to boil. Simmer for 15 to 20 mins, stirring occasionally.

STEP 5

Finally, sprinkle in the garam masala and stir in well for the final 2 mins before serving.

Sea trout with samphire, potted shrimp & lemon

Prep:10 mins **Cook:**25 mins

Serves 2

Ingredients

- 350g Jersey Royal potato or small Charlotte potatoes - larger ones halved lengthways
- 2 sea trout or salmon fillets, skin on but scales removed
- pinch of cayenne pepper
- 1 tsp sunflower or vegetable oil
- 85g samphire , well washed
- 25g unsalted butter
- 1 tbsp finely chopped shallot
- 4 tbsp white wine (I used white Burgundy)
- 57g tub potted shrimp (see tip, below)
- 1 tarragon sprig, chopped
- juice 1 lemon

Method

STEP 1

Steam the potatoes for 15-20 mins, either using a steamer basket or a simple metal colander over a pan of boiling water, with a lid on top. Put 3 plates in a low oven to warm.

STEP 2

Slash the fish skin a few times, then season generously and sprinkle with the cayenne. Put a heavy-based frying pan over a medium heat, adding the oil once the pan is hot. Cook the fish, skin-side down, for 6 mins, until the skin is golden and crisp. Avoid the urge to move it about.

STEP 3

Season the fish on the upper side, then carefully turn the fillets using a fish slice or spatula. Cook for 2 mins more until the fish has changed from dark to pale pink all over, with a little blush remaining in the thickest part. Transfer to a warm plate. Wipe out the pan with kitchen paper.

STEP 4

Scatter the samphire over the cooked potatoes, return the lid and steam for 2-3 mins until just tender.

STEP 5

Melt the butter in the frying pan and sizzle the shallot for 1 min. Splash in the wine, boil to reduce by half, then add the shrimps, tarragon and lemon juice to taste. Swirl the pan off the heat to melt the potted shrimp butter and make a buttery sauce, then season to taste. Spoon the veg onto warm plates, drizzle with a little sauce, then top with the fish, the rest of the sauce and the shrimps.

Slow cooker vegetable curry

Prep: 10 mins **Cook:** 6 hrs

Serves 2

Ingredients

- 400ml can light coconut milk
- 3 tbsp mild curry paste
- 2 tsp vegetable bouillon powder
- 1 red chilli, deseeded and sliced
- 1 tbsp finely chopped ginger
- 3 garlic cloves, sliced
- 200g butternut squash (peeled weight), cut into chunks
- 1 red pepper, deseeded and sliced
- 1 small aubergine (about 250g), halved and thickly sliced
- 15g coriander, chopped
- 160g frozen peas, defrosted
- 1 lime, juiced, to taste
- wholemeal flatbread, to serve

Method

STEP 1

Put the coconut milk, curry paste, bouillon powder, chilli, ginger, garlic, butternut squash, pepper and aubergine into the slow cooker pot and stir well. Cover with the lid and chill overnight.

STEP 2

Cook on low for 6 hrs until the vegetables are really tender, then stir in the coriander and defrosted peas. The heat of the curry should be enough to warm them through. Taste and add a good squeeze of lime juice, if you fancy extra zing. Serve with a wholemeal flatbread.

Salted caramel choc pots

Prep: 30 mins **Cook:** 5 mins

Makes 2

Ingredients

- 4 tbsp dulce de leche or canned caramel (we used Carnation)
- ½ tsp sea salt , plus extra to serve
- 85g each milk and dark chocolate , broken into squares
- 1-2 long, thin, plain grissini
- 2 tbsp demerara sugar
- 100ml double cream , at room temperature
- 50ml milk

Method

STEP 1

Mix the caramel with the salt, divide between 2 small glasses and chill.

STEP 2

Melt the chocolates together in a glass bowl set over a pan of barely simmering water. Snap the grissini into short lengths, then dip each end into the chocolate to coat a little. Sit on a wire rack for the chocolate to drip and set a little, then dip the chocolate ends into the sugar to coat. Sit in an airtight container lined with baking parchment and chill to set until ready to serve.

STEP 3

Stir the double cream and milk into the remaining melted chocolate until smooth, then scrape into a jug. Slowly pour on top of the caramel, around the edges first. Chill the pots for at least 2 hrs, or up to 24 hrs.

STEP 4

To serve, scatter a little more sea salt on top of each pot, then add one or two sugar-tipped grissini.

Mushroom brunch

Prep: 5 mins **Cook:** 12 mins - 15 mins

Serves 4

Ingredients

- 250g mushrooms
- 1 garlic clove
- 1 tbsp olive oil

- 160g bag kale
- 4 eggs

Method

STEP 1

Slice the mushrooms and crush the garlic clove. Heat the olive oil in a large non-stick frying pan, then fry the garlic over a low heat for 1 min. Add the mushrooms and cook until soft. Then, add the kale. If the kale won't all fit in the pan, add half and stir until wilted, then add the rest. Once all the kale is wilted, season.

STEP 2

Now crack in the eggs and keep them cooking gently for 2-3 mins. Then, cover with the lid to for a further 2-3 mins or until the eggs are cooked to your liking. Serve with bread.

Egyptian courgettes with dukkah sprinkle

Prep: 10 mins **Cook:** 25 mins

Serves 4

Ingredients

- 1 tbsp rapeseed oil
- 2 onions , halved and sliced
- 2 tsp ground coriander
- 2 tsp smoked paprika
- 400g can chopped tomatoes
- 2 tsp vegetable bouillon powder

- 2 large courgettes , sliced
- 400g can butter beans , drained
- 180g cherry tomatoes
- 160g frozen peas
- 15g coriander , chopped
- For the dukkah

- 1 tsp coriander seeds
- 1 tsp cumin seeds
- 1 tbsp sesame seeds
- 25g flaked almonds

Method

STEP 1

Heat the oil in a large non-stick pan and fry the onions for 5 mins, stirring occasionally until starting to colour. Stir in the ground coriander and paprika, then tip in the tomatoes with a can of water. Add the bouillon powder and courgettes, cover and cook for 6 mins.

STEP 2

Meanwhile, make the dukkah. Warm the whole spices, sesame seeds and almonds in a pan until aromatic, stirring frequently, then remove the pan from the heat.

STEP 3

Add the butter beans, tomatoes and peas to the courgettes, cover and cook for 5 mins more. Stir in the coriander, then spoon into bowls. Crush the spices and almonds using a pestle and mortar and scatter on top. If you're cooking for two people, put half the seed mix in a jar and chill half the veg for another day.

Three-hour shoulder of lamb

Prep: 10 mins **Cook:** 3 hrs and 30 mins

Serves 4

Ingredients

- 2 garlic cloves, finely chopped
- 1 tbsp oregano, roughly chopped
- 1 tbsp olive oil
- 1 shoulder of lamb, boned and tied, approx 1.5kg/3lb 5oz
- 400g pearl onions or shallots
- 250ml lamb stock
- 100g fresh peas
- 100g fresh broad beans
- 2 Little Gem lettuces, cut into quarters
- juice 1 lemon

- small handful mint or coriander, roughly chopped

Method

STEP 1

Heat oven to 140C/120C fan/gas 1. Mix the garlic, oregano and olive oil with some salt and pepper. Slash the lamb all over and rub the mixture into the meat. Place into a deep casserole dish with the onions and pour over the stock, cover with a tight-fitting lid and cook 3 hrs.

STEP 2

Remove the lamb from the pot, stir through the peas and broad beans. Sit the lamb back on top of the vegetables and return to the oven. Increase temperature to 180C/160C fan/gas 4 and roast, uncovered, for another 20-30 mins until the lamb is browned, adding the lettuce for the final 5 mins. Allow to rest for 20 mins, then add the lemon juice and mint to the cooking juices around the lamb. Remove the string, carve into thick slices and lay them back on top of the veg to make serving easier.

Prawn jambalaya

Prep:10 mins **Cook:**35 mins

Serves 2

Ingredients

- 1 tbsp rapeseed oil
- 1 onion , chopped
- 3 celery sticks , sliced
- 100g wholegrain basmati rice
- 1 tsp mild chilli powder
- 1 tbsp ground coriander
- ½ tsp fennel seeds
- 400g can chopped tomatoes

- 1 tsp vegetable bouillon powder
- 1 yellow pepper , roughly chopped
- 2 garlic cloves , chopped
- 1 tbsp fresh thyme leaves
- 150g pack small prawns , thawed if frozen
- 3 tbsp chopped parsley

Method

STEP 1

Heat the oil in a large, deep frying pan. Add the onion and celery, and fry for 5 mins to soften. Add the rice and spices, and pour in the tomatoes with just under 1 can of water. Stir in the bouillon powder, pepper, garlic and thyme.

STEP 2

Cover the pan with a lid and simmer for 30 mins until the rice is tender and almost all the liquid has been absorbed. Stir in the prawns and parsley, cook briefly to heat through, then serve.

Sticky Chinese chicken traybake

Prep: 10 mins **Cook:** 40 mins

Serves 4

Ingredients

- 8 chicken thighs, skin on and bone in
- 4 tbsp hoisin sauce
- 2 tsp sesame oil
- 2 tbsp clear honey
- 1 ½ tsp Chinese five-spice powder
- thumb-sized knob of ginger, grated
- 2 garlic cloves, grated
- bunch spring onions, chopped
- 50g cashew nuts, toasted
- cooked brown rice, to serve

Method

STEP 1

Heat oven to 200C/180C fan/gas 6. Arrange the chicken thighs in a large roasting tin and slash the skin 2-3 times on each thigh. Mix together the hoisin, sesame oil, honey, five-spice, ginger, garlic and some seasoning. Pour over the chicken and toss to coat – you could now marinate the chicken for 2 hrs, or overnight if you have time. Roast, skin-side up, for 35 mins, basting at least once.

STEP 2

Stir through the cashew nuts and sprinkle the spring onions over the chicken. Return to the oven for 5 mins, then serve with brown rice.

Double chocolate cardamom pots

Prep: 15 mins **Cook:** 5 mins

Makes 4

Ingredients

- 25g white chocolate
- 50g dark chocolate , chopped
- 2 large egg whites

- 1 tbsp caster sugar
- generous pinch ground cardamom

Method

STEP 1

Make chocolate curls with the white chocolate by running a swivel peeler over the surface. When you have enough to sprinkle over 4 chocolate pots, set these aside, then chop the remainder.

STEP 2

Melt the dark chocolate in a bowl over simmering water or in the microwave on Medium for 1½-2 mins. Leave to cool slightly. Whisk the egg whites until stiff, then whisk in the sugar and cardamom. Fold in the melted chocolate, then gently fold in the chopped white chocolate.

STEP 3

Divide between 4 small dishes or cups, about 100ml in size. Sprinkle over the white chocolate curls and chill until ready to serve, at least 1 hr.

Veggie noodle pot

Prep: 10 mins **Cook:** 10 mins

Serves 2

Ingredients

- 100g noodles (rice, soba or egg)
- 3 tbsp frozen peas

- handful sugar snap peas or mangetout, halved lengthways

- handful baby corn , halved lengthways
- 1 spring onion , sliced

For the dressing

- 1 tbsp reduced-salt soy sauce
- 1 tsp clear honey
- ½ garlic clove , crushed

For the omelette

- 1 tbsp olive oil
- splash of milk

- ½ red pepper , deseeded and chopped

- juice 1/2 lemon
- grating of fresh ginger (optional)

- 2 eggs , beaten

Method

STEP 1

To make the omelette, heat the olive oil in a small non-stick frying pan. Add a splash of milk to the beaten eggs, then tip into the pan. Stir once and allow to cook over a gentle heat until almost set. Flip (using a plate if necessary) and cook on the other side until cooked through. Tip onto a board and cut into strips. (You can roll the omelette up and cut slices to give you spirals, if you like.)

STEP 2

Cook the noodles following pack instructions. Drain and rinse under cold water, then set aside. Meanwhile, mix the dressing ingredients together. Blanch the peas and sugar snap peas, then drain and run under cold water to stop them cooking any further.

STEP 3

To assemble the salad, mix the noodles with the baby corn, spring onion, red pepper and green veg, then toss with the dressing and top with strips of omelette.

One-pan glazed rack of lamb with spiced red onions & potatoes

Prep:15 mins **Cook:**1 hr and 10 mins

Serves 6

Ingredients

- 600g new potatoes , halved lengthways
- 3 red onions , each cut into 6 wedges
- 2 tsp ras el hanout
- 8 tbsp olive oil
- 2 racks of lamb , French trimmed (get your butcher to do this for you)
- 1 tbsp pomegranate molasses
- 2 tsp lemon thyme leaves

Method

STEP 1

Heat oven to 200C/180C fan/gas 6. Tip the potatoes and onions into a large roasting tin. Scatter over half the ras el hanout, drizzle with 2 tbsp of the oil and toss together until completely coated. Put in the oven for 40 mins to roast, turning everything over once or twice so it cooks evenly.

STEP 2

Meanwhile, heat 1 tbsp of oil in a frying pan and, one at a time, fry the fat side of the lamb well until dark brown, then remove from the pan. Remove the roasted veg from the oven. Season the lamb fat with the remaining ras el hanout, then drizzle or brush over the molasses. Put the lamb, fat-side up, among the potatoes and return to the oven. Cook for 20 mins for rare, 25 mins for pink and 30 mins for well done. Remove and leave to rest for 10 mins.

STEP 3

Meanwhile, mix the thyme with the remaining oil and set aside. To serve, either bring the roasting tin to the table, carve the racks into chops and serve the potatoes straight from the pan, or remove the racks, cut them into thick three-boned chops, then spoon some of the potatoes onto each plate and rest a thick chop against them. Drizzle everything with the lemon thyme oil to serve.

Spicy Spanish rice

Prep: 10 mins **Cook:** 45 mins

Serves 2

Ingredients

- 1 tbsp rapeseed oil
- 1 large onion , finely chopped
- 200g lean pork tenderloin fillet , diced into cubes roughly 1.5cm
- 2 large garlic cloves , chopped
- 100g brown basmati rice
- ½ -1 tsp smoked paprika (depending on how much heat you want)
- generous pinch saffron
- 500ml hot vegetable bouillon
- 1 large red pepper , deseeded, quartered and sliced
- 160g fine green beans , trimmed and halved
- 60g large prawns
- large handful parsley , chopped
- ½ lemon , cut into wedges

Method

STEP 1

Heat the oil in a frying pan and cook the onion for 5 mins until soft. Add the pork and fry a few mins to brown it a little.

STEP 2

Tip in the garlic, rice and paprika, stirring briefly. Stir the saffron into the bouillon, then pour this in as well. Add the pepper, cover the pan, reduce the heat and simmer for 25 mins before mixing in the beans. Cover and cook for 10 mins more.

STEP 3

Add the prawns, cover again and cook for 2 mins until the rice has absorbed all the liquid. Stir in the parsley and serve with lemon wedges.

Creamy prawn & spring vegetable pot

Prep:10 mins **Cook:**30 mins

Serves 8

Ingredients

- 850ml low-salt chicken or vegetable stock
- 100g pearl barley
- 750g new potato , sliced
- ½ spring green cabbage , shredded
- 140g frozen broad or soya beans
- 100g frozen pea
- 250g broccoli florets

- 200g tub crème fraîche
- small bunch dill , snipped
- zest 1 lemon , plus squeeze of juice
- 600g cooked, peeled prawn

Method

STEP 1

Bring the stock to a simmer in a large frying pan or shallow casserole covered with a lid. Add the pearl barley, cover and cook for 10 mins. Then add the potatoes and cook covered for 12-15 mins until tender.

STEP 2

Remove the lid, increase the heat and bubble the stock for a few mins to reduce. Stir in the greens, crème fraîche, dill, zest and juice. If you're freezing, cool at this stage. If eating straight away, simmer for 3-4 mins until veg is just tender.

STEP 3

Just before serving, stir in the prawns to heat through and season to taste. If freezing, cool completely then scatter the prawns on top and freeze. Defrost fully in the fridge overnight then gently bring back to a simmer, uncovered, until veg is tender and prawns hot through.

Charred cauliflower, lemon & caper orzo

Prep:5 mins **Cook:**20 mins

Serves 1, plus 1 lunchbox for leftovers

Ingredients

- ½ cauliflower , broken into florets, stalk chopped into cubes
- 2 tsp olive oil
- 100g orzo
- 2 tsp capers , drained and rinsed
- 1 small garlic clove , sliced
- ½ lemon , zested and juiced
- 100ml low-salt vegetable stock (check it's vegan, if required)
- handful of rocket leaves , to serve

Method

STEP 1

Heat the grill to high. Toss the cauliflower with half the oil and some seasoning. Tip onto a baking tray and grill for 15-20 mins until golden, charred, and tender all the way through.

STEP 2

Meanwhile, cook the orzo in a pan of boiling salted water for 8 mins, or until al dente. Drain.

STEP 3

Heat the remaining oil in a frying pan and sizzle the capers and garlic until golden. Stir in the orzo, cauliflower, lemon zest and juice and the stock. Bubble for 1 min, then spoon half into a bowl and top with the rocket. Leave the leftovers to cool for the lunchbox, see tip below.

Christmas dinner Wellington

Prep:30 mins **Cook:**1 hr and 15 mins

Serves 8

Ingredients

- 1 tbsp oil
- 1 onion , finely chopped
- 6 chicken breasts
- 400g sausagemeat
- small bunch winter herbs (we used rosemary, thyme and sage), chopped
- 100g fresh breadcumbs
- 10 slices prosciutto or parma ham
- 250g jar cranberry sauce
- 2 x 500g blocks all-butter puff pastry
- plain flour , for rolling
- 1 egg , plus 1 yolk
- roast potatoes , vegetables and gravy, to serve (optional)

Method

STEP 1

Heat the oil in a pan. Add the onion and cook for 8-10 mins until soft. Tip into a bowl and leave to cool.

STEP 2

Cover a chopping board with cling film and place a chicken breast on top. Cover the chicken with more cling film. Use a rolling pin to gently bash the thicker part of the chicken until the whole chicken breast is an even thickness of about ½cm. Repeat with the remaining breasts.

STEP 3

Mix the sausagemeat, herbs and breadcrumbs into the cooled onions. On your worktop, make a double layer of cling film, about 30 x 40cm in size. Lay the prosciutto on top, covering as much of the cling film's surface area as possible. Top with the chicken breasts, placing them to fit together (cut into smaller pieces if you need to) and arranging them to completely cover the prosciutto. Season the chicken.

STEP 4

Cover the chicken with the sausagemeat mixture, spreading it right to the edges. Stir the cranberry sauce to loosen it, then spread over the sausagemeat. Roll the chicken up tightly from one of the longer sides (using the cling film to help you but keeping the cling film on the outside), encasing the fillings in a spiral inside. The prosciutto should be the outermost layer. Wrap the roulade in a large sheet of cling film and twist at the ends to seal, then freeze for 30 mins.

STEP 5

On a floured surface, roll out one block of pastry to the thickness of a £1 coin. Place on a baking tray lined with parchment. Unwrap the chicken roulade and place on top of the pastry. Trim the pastry to a rectangle, leaving 2-3cm all the way around the base of the roulade. Save the off-cuts for decorating the top.

STEP 6

Roll out the second piece of pastry to the same thickness as the first. Whisk together the egg and extra yolk and brush a little around the edge of the pastry base. Drape the second piece of pastry over the roulade, moulding it tightly around the meat and pushing out any air pockets. Trim off any excess pastry, leaving a border of about 2cm.

STEP 7

Crimp the border with your thumb and forefingers, or use a fork to press around the edge to seal (flour the fork if the pastry begins to stick). Brush the Wellington all over with the egg wash. Use the reserved pastry off-cuts to decorate the Wellington as you like, or score through the top layer with a sharp knife. Cover and chill for at least 1 hr, or for up to 48 hrs. *Can be frozen at this stage for up to two months (defrost in the fridge before cooking).* When you're ready to cook, heat oven to 200C/180C fan/gas 6.

STEP 8

If you have any egg wash left over, brush the Wellington with a little more just before baking. Cook for 1 hr 15 mins until the pastry is golden and crisp. If you've previously frozen the Wellington, make sure it's cooked through by poking a sharp knife into the centre and checking the tip comes out very hot. Serve with mash or roast potatoes, veg and gravy, if you like. Chicken is much juicier than beef, so have some kitchen paper to hand ready for when you cut into the Wellington.

How to make oat milk

Prep:25 mins plus at least 4 hrs soaking + 1 hr straining

Makes approximately 750ml

Ingredients

- 100g porridge oats

Method

STEP 1

Put the porridge oats in a bowl and cover with tap water until the oats are submerged. Cover the bowl (a shower cap or teatowel work well) and leave for 4 hrs or overnight, somewhere cool, but not in the fridge.

STEP 2

Sieve the mixture, discarding the water, and rinse under the tap for a few seconds.

STEP 3

Tip the oats into a liquidiser, or food processor. Cover with 750ml cold water and ½ tsp fine sea salt. Blend for 2-4 mins until completely smooth, and there are no oats visible. The finer you make the mixture, the creamier the milk will be.

STEP 4

Line a sieve with a clean piece of muslin, or a cloth with a mesh – it needs to have small holes, so a j-cloth or teatowel might not work. (You could also try a fine strainer or meshed coffee filter.)

STEP 5

Put the lined sieve over a bowl or jug, and pour in the oat milk. Leave to strain for 1 hr. Every once in a while, use a spoon to scrape the bottom of the cloth to disperse some of the sediment, this will help speed up the straining.

STEP 6

When most of the liquid is in the jug, gather the sides of the muslin together and squeeze tightly with both hands to extract the last of the milk. Discard leftover oat pulp (or make a body scrub by adding used coffee grounds).

STEP 7

If you want thinner consistency, add 50ml cold water to the mix, before pouring into a bottle or container. See our troubleshooting tips below. *Will keep for 2-3 days in the fridge. Shake well before use.*

All-in-one roast chicken & veg

Prep: 10 mins **Cook:** 50 mins

Serves 2

Ingredients

- 8 baby new potatoes , halved
- 2 tsp olive oil
- 2 carrots , sliced
- 1 courgette , sliced
- 1 leek , sliced
- 1 tsp each chopped thyme and rosemary, plus a sprig or two
- 2 small skinless chicken breasts
- 150ml low-sodium chicken stock

Method

STEP 1

Heat oven to 200C/180C fan/gas 6. In a small roasting tray toss the potatoes with the oil, carrots, courgette, leek, herbs and seasoning. Roast for 30 mins until starting to brown. Remove from the oven and give the veg a stir, nestle in the chicken, then return to the oven for 15 mins. Pour over the stock, then cook for 5 mins more or until the chicken and veg are cooked through.

Thai fried prawn & pineapple rice

Prep: 10 mins **Cook:** 15 mins

Serves 4

Ingredients

- 2 tsp sunflower oil
- bunch spring onions , greens and whites separated, both sliced
- 1 green pepper , deseeded and chopped into small chunks
- 140g pineapple , chopped into bite-sized chunks
- 3 tbsp Thai green curry paste
- 4 tsp light soy sauce , plus extra to serve

- 300g cooked basmati rice (brown, white or a mix - about 140g uncooked rice)
- 2 large eggs , beaten
- 140g frozen peas
- 225g can bamboo shoots , drained
- 250g frozen prawns , cooked or raw
- 2-3 limes , 1 juiced, the rest cut into wedges to serve
- handful coriander leaves (optional)

Method

STEP 1

Heat the oil in a wok or non-stick frying pan and fry the spring onion whites for 2 mins until softened. Stir in the pepper for 1 min, followed by the pineapple for 1 min more, then stir in the green curry paste and soy sauce.

STEP 2

Add the rice, stir-frying until piping hot, then push the rice to one side of the pan and scramble the eggs on the other side. Stir the peas, bamboo shoots and prawns into the rice and eggs, then heat through for 2 mins until the prawns are hot and the peas tender. Finally, stir in the spring onion greens, lime juice and coriander, if using. Spoon into bowls and serve with extra lime wedges and soy sauce.

Chocolate & raspberry pots

Prep: 15 mins **Cook:** 10 mins

Serves 6

Ingredients

- 200g plain chocolate (not too bitter, 50% or less)
- 100g frozen raspberry , defrosted or fresh raspberries
- 500g Greek yogurt
- 3 tbsp honey
- chocolate curls or sprinkles, for serving

Method

STEP 1

Break the chocolate into small pieces and place in a heatproof bowl. Bring a little water to the boil in a small saucepan, then place the bowl of chocolate on top, making sure the bottom of the bowl does not touch the water. Leave the chocolate to melt slowly over a low heat.

STEP 2

Remove the chocolate from the heat and leave to cool for 10 mins. Meanwhile, divide the raspberries between 6 small ramekins or glasses.

STEP 3

When the chocolate has cooled slightly, quickly mix in the yogurt and honey. Spoon the chocolate mixture over the raspberries. Place in the fridge to cool, then finish the pots with a few chocolate shavings before serving.

Chocolate & berry mousse pots

Prep: 15 mins **Cook:** 5 mins

Serves 4

Ingredients

- 75g dark chocolate 70% grated
- 4 tbsp low-fat yogurt
- 2 large egg whites
- 2 tsp caster sugar
- 350g berries (try blueberries, raspberries, cherries or a mix)

Method

STEP 1

Melt the chocolate in a heatproof bowl over a pan of simmering water, making sure the bowl doesn't directly touch the water. Once melted, allow it to cool for 5-10 mins, then stir in the yogurt.

STEP 2

Whisk the egg whites until stiff, then whisk in the sugar and beat until stiff again. Fold the whites into the chocolate mix – loosen the mixture first with a spoonful of egg white, then carefully fold in the rest, keeping as much air as possible.

STEP 3

Put berries into small glasses or ramekins, then divide mousse on top. Chill in the fridge until set.

Oat & chia porridge

Prep: 10 mins **Cook:** 4 mins

Serves 4

Ingredients

- 150g gluten-free porridge oats
- 50g milled seeds with flax and chia
- 400ml almond or oat milk
- 200g dairy-free coconut yogurt
- 40g toasted flaked almonds
- 2 pink grapefruit , segmented and chopped (4 portions)

Method

STEP 1

Soak the oats and seeds in 800ml water overnight.

STEP 2

Tip into a pan with 200ml milk and heat, stirring, until bubbling and thick. If you're following our Healthy Diet Plan, save half for the next day. *Will keep in the fridge for two days.* Divide the rest between two bowls, along with 50ml milk each and topping with a quarter portion each of the yogurt, almonds and grapefruit.

STEP 3

The next day, prepare the second grapefruit and reheat the leftover porridge in a pan with a splash more milk before serving with the toppings as described in step 2.

Chocolate hazelnut ice cream cheesecake

Prep: 15 mins plus overnight freezing, no cook

Serves 12

Ingredients

- 200g honey nut cornflakes
- 2 x 400g jars chocolate hazelnut spread
- 2 x 180g tubs full-fat cream cheese
- 1 tbsp roasted and chopped hazelnuts

- 200g honey nut cornflakes
- 2 x 400g jars chocolate hazelnut spread
- 2 x 180g tubs full-fat cream cheese
- 1 tbsp roasted and chopped hazelnuts

Method

STEP 1

Put the cornflakes and half a jar of chocolate hazelnut spread in a bowl and beat to combine – don't worry about breaking up the cornflakes. Press the mix into the base of a 23cm springform tin.

STEP 2

In a separate bowl, beat the cream cheese until smooth, then fold in the remaining chocolate hazelnut spread. Smooth onto the cornflake base, wrap tightly in cling film and freeze overnight.

STEP 3

Remove from the freezer 30 mins before serving, or until you can cut it easily with a sharp knife. Serve in slices with hazelnuts sprinkled over. *Will keep in the freezer for up to 1 month.*

STEP 4

Put the cornflakes and half a jar of chocolate hazelnut spread in a bowl and beat to combine – don't worry about breaking up the cornflakes. Press the mix into the base of a 23cm springform tin.

STEP 5

In a separate bowl, beat the cream cheese until smooth, then fold in the remaining chocolate hazelnut spread. Smooth onto the cornflake base, wrap tightly in cling film and freeze overnight.

STEP 6

Remove from the freezer 30 mins before serving, or until you can cut it easily with a sharp knife. Serve in slices with hazelnuts sprinkled over. *Will keep in the freezer for up to 1 month.*

Pot-roast pheasant with cider & bacon

Prep: 15 mins **Cook:** 45 mins

Serves 4

Ingredients

- 50g butter
- 2 pheasants , cleaned
- 100g bacon lardon
- 1 onion , chopped
- 1 celery stick, chopped
- 4 sage sprigs, leaves chopped

- 2 eating apples , cored and cut into large chunks
- 500ml cider
- 300ml chicken stock
- 1 Savoy cabbage , finely shredded
- 100ml double cream
- mashed potato , to serve (optional)

Method

STEP 1

Heat oven to 190C/170C fan/gas 5. Melt the butter in a large non-stick flameproof dish. Season the pheasants, add to the dish and brown on all sides. Remove from the dish and set aside.

STEP 2

Add the bacon, onion, celery and sage to the dish and cook for 10 mins until the onion is soft and the bacon is crisp. Carefully pour off any excess fat.

STEP 3

Return the pheasants to the dish and scatter over the apples. Pour over the cider and the chicken stock, bring to a simmer, cover with a lid and cook in the oven for 25 mins until the birds are cooked through.

STEP 4

Remove the birds from the dish and keep warm. Return dish to the hob over a high heat. Let the liquid bubble until reduced by half, then add the cabbage, cover with a lid and cook for 3 mins. Add the cream, check the seasoning, and continue cooking for 1 min more. Serve the pheasant on top of the cabbage mixture with some mashed potato, if you like.

Lentil & cauliflower curry

Prep: 10 mins **Cook:** 40 mins

Serves 4

Ingredients

- 1 tbsp olive oil
- 1 large onion, chopped
- 3 tbsp curry paste
- 1 tsp turmeric
- 1 tsp mustard seeds
- 200g red or yellow lentil
- 1l low-sodium vegetable or chicken stock (made with 2 cubes)
- 1 large cauliflower, broken into florets
- 1 large potato, diced
- 3 tbsp coconut yogurt
- small pack coriander, chopped
- juice 1 lemon
- 100g cooked brown rice

Method

STEP 1

Heat the oil in a large saucepan and cook the onion until soft, about 5 mins. Add the curry paste, spices and lentils, then stir to coat the lentils in the onions and paste. Pour over the stock and simmer for 20 mins, then add the cauliflower, potato and a little extra water if it looks a bit dry.

STEP 2

Simmer for about 12 mins until the cauliflower and potatoes are tender. Stir in the yogurt, coriander and lemon juice, and serve with the brown rice.

Beetroot & apple salad pots

Prep: 15 mins No cook

Serves 6 - 8

Ingredients

- 250g cooked beetroot , diced into 1cm cubes
- 2 apples , diced into 1cm cubes
- 2 celery sticks, finely sliced
- 50g walnut , roughly chopped
- handful parsley , chopped
- 3 tbsp walnut oil
- 1 tbsp red wine vinegar

Method

STEP 1

Put the beetroot, apples, celery, walnuts and parsley in a bowl. Whisk together the walnut oil, vinegar and some seasoning, pour over the beetroot salad and mix well. Divide between small glasses or teacups and chill until ready to serve. Can be made up to 3 hrs ahead.

Spicy baby aubergine stew with coriander & mint

Prep: 10 mins **Cook:** 45 mins

Serves 4

Ingredients

- 2 tbsp olive oil
- 2 red onions , sliced
- 4 garlic cloves , smashed
- 2 red chillies , deseeded and sliced, or 2-3 dried red chillies left whole
- 2 tsp coriander seeds , toasted and crushed
- 2 tsp cumin seeds , toasted and crushed
- 16 baby aubergines , left whole with stalk intact
- 2 x 400g cans chopped tomatoes
- 2 tsp sugar
- bunch mint leaves, roughly chopped
- bunch coriander , roughly chopped
- couscous and yogurt to serve

Method

STEP 1

Heat oil in a heavy-based saucepan, add the onions and garlic and cook until they begin to colour. Add the chillies, coriander and cumin seeds. When the seeds give off a nutty aroma, toss in the whole aubergines, coating them in the onion and spices.

STEP 2

Tip in tomatoes and sugar, cover and gently cook for 40 mins, until aubergines are tender.

STEP 3

Season sauce and toss in half the mint and coriander. Cover and simmer for 2 mins. Sprinkle over remaining herbs and serve with couscous and yogurt.

Chia & oat breakfast scones with yogurt and berries

Prep:8 mins **Cook:**20 mins

Serves 4

Ingredients

- 2 tsp cold pressed rapeseed oil , plus a little for the ramekins
- 50ml milk
- 1 tbsp lemon juice
- 2 tsp vanilla extract
- 160g plain wholemeal spelt flour

- 2 tbsp chia seeds
- 25g oats
- 2 tsp baking powder
- 2 x 120g pots bio Greek yogurt
- 400g strawberries , hulled and sliced

Method

STEP 1

Heat oven to 200C/180C fan/gas 6 and line the base of 4 x 185ml ramekins with a disc of baking parchment and oil the sides with the rapeseed oil. Measure the milk in a jug and make up to 300ml with water. Stir in the lemon juice, vanilla and the 2 tsp oil. Mix the flour, seeds and oats then blitz in a food processor to make the mix as fine as you can. Stir in the baking powder.

STEP 2

Pour in the liquid, then stir in with the blade of a knife until you have a very wet batter like dough. Spoon evenly into the ramekins then bake on a baking sheet for 20 mins until risen – they don't have to be golden but should feel firm. Cool for a few mins then run a knife round the inside of the ramekins to loosen the scones then carefully ease out.

STEP 3

The scones can be eaten immediately or cooled and stored for later. If you're following our Healthy Diet Plan, this recipe can be used for two people over two meals, use two scones straight away split in half and served topped with half the yogurt and two portions of the berries. Cool and pack the remainder to eat on another day on the plan.

Kleftiko-style lamb shanks

Prep:30 mins **Cook:**3 hrs

Serves 4

Ingredients

- 4 lamb shanks
- 4 garlic cloves , roughly chopped
- 1 tsp dried rosemary
- 1 tsp dried thyme
- 2 tsp dried oregano
- large pinch of ground cinnamon
- 3 bay leaves
- 1 large lemon , juiced
- 2 tbsp olive oil , plus extra for drizzling, if needed
- 1 ½kg waxy potatoes , chopped into large chunks
- 1 red pepper , deseeded and chopped into chunks
- 100ml white wine (or use water)
- To serve (optional)
- 150g feta , crumbled into large chunks

Method

STEP 1

Put the lamb shanks in a large bowl with the garlic, rosemary, thyme, dried oregano, cinnamon, bay leaves, lemon juice (drop in the juiced halves as well), and olive oil. Season well, then toss everything together. If you have time, chill overnight.

STEP 2

Heat the oven to 190C/170C fan/ gas 5. Tip the potatoes and peppers into a large roasting tin, then pour over the wine. Remove the lamb from the marinade and set aside, then pour the leftover marinade over the veg. Toss to combine, then arrange the lamb on top of the veg. Cover tightly with foil and bake for 2 hrs 30 mins. Remove the lamb from the tin, turn all the veg over, then turn the lamb over and return to the tin on top of the veg. Drizzle over a little more oil, if the tin seems dry. Bake for 30 mins more, uncovered, until the lamb is falling off the bone and the potatoes are golden around the edges. Leave to rest for 5 mins, then scatter over the feta and fresh oregano, if using.

Spiced cauliflower hummus

Prep:5 mins **Cook:**25 mins

Serves 2

Ingredients

- ½ small cauliflower
- 1 tsp ground turmeric
- 2 tsp cumin seeds
- 2 tbsp olive oil

- 200g tub plain hummus
- 1 tbsp Bombay mix
- generous pinch of salt and pepper

Method

STEP 1

Heat oven to 220C/200C fan/gas 7. Cut the cauliflower into florets, saving the leaves. Tip the florets into a bowl and toss with the ground turmeric, cumin seeds, olive oil and a generous pinch of salt and pepper. Tip the cauliflower onto a baking tray, cook for 20 mins, then add the cauliflower leaves, give everything a good mix and cook for a further 5 mins. Spread the plain hummus onto a plate. Top with the roasted cauliflower and Bombay mix.

Pot-roast veal with new-season carrots & orange

Prep:20 mins **Cook:**2 hrs and 30 mins

Serves 6

Ingredients

- 1 ½kg piece rolled and tied veal shoulder
- 3 garlic cloves , 1 finely sliced, 2 bashed
- bunch of thyme
- 1 tbsp olive oil
- 25g butter
- 800g new-season bunch of carrot , trimmed with stalks still attached
- 1 large shallot , roughly chopped
- sprinkling of icing sugar
- zest 1 orange , ½ pared into strips, ½ finely grated
- 150ml white wine
- 350ml chicken stock

Method

STEP 1

Heat oven to 180C/160C fan/gas 4. Stud the gaps in the veal joint with the sliced garlic and some thyme, then season well.

STEP 2

Heat oil and butter in a deep flameproof casserole dish and spend a good 15 mins slowly sizzling the veal until brown all over. Remove the joint to a plate and add the carrots, shallot and icing sugar, then cook for 5 mins until everything is slightly caramelised. Lift out the carrots but leave everything else in the dish. Add the rest of the thyme, bashed garlic and the pared orange zest. Nestle the veal back in the dish and pour over the wine, then the stock. Cover and put in the oven for 1 hr.

STEP 3

Remove the dish from the oven, uncover, and scatter the carrots around the meat. Return the dish to the oven for 1 hr, uncovered. Cook until the meat is very tender, then leave to cool slightly. Lift the meat onto a board and carve into slices. Serve with the juices from the dish and the tender carrots.

Ploughman's pork & cheese picnic pie

Prep: 1 hr **Cook:** 1 hr and 15 mins

Serves 8-10

Ingredients

- butter , for the tin
- For the pastry

- 500g plain flour
- 175g lard , diced
- 1 egg yolk , beaten to glaze
- For the filling
- 400g shredded ham meat, or 8 thick slices of ham
- 200g fatty pork mince or good-quality sausagemeat
- 300g smoked chicken , or regular chicken if you have it leftover
- 100g pickled silverskin onions , halved
- 1 tbsp coarse grain mustard
- 2 tbsp chopped tarragon or parsley
- 200g red leicester or cheddar, cut into 1cm thick slices

Method

STEP 1

To make the pastry, tip the flour into a bowl with ½ tsp salt. Pour 200ml water into a saucepan and bring up to the boil, then take off the heat, add the lard and leave to melt. Pour the mixture into the flour, beat with a wooden spoon and work into a dough. Cut a third of the pastry off for the top and wrap in cling film then, while still warm, roll out the other two-thirds of the pastry to the thickness of a £1 coin. Butter a 20cm springform cake tin and line with the pastry, leaving a good amount of excess hanging over the side.

STEP 2

Heat oven to 200C/180C fan/gas 6 with a sturdy baking tray in it. Make the filling by mixing all the ingredients, except the cheese, together in a bowl and season generously with cracked pepper and a little salt. Pack half the filling well into the lined tin, cover with a layer of cheese slices, then pack over the rest of the filling. Roll the remaining pastry out and lay on top of the filled pie tin, trim the edges leaving a little overhang, and save the trimmings. Crimp the pie all the way around the edge, then brush the top with the beaten egg. Score the top of the pie with the back of a knife to decorate then, using a small cutter, press a hole into the middle of the pie to let steam escape.

STEP 3

Bake for 15 mins, then reduce the heat to 180C/160C fan/gas 4 and cook for a further 50 mins-1 hr until golden brown. Leave until cold. Can be made the day before and kept at room temperature or chilled for two days. Wrap the pie well and take to the picnic in the tin, with a board and a large knife for serving.

Quick & spicy nasi goreng

Prep:10 mins **Cook:**10 mins

Serves 1

Ingredients

- 2 tbsp vegetable oil
- 1 small onion, finely sliced
- 2 garlic cloves, crushed
- 1 carrot, grated
- ½ small Chinese or Savoy cabbage, shredded

- 175g cooked brown rice
- 1 tbsp fish sauce (optional)
- 1 tbsp soy sauce
- 1 egg
- hot sriracha chilli sauce, to serve

Method

STEP 1

Heat the oil in a wok over a high heat. Add the onion and cook for 3-4 mins until softened and slightly caramelised. Add the garlic and stir for 1 min.

STEP 2

Toss in the carrot and cabbage, then cook for 1-2 mins. Add the rice and stir to warm through. Pour in the fish sauce, soy sauce and some seasoning. Make a well in the centre of the wok and crack in the egg. Fry until the white is nearly set.

STEP 3

Serve the rice in a large bowl, topped with the fried egg and drizzled with chilli sauce.

Steak & chips pie

Prep:20 mins **Cook:**3 hrs and 30 mins

Serves 6

Ingredients

For the beef

- 2 tbsp sunflower oil , plus extra for the dish

- 750g-1kg braising steak (or topside) sliced into 6 thin steaks (buy a joint and do it yourself if you can't find any already sliced)

- 2 onions , chopped
- 4 medium carrots , chopped
- 1 tsp treacle , sugar or golden caster sugar
- 1 tbsp plain flour

For the pastry

- 500g block of shortcrust pastry
- flour , for dusting
- 1 tsp dried porcini mushroom powder (optional)

For the chips

- 800g frozen oven chips

- 175ml red wine
- 2 beef stock cubes diluted in 600ml hot water
- small bunch thyme , half of the leaves picked for the pastry and reserved
- 3 bay leaves , tied together

- thyme leaves , from the bunch used for the beef

Method

STEP 1

Up to three days before, braise the steak. Heat oven to 160C/140C fan/gas 3. Heat half the oil in a flameproof casserole pan and brown the steaks really well on either side, then set aside. Add the onions and carrots to the pan, drizzle over a little more oil, then cook over a low heat for 5 mins until coloured. Drizzle over the treacle or add the sugar, and scatter in the flour, stirring until you have a brown paste clinging to the vegetables. Tip the meat and any juices back into the pan and give it all a good stir. Pour over the wine and stock, season, tuck in the herbs and bring everything to a simmer. Cover with a lid and cook in the oven for about two hours, or until the meat is tender, then leave to cool and chill until needed. *Can be prepared up to two days ahead and chilled.*

STEP 2

To make the pastry, roll out the block on a floured surface to the thickness of a £1 coin and scatter over the thyme leaves and mushroom powder. Fold the pastry into quarters and chill until needed. Or, to give the pastry a more interesting finish, scatter over the thyme and mushroom powder when you roll the pastry out to line the dish, rolling over them firmly so they stick. *Can be prepared a day ahead and chilled.*

STEP 3

Heat oven to 220C/200C fan/gas 7 and put a baking sheet in the oven. Oil a 24-28cm pie dish or tin (ideally with a lip) and dust well with flour. Roll out the pastry to a thick-ish round that will easily line the pie dish with a slight overhang, then line the dish. Lift the steak out of the gravy, then spoon in the vegetables and a little of the gravy and lay the steaks over the top to form an overlapping layer (serve any leftover gravy alongside in a small jug for pouring over). Pile the chips over the meat. Trim the edges of the pastry and crimp the edge. Bake for 40 mins until the chips and pie crust are golden – cover the chips loosely with foil if they are browning too quickly. Scatter over some salt then serve straight from the dish with the leftover gravy (reheated), and the rest of that bottle of red wine.

Halloween cheeseboard with creepy crackers

Prep:20 mins **Cook:**15 mins plus cooling

Makes 30

Ingredients

- selection of cheeses , including an orange one, blue-veined variety, white one, and if you can find it, a charcoal-coated cheese
- figs , black grapes and celery, to serve

For the creepy crackers

- 2 tbsp olive oil
- 150g plain flour , plus extra for sprinkling
- 1 tsp sea salt flakes

- 1 tsp golden caster sugar
- 1 tbsp black sesame seeds , plus 1 tsp for sprinkling
- black food colouring

Method

STEP 1

Heat the oven to 220C/200C fan/gas 7. Mix the olive oil with 60ml water, then put in a bowl with the flour, salt, sugar, sesame seeds and a few drops of the food colouring. Mix with your hands until you have a rough dough. If it's too sticky, add a little more flour until it's smooth.

STEP 2

Sprinkle a non-stick baking mat or a sheet of baking parchment with some flour, roll the dough out to the thickness of a £1 coin, then use a pizza cutter or knife to cut it into skinny strips. Brush the strips with a little water and sprinkle with some salt and extra sesame seeds. Prick each strip with a fork.

STEP 3

Transfer the strips with the mat to a baking sheet, separating the strips with a palette knife, and bake for 12-15 mins, or until the crackers are firm and feel hard. Leave to cool. *Will keep in an airtight container for up to two weeks.* Arrange your selection of cheeses with the fruit and crackers on a serving board.

Coconut & tamarind chicken curry

Prep:30 mins **Cook:**50 mins Plus marinating

Serves 10

Ingredients

- 20 skinless, boneless chicken thighs
- juice 3 limes
- 2 tsp coarsely ground black pepper
- 2 tsp turmeric
- 6 tbsp vegetable oil , for frying

- 3 tbsp tamarind pulp
- 400ml coconut milk
- 1 x 160ml can coconut cream
- 2 tbsp coriander , chopped

For the sauce

- 4-6 tbsp vegetable oil
- 3 tsp mustard seed
- 3 tbsp fresh or dried curry leaf
- 4 onions , finely diced
- 8 garlic cloves , crushed

- 75g ginger , finely shredded
- 1 tbsp paprika
- 3 x 400g cans chopped tomatoes
- 450ml chicken stock
- 2 tbsp golden muscovado sugar

Method

STEP 1

Put the chicken in a big mixing bowl, add the lime juice, pepper and turmeric, and mix well. (It's best to use gloves for this as the turmeric stains fingers.) Set aside for 1 hr.

STEP 2

Make the sauce. Heat the oil in a big pan, toss in the mustard seeds followed by the fresh curry leaves (if you are using dried leaves, add them later with the tomatoes) and fry until it releases a warm, nutty aroma – about 30 secs.

STEP 3

Add the onions, put on the lid, and cook over a low heat for 10-15 mins until meltingly soft, stirring now and then. Take the lid off, turn up the heat, add the garlic and ginger, and fry for 1 min until it gives off a toasty aroma. Stir in the paprika and continue cooking for another 30 secs.

STEP 4

Add the tomatoes, stock and sugar (and dried curry leaves if using). Cook, uncovered, for 15-20 mins until the sauce has thickened and reduced by one-third.

STEP 5

Heat oven to 180C/160C fan/gas 4. Meanwhile, fry the chicken. Heat 6 tbsp oil in a frying pan and cook in batches until golden. You may need a little extra oil. Keep warm.

STEP 6

Pour any excess oil from the frying pan and add a ladleful of water – swirl it around and scrape up any juices with a spoon before adding to the tomato sauce.

STEP 7

Put the chicken in a deep roasting tin or ovenproof casserole and pour over the sauce. Cover with foil and oven cook for 15 mins until the chicken is tender. Skim off any oil from the top of the sauce.

STEP 8

Take the chicken pieces out of the tin and transfer to a serving dish. Pour the sauce into a pan and bring to a simmer. Stir in the tamarind pulp, coconut milk and half the coconut cream. Adjust the flavour by adding more sugar or tamarind. Ladle the sauce over the chicken, drizzle with the remaining coconut cream, and scatter with coriander before serving.

Super speedy chilli

Prep: 10 mins **Cook:** 20 mins - 25 mins

Serves 4

Ingredients

- 180g jar fiery chilli pesto (we used Sacla)
- 450g lean beef mince
- 2 tsp ground cumin
- 1 beef stock cube
- 2 red peppers , sliced
- 400g can kidney bean , drained
- 8 small bunch coriander , chopped
- 8 flour tortillas
- 2 avocados , stoned and thickly sliced
- 1 red onion , thinly sliced
- reduced-fat mayonnaise , to serve

Method

STEP 1

Tip the pesto into a large pan with the mince and cumin, and fry for a few mins. Crumble in the stock cube, add the peppers and kidney beans, then fill the empty can with water and add this to the pan, too. Cover and simmer for 10 mins, then remove the lid and continue to cook for 5-10 mins or until all the liquid has been absorbed. Remove from the heat and stir in the coriander.

STEP 2

Heat the tortillas following pack instructions and serve with the chilli, avocados, onion and a dollop of mayo.

One-pan prawn & tomato curry

Prep: 10 mins **Cook:** 20 mins

Serves 4

Ingredients

- 2 tbsp sunflower oil
- 1 large onion , chopped
- large piece ginger , crushed
- 4 garlic cloves , crushed
- ½ red chilli , finely chopped
- 1 tsp golden caster sugar
- 1 tsp black mustard seeds
- 1 tsp ground cumin
- 1 tsp ground coriander
- 1 tsp turmeric

- 1 tbsp garam masala
- 2 tsp malt vinegar
- 400g can chopped tomato
- 400g raw king prawns
- small bunch coriander , chopped
- basmati rice , yogurt, mango chutney and Carrot & cumin salad, to serve

Method

STEP 1

Heat the oil in a deep-sided frying pan and cook the onion for 8-10 mins until it starts to turn golden. Add the ginger, garlic and chilli and cook for 1-2 mins. Stir in the sugar and spices for 1 min, then splash in the vinegar and tomatoes. Season with salt and simmer for 5 mins, stirring, until the sauce thickens.

STEP 2

Stir in the prawns, reduce the heat and cook for 8-10 mins until cooked through – if the sauce gets really thick, add a splash of water. Remove from the heat, stir though most of the coriander. Serve straight from the dish scattered with the remaining coriander and the rice, yogurt, chutney and salad in separate bowls.

20-minute beef in red wine

Prep: 5 mins **Cook:** 15 mins

Serves 1

Ingredients

- 1 tbsp olive oil
- 200g sirloin or rump steak
- 1 small onion , sliced
- 1 garlic clove , finely sliced
- pinch dried oregano
- glass red wine
- 200g can chopped tomato

Method

STEP 1

Heat the oil in a pan. Fry steak for 2 mins on each side until brown. Remove steak to a plate, then throw the onion, garlic and oregano into the pan. Fry for 5 mins until starting to turn golden.

STEP 2

Tip the wine and tomatoes into the pan, then simmer for 10 mins until thickened and rich. Slice the steak into chunks, return to the pan with any juices, then simmer for a few mins to reheat. Serve with pasta, chips or some fried potatoes.

Baked fennel pork with lemony potatoes & onions

Prep:15 mins **Cook:**50 mins

Serves 4

Ingredients

- 2 tbsp fennel seeds
- 1 tbsp olive oil
- 4 pork loin steaks , trimmed of fat
- 1 large onion , sliced
- 2 garlic cloves , thinly sliced

- 750g baby new potatoes , halved lengthways
- 2 fennel bulbs , thinly sliced, green fronds reserved
- juice 2 lemons
- 340g broccoli , broken into florets

Method

STEP 1

Crush the fennel seeds lightly in a pestle and mortar. Mix with half the oil and a little seasoning. Rub into the pork and set aside.

STEP 2

Heat oven to 200C/180C fan/gas 6. Heat remaining oil in a shallow ovenproof dish. Soften the onion and garlic for about 5 mins, then tip in the potatoes and brown for a few mins. Add the fennel, lemon juice and about 100ml water. Season, cover with the lid and cook in the oven for 35 mins.

STEP 3

Remove the lid, stir the potatoes and place the meat on top. Return to the oven, uncovered, and cook for another 10 mins or until the pork is cooked to your liking. Meanwhile, cook the broccoli.

STEP 4

Scatter over the reserved fennel fronds and serve with the broccoli.

Chicken fajitas

Prep:20 mins **Cook:**25 mins

Serves 8

Ingredients

- 24 flour tortillas
- 300g soured cream
- For the chicken
- 6 chicken breasts
- 4 tbsp olive oil
- 2 garlic cloves , crushed

- 2 limes , juiced
- 1 tsp chilli powder
- 1 tsp ground cumin
- small pack coriander , finely chopped

For the pepper mix

- 2 tbsp olive oil
- 1 large red onion , cut into thin wedges

- 2 red and 2 yellow peppers , cut into thin strips
- 200g cherry tomatoes , halved

Method

STEP 1

Slice the chicken breasts in half horizontally, then cut them into thin strips. Put them in a bowl, add the remaining ingredients and rub into the chicken with your hands.

STEP 2

Heat the oil for the pepper mix in a large frying pan and fry the onion wedges for 6 mins or until softened. Turn the heat up high so the wedges char slightly at the edges, season well and, using a slotted spoon, lift them onto a baking tray and keep warm.

STEP 3

Add the peppers in batches, cook them the same way, then transfer to the baking tray with the onions. Cook the tomatoes in the same way and add them to the peppers.

STEP 4

Heat a griddle pan or use the same frying pan and cook the chicken in batches over a high heat – allow them to catch a little on the edges but don't overcook them. Add them to the baking tray to keep warm.

STEP 5

Heat the tortillas on the griddle, then wrap in foil and keep warm in the oven, or heat in the microwave following pack instructions.

Super-easy birthday cake

Prep:20 mins **Cook:**25 mins

Serves 8

Ingredients

- 225g butter , at room temperature
- 225g golden caster sugar
- 4 large eggs
- 225g self-raising flour

- 3 tbsp whole milk
- 1 tsp vanilla extract
- 2 tbsp cocoa powder

For the pink icing

- 150g butter , very soft
- 300g icing sugar , sifted

- pink food colouring

Method

STEP 1

Heat oven to 180C/160C fan/gas 4. Butter two 18cm loose-based cake tins and line the bases with baking parchment. Beat the butter and sugar in a mixer or by hand, then add the eggs, one at a time, mixing well after each. Fold in the flour, milk and vanilla extract until the mixture is smooth.

STEP 2

Divide the mixture between two bowls. Sift the cocoa powder into one of the bowls. Scrape the vanilla batter into one tin and the chocolate batter into the other and level the tops. Bake for 20-25 mins or until a skewer comes out clean. Cool for 5 mins, then transfer to a wire rack and cool completely.

134

STEP 3

To make the icing, beat the butter and add the icing sugar a little at a time, beating each lot in until you have a smooth, creamy icing. Add a little pink colour and beat it in (add more if you want a stronger colour). Sandwich the two cakes together with icing and spread the rest on top using a palette knife. Will keep in an airtight container for three days.

All-in-one chicken traybake

Total time 30 mins Ready in 30 mins

Serves 4

Ingredients

- 2 tbsp olive oil
- 4 chicken breasts, skin on
- 750g new potato , sliced
- large pinch dried thyme or fresh if you have it
- 4 garlic cloves , peeled, but left whole
- 450g jar mixed roasted peppers , cut into bite-size pieces
- 2 oranges , each cut into eight segments
- 200g jar pitted black olives in brine, drained

Method

STEP 1

Heat oven to 200C/180C fan/gas 6. Heat 2 tbsp of oil in a large flameproof roasting tin, then fry the chicken, skin side down, and the potatoes for 8 mins or until the chicken skin is crisp and golden. Turn the chicken and potatoes, then continue to cook for a further minute.

STEP 2

Add the thyme and garlic, then stir to coat everything.

STEP 3

Roast everything for 15 mins until the potatoes are soft. Remove the tray from the oven and throw in the peppers, orange segments and olives and roast for 5 mins more until the chicken and potatoes are completely cooked. To serve, bring the tray to the table and let everyone help themselves.

Cherry chocolate meringue pots

Prep:8 mins **Cook:**5 mins

Serves 4

Ingredients

- 300ml pot double cream
- 4 shop-bought meringues nests, roughly broken
- 50g dark chocolate
- 8 tbsp cherry compote (we used Bonne Maman)

Method

STEP 1

Whip the cream to soft peaks, then fold in the meringue pieces. Heat the chocolate in the microwave for 30-45 secs or until melted, stirring halfway through. Spoon 2 tbsp cherry compote into each of 4 glasses, then top with the meringue mix. Drizzle melted chocolate on top of each glass and serve.

Easy pulled beef ragu

Prep:20 mins **Cook:**4 hrs

8 (or 2 meals for 4)

Ingredients

- 2 tbsp olive oil
- 1kg boneless beef brisket
- 2 onions , finely chopped
- 4 garlic cloves , finely chopped
- 5 carrots , thickly sliced
- 250ml red wine
- 2 x 400g cans chopped tomatoes
- 2 tbsp tomato purée
- 4 bay leaves
- 450g large pasta shapes (such as paccheri, rigate or rigatoni)
- large handful basil leaves , to serve
- grated parmesan , to serve

Method

STEP 1

Heat oven to 150C/130C fan/gas 2. Heat 1 tbsp oil in a flameproof casserole dish and brown the beef all over. Take the beef out of the dish, add the remaining oil and gently cook the onions and garlic for 10 mins until softened.

STEP 2

Add the browned beef back to the dish with the carrots, red wine, tomatoes, tomato purée and bay leaves. Cover with foil and a lid, and slowly cook for 3 - 3 1/2 hrs or until the meat falls apart. Check on it a couple of times, turning the beef over and giving it a good stir to make sure it's coated in the sauce.

STEP 3

Cook the pasta following pack instructions, then drain. Shred the beef – it should just fall apart when you touch it with a fork – then spoon the beef and tomato sauce over the pasta. Scatter with basil and Parmesan before serving.

Meal prep: pasta

Prep:20 mins **Cook:**30 mins

Each box serves 1

Ingredients

For the pasta base

- 2 red onions , halved and thinly sliced
- 150g wholemeal penne
- 1 lemon , zested and juiced
- 1 tbsp rapeseed oil , plus a little extra for drizzling
- 2 large garlic cloves , finely grated
- 30g pack basil , chopped, stems and all

For the salmon pasta box

- ½ red pepper , sliced
- 1 salmon fillet
- 1 tsp capers
- big handful rocket

For the chicken pasta box

- 1 large courgette , sliced
- 1 skinless chicken breast fillet, thickly sliced (150g)
- 2 tsp pesto
- 5 large cherry tomatoes , halved (80g)

For the aubergine pasta box

- 1 small aubergine , sliced then diced (about 275g)
- 5 large cherry tomatoes , quartered (80g)
- 5 kalamata olives , halved

Method

STEP 1

Heat oven to 200C/180C fan/gas 6. Arrange the red onions, red pepper, courgette and aubergine in lines on a large baking sheet. Drizzle with a little oil and roast for 15 mins.

STEP 2

Cook the pasta for 10-12 mins until al dente. While the pasta is cooking, loosely wrap the salmon fillet in foil and do the same with the chicken and pesto in another foil parcel, then put them on another baking tray.

STEP 3

When the veg have had their 15 mins, put the salmon and chicken in the oven and cook for a further 12 mins (or until the chicken is cooked through). Drain the pasta, put in a bowl and toss really well with the lemon zest and juice, rapeseed oil, garlic and two-thirds of the basil. When everything is cooked, add the red onions to the pasta. Toss together and divide between three lunch boxes.

STEP 4

Top the first box with the salmon fillet (remove the skin first), then add the red pepper from the tray. Scatter over the capers and add the rocket. To the second box, add the chicken and pesto with any juices, the roasted courgette and the halved cherry tomatoes. In the third box, toss the aubergine into the pasta with the quartered cherry tomatoes, olives and the remaining basil. Seal up each container and chill. Eat within three days, preferably in the order of the salmon, then the chicken and then the aubergine.

Italian aubergine traybake

Prep:10 mins **Cook:**50 mins

Serves 4

Ingredients

- 2 aubergines , sliced into half moons
- 2 tbsp olive oil
- 2 x 400g cans chopped tomatoes
- 2 garlic cloves , crushed
- 70g pack black olives (we used Crespo dry black olives with herbs)
- small pack basil , leaves picked, 3/4 torn
- 2 ciabatta rolls, torn into chunks
- 150g ball of mozzarella , torn

Method

STEP 1

Heat oven to 200C/180C fan/gas 6. In a roasting tin, toss the aubergine with the oil and roast for 15 mins, then stir in the tomatoes, garlic, olives and torn basil leaves, and cook for another 10 mins.

STEP 2

Top with the bread and dot with the chunks of mozzarella. Bake for a further 25 mins, then scatter over the remaining basil leaves before serving.

Beetroot hummus party platter

Prep:15 mins **Serves 8**

Ingredients

- 2 x 400g can chickpeas , drained
- 2 x 300g pack cooked beetroot , drained
- 2 small garlic cloves
- 2 tbsp tahini
- 100ml extra virgin olive oil , plus a drizzle to serve
- good squeeze of lemon juice
- 2 tbsp toasted hazelnuts , roughly chopped
- 2 tbsp pumpkin seeds , roughly chopped
- 2 tsp nigella seeds
- 1 tsp sumac (optional)
- pinch of chilli flakes (optional)

To serve (optional)

- crunchy summer veg , cut into batons (we used fennel, sugar snap peas, baby heritage carrots & radishes)
- bread , toasted and cut into fingers for dipping
- mini mozzarella balls

- olives
- prosciutto-wrapped breadsticks

Method

STEP 1

Set about 2 tbsp chickpeas aside. Tip the rest of the chickpeas, the beetroot, garlic, tahini, oil and lemon juice into a food processor with a good pinch of salt. Blend until smooth, then check the seasoning, adding a little more salt or lemon if it needs it. Chill the hummus until you're ready to serve (it will keep for up to two days).

STEP 2

Transfer the hummus to a wide, shallow bowl or spread over a platter. Drizzle with some oil, scatter with the reserved chickpeas, hazelnuts, seeds, sumac and chilli (if using). Arrange the crunchy veg and other accompaniments around the platter and let everyone dig in.

Coconut chai traybake

Prep:25 mins **Cook:**25 mins - 30 mins

Cuts into 15 squares

Ingredients

- 100ml vegetable oil , plus a little for greasing
- 300ml coconut milk (not low-fat) - if the cream has separated in the can, give it a good mix before measuring
- 4 large eggs
- 2 tsp vanilla extract
- 280g light brown soft sugar
- 250g self-raising flour
- 75g desiccated coconut
- 1 tsp ground ginger
- 1 tsp ground cinnamon
- ¼ nutmeg , finely grated
- ¼ tsp ground cloves
- 10 cardamom pods , seeds removed and crushed using a pestle and mortar
- 4 tbsp ginger syrup

For the topping and icing

- 3-4 tbsp coconut milk
- 140g icing sugar
- 2 balls stem ginger , finely chopped
- chopped pistachios and coconut flakes (optional)

Method

STEP 1

Grease a 20 x 30cm baking tin with a little oil, and line the base and sides with baking parchment. Heat oven to 180C/160C fan/gas 4. Measure the coconut milk and oil into a jug. Crack in the eggs, add the vanilla and whisk with a fork to combine.

STEP 2

In a large bowl, mix the sugar, flour, coconut, spices and a pinch of salt. Squeeze any lumps of sugar through your fingers, shaking the bowl a few times so they come to the surface. Pour in the wet ingredients and use a large whisk to mix to a smooth batter. Pour into the tin, scraping every drop of the mixture out of the bowl with a spatula.

STEP 3

Bake on the middle shelf of the oven for 25 mins or until a skewer inserted into the middle comes out clean. If there is any wet mixture clinging to it, bake for a further 5 mins, then check again. Leave to cool for 15 mins in the tin, then transfer to a wire rack and drizzle over the ginger syrup.

STEP 4

To make the icing, mix the coconut milk with the icing sugar until smooth. Drizzle the icing over the cake in squiggles, then scatter with the chopped ginger, pistachios and coconut flakes, if using. Eat warm or cold. Will keep for 3 days in an airtight container.

Chorizo hummus bowl

Prep: 5 mins **Cook:** 10 mins

Serves 1

Ingredients

- 400g can chickpeas
- 2 tbsp olive oil
- ¼ lemon , juiced

- 1-2 small cooking chorizo , chopped
- 2 handfuls chopped kale
- flatbread , to serve

Method

STEP 1

Warm the chickpeas in a microwave or frying pan in their liquid. Drain and reserve the liquid. Tip half the chickpeas into a small food processor with 1 tbsp oil, the lemon juice and a splash of the liquid from the tin and whizz to a paste. Season.

STEP 2

Put the chorizo in a small frying pan and cook over a low heat until it starts to release its oils, then turn up the heat and continue cooking until the chorizo starts to crisp. Add the remaining chickpeas and stir for a couple of mins. Stir in the kale and cook until it wilts.

STEP 3

Spoon the warm hummus into a bowl and tip the chorizo, chickpeas and kale on top. Drizzle over the remaining oil, season well and serve with flatbread for scooping up.

Sweet potato jackets with guacamole & kidney beans

Prep: 10 mins **Cook:** 45 mins

Serves 2

Ingredients

- a drop of rapeseed oil
- 2 sweet potatoes
- 1 large avocado
- juice 1 lime, plus 2 wedges
- 1 red chilli, deseeded and finely chopped
- 2 tomatoes, finely chopped
- ⅓ small pack coriander, leaves roughly chopped
- 1 small red onion, finely chopped
- 400g can red kidney beans in water, drained

Method

STEP 1

Heat oven to 220C/200C fan/gas 7, oil the sweet potatoes, then put them straight on the oven shelf and roast for 45 mins or until tender all the way through when pierced with a knife.

STEP 2

Meanwhile, mash the avocado with the lime juice in a small bowl, then stir in the chilli, tomatoes, coriander and onion.

STEP 3

Cut the potatoes in half and top with the beans and guacamole. Serve with the lime wedges for squeezing over.

Peach Melba pots

Prep: 15 mins No cook

Makes 6

Ingredients

- 140g mascarpone
- 200g Greek-style yogurt
- 3 tbsp icing sugar , sifted
- pinch of ground cloves
- few drops of vanilla extract
- 300ml double cream

- 300ml Peach Melba jam (see 'goes well with...' below, or use a mixture of raspberry and peach jams)
- 3 peaches , each sliced into 8
- 150g punnet raspberries
- 1 ½ tbsp roasted chopped hazelnut
- biscotti or amaretti biscuit , to serve

Method

STEP 1

Put the mascarpone, yogurt, sugar, ground cloves and vanilla extract in a large bowl. Using a balloon whisk, beat until smooth. Pour in the cream and whisk again until the mixture just holds its shape – you want it to be soft and pillowy, so be careful not to take it too far.

STEP 2

Put a little jam in the bottom of 6 small glasses or pots, top with some of the cream mixture, then 4 peach slices and more jam. Follow this with another layer of the cream, a drizzle of jam and finally the raspberries. Can be chilled for up to 5 hrs. Scatter over the hazelnuts and serve with biscotti or amaretti biscuits on the side.

All-in-one gammon, egg & chips

Prep: 5 mins **Cook:** 45 mins

Serves 1

Ingredients

- 1 large baking potato , unpeeled, cut into chunky chips
- 1 tsp olive oil
- 1 small gammon steak
- 1 egg
- ketchup , to serve

Method

STEP 1

Heat oven to 200C/180C fan/gas 6. Drizzle the potatoes with the oil and some salt and pepper. Bake on a roasting tray for 25 mins, until starting to go brown.

STEP 2

Remove and turn the chips. Push to edges of the tray, put the gammon in the centre and cook for 7 mins more. Take the tray out of the oven and turn the gammon over, then crack the egg into the corner of the tray. Cook for 7 mins more until the egg is set and the gammon is cooked through. Serve with ketchup, if you like.

Roast cod with curried cauliflower purée & onion bhaji

Prep:30 mins **Cook:**1 hr and 10 mins

Serves 4

Ingredients

- 200g spinach , washed
- olive oil , for frying
- 4 x 150g portions skinless cod fillet (from the head end if possible)
- For the dressing
- ½ onion , finely chopped
- vegetable oil , for frying
- 1 tbsp golden raisins
- 2 tsp nonpareilles capers
- 50ml apple juice
- ½ lime zested and juiced
- 1 tsp chopped coriander
- pinch of golden caster sugar

For the bhaji

- 125g gram flour
- 1 egg
- 125ml milk
- 1 red onion , very finely sliced

- ½ red chilli , finely chopped
- 1 tsp chopped coriander

For the purée

- 25g unsalted butter
- ½ onion , finely sliced
- 1 tsp mild curry powder

- vegetable oil , for frying

- 150g cauliflower , chopped
- 100ml double cream

Method

STEP 1

To make the dressing, fry the onion in a small, non-stick pan with a splash of oil for 5 mins. Transfer to a bowl and add the rest of the dressing ingredients with a pinch of salt, and leave to macerate for 2 hrs.

STEP 2

To make the bhaji, whisk the flour, egg and milk into a light batter. Add the onion, chilli and coriander with a pinch of salt and set aside for 30 mins.

STEP 3

For the purée, melt the butter over a medium heat in a heavy-based saucepan. Add the onion, a generous pinch of salt and fry for 5 mins until soft and translucent. Add the curry powder and cook for another 5 mins, then stir in the cauliflower and cook for a few mins more. Pour in the cream, bring to the boil, then turn the heat right down. Cover with a lid and cook gently for 25-30 mins. Transfer to a blender and blend to a smooth purée. Check the seasoning.

STEP 4

Half an hour before you want to serve, heat oven to 160C/140C fan/ gas 3. To fry the bhaji, heat enough oil to half-fill a large pan to 160C. Using a slotted metal spoon, lift the onion mix from the batter and let the excess liquid drain away. Lower into the oil and fry until the slices are crisp and golden. Drain on kitchen paper, then spread out on a baking tray and keep warm in the oven while you prepare the other elements.

STEP 5

Wilt the spinach in a splash of olive oil, seasoning as you do so, and warm your purée through. Keep both on a low heat while you cook the cod.

STEP 6

Put a non-stick ovenproof pan over a high heat. Season the top of the cod with salt. Add a splash of oil to the pan and put the seasoned side of the cod into the oil. Fry until golden brown, turn down the heat, turn the fish over and roast in the oven for 2-3 mins until just cooked.

STEP 7

To serve, spoon some purée onto four heated plates. Put the spinach alongside and top with a piece of cod. Spoon a generous amount of the dressing onto the cod and garnish the fish with a bhaji.

Quick prawn, coconut & tomato curry

Prep: 10 mins **Cook:** 20 mins

Serves 4

Ingredients

- 2 tbsp vegetable oil
- 1 medium onion , thinly sliced
- 2 garlic cloves , sliced
- 1 green chilli , deseeded and sliced
- 3 tbsp curry paste
- 1 tbsp tomato purée
- 200ml vegetable stock
- 200ml coconut cream
- 350g raw prawn
- coriander sprigs and rice, to serve

Method

STEP 1

Heat the oil in a large frying pan. Fry the onion, garlic and half the chilli for 5 mins or until softened. Add the curry paste and cook for 1 min more. Add the tomato purée, stock and coconut cream.

STEP 2

Simmer on medium heat for 10 mins, then add the prawns. Cook for 3 mins or until they turn opaque. Scatter on the remaining green chillies and coriander sprigs, then serve with rice.

Easy risotto with bacon & peas

Prep:5 mins **Cook:**40 mins

Serves 4

Ingredients

- 1 onion
- 2 tbsp olive oil
- knob of butter
- 6 rashers streaky bacon, chopped
- 300g risotto rice
- 1l hot vegetable stock
- 100g frozen peas
- freshly grated parmesan, to serve

Method

STEP 1

Finely chop 1 onion. Heat 2 tbsp olive oil and a knob of butter in a pan, add the onions and fry until lightly browned (about 7 minutes).

STEP 2

Add 6 chopped rashers streaky bacon and fry for a further 5 minutes, until it starts to crisp.

STEP 3

Add 300g risotto rice and 1l hot vegetable stock, and bring to the boil. Stir well, then reduce the heat and cook, covered, for 15-20 minutes until the rice is almost tender.

STEP 4

Stir in 100g frozen peas, add a little salt and pepper and cook for a further 3 minutes, until the peas are cooked.

STEP 5

Serve sprinkled with freshly grated parmesan and freshly ground black pepper.

5-a-day chicken with kale & pistachio pesto

Prep:20 mins **Cook:**45 mins

Serves 3-4

Ingredients

- olive oil
- 500g butternut squash , peeled and cut into thin slices (keep the seeds if you like and toast them on a separate tray to scatter over the finished dish)
- 200g shallots , peeled and halved
- 300g leeks , use baby leeks or cut large ones into lengths and halve them

For the pesto

- 200g chopped kale , woody stalks removed
- 1 garlic clove , crushed
- 2 tbsp pistachio kernels

- 300g carrots , use baby ones or cut them into long batons
- 400g fennel , cut into long wedges
- 1 garlic bulb , halved through the middle
- 3-4 large or 6-8 small chicken thighs (depending on whether you're serving 3 or 4), skin patted dry

- 2 tbsp grated parmesan
- ½ lemon , juiced
- 60ml olive oil

Method

STEP 1

Heat oven to 200C/180C fan/gas 6. Put all the veg for the bake except the garlic in a large bowl and add 1 tbsp olive oil, then carefully turn everything over with your hands so the oil adds a very thin coating. Lightly oil the tray as well if you are worried about things sticking.

STEP 2

Arrange the veg in piles on the tray, or scatter it all over if you prefer. Add the garlic halves and the chicken, sitting the chicken on top of the veg. Season well and bake for 40 mins then, if the chicken skin is still pale, either turn the oven up or turn it onto the grill setting, and cook or grill until it is nicely browned.

STEP 3

Meanwhile, make the pesto. Whizz the kale, garlic and pistachios until everything is finely chopped. Add the parmesan, lemon juice and olive oil and whizz again. Add a splash of water to loosen. Any left over will keep in a jar for up to three days in the fridge. Serve the chicken and veg with the pesto spooned over.

Mini nut roasts with candied carrots

Prep: 35 mins **Cook:** 40 mins

Serves 6

Ingredients

- 250g bunch thin baby carrots
- 3 tbsp olive oil, plus extra for the tin
- 5 tbsp maple syrup
- 2 tbsp milled flaxseed
- 1 large onion, finely chopped
- 1 celery stick, finely chopped
- 2 garlic cloves, chopped
- 350g mixed mushrooms, finely chopped
- 3 rosemary sprigs, leaves picked and finely chopped

- 1 tsp tomato purée
- 2 tsp tamari or dark soy sauce
- 1 tbsp smoked paprika
- 100g pecans
- 50g hazelnuts
- 400g can green lentils, drained
- 400g can chickpeas, drained
- 40g ground almonds
- handful of sage and thyme leaves

You will need

- 6 mini loaf tins (silicone ones work well)

Method

STEP 1

Heat the oven to 200C/180C fan/gas 6. Scrub and trim the carrots, and cut them in half lengthways or into quarters if large. Toss the carrots with 1 tbsp olive oil and 2 tbsp maple syrup in a bowl. Season well, and tip onto a baking tray. Roast for 20-25 mins until tender and starting to caramelise.

STEP 2

Meanwhile, mix the flaxseed with 4 tbsp water and leave to thicken. Heat 1 tbsp olive oil in a frying pan, and fry the onion and celery until soft and translucent, about 10 mins. Add a splash of water if you need to, to stop them from catching. Stir in the garlic, mushrooms, rosemary, tomato purée, tamari and paprika, and fry for another 10 mins until the mushrooms are tender. Remove from the heat and leave in a bowl to cool slightly.

STEP 3

Put the pecans and hazelnuts in a food processor and blitz until roughly chopped. Add the lentils and chickpeas and blend again until you get a thick, dry paste.

STEP 4

Combine the nuts and pulses, mushroom mixture, ground almonds, 2 tbsp maple syrup and soaked flaxseed in a bowl with a good amount of seasoning. Mix everything well using your hands.

STEP 5

Oil six holes of a mini loaf tin and line each with a strip of baking parchment. Trim and cut the carrots to fit in the base in a snug single layer, cut-side down. Roughly chop any remaining carrots and mix them through the nut roast mixture. Pack it firmly into the tins and smooth over. Bake, uncovered, for 20 mins. Leave to rest for 10 mins before inverting onto a serving plate, or plates. Fry the sage and thyme in the remaining 1 tbsp olive oil until crisp, then stir through the remaining 1 tbsp maple syrup. Spoon over the nut roasts to serve.

Baked ginger & spinach sweet potato

Prep: 10 mins **Cook:** 45 mins

Serves 1

Ingredients

- 1 sweet potato
- 2 tsp oil
- ½ onion , finely chopped
- 1 garlic clove , crushed
- small knob of ginger , grated

- 1-2 tsp curry paste (use what you have or buy a Madras or red curry paste)
- knob of butter
- handful of spinach

Method

STEP 1

Heat oven to 200C/180C fan/gas 6. Prick the potato and bake it for 40-45 mins or until soft when you squeeze the sides.

STEP 2

Meanwhile, heat the oil in a small frying pan and fry the onion until softened, add the garlic and cook for 1 min, then add the ginger and curry paste and cook for another min. Stir in the butter and spinach, and continue stirring until the spinach wilts. Season well.

STEP 3

Cut open the top of the sweet potato, scoop out some of the flesh, add it to the mix in the pan and stir through, then spoon the mixture back into the potato.

Mix & match seafood tacos

Prep: 15 mins **Cook:** 5 mins

Serves 4

Ingredients

- 8 crispy corn taco shells

For the salmon

- 2 sushi-grade skinless salmon fillets (about 250g), cut into 1cm cubes (ask your fishmonger)
- 2 tbsp soy sauce
- 2 tbsp Yuzu juice or lime juice
- 1 tsp sesame oil
- 1 avocado , stoned, peeled and cubed
- nori seaweed , sliced, to serve

For the prawns

- 1 tsp olive oil
- 1 crushed garlic
- 1 tsp crushed ginger
- 3 spring onions , sliced, plus extra to serve
- 1/2 tsp finely chopped red chilli
- 250g raw king prawns , roughly chopped
- 1 lime , zested and juiced, plus wedges to serve
- 1/2 small bunch coriander , leaves picked

Method

STEP 1

For the salmon, combine all the ingredients, except the avocado and seaweed, in a bowl and mix well. Cover and leave to marinate in the fridge while you prepare the other ingredients.

STEP 2

For the prawns, heat the olive oil in a pan over a high heat. Add the garlic, ginger, spring onions and chilli, stirring into the oil for 20 secs. Add the prawns and stir constantly until cooked through and pink. Remove from the heat and stir through the lime zest and juice.

STEP 3

Stir the avocado into the salmon and warm the taco shells following pack instructions. Fill each taco with the prawns or the salmon. Top the salmon tacos with the seaweed and the prawn tacos with coriander and extra spring onions. Squeeze over lime wedges to serve.

Roast potato, turkey, sausage & stuffing pie

Prep: 10 mins **Cook:** 1 hr and 10 mins

Serves 6

Ingredients

- 1 tbsp olive oil or rapeseed oil
- knob of butter
- 1 large onion , halved and sliced
- 6 sausages or 8 chipolatas (leftover pigs in blankets are fine too)
- 2 tsp English mustard powder
- 50g plain flour
- 1 chicken stock cube , crumbled
- 150ml white wine
- 500ml chicken stock or leftover gravy
- 6 stuffing balls, leftover or shop-bought
- 300g cooked turkey , shredded
- 1 tbsp wholegrain mustard
- 100g low-fat crème fraîche
- small bunch parsley , chopped
- 800g leftover roast potatoes
- 20g mature cheddar , grated

Method

STEP 1

Heat the oil and butter in a large, shallow ovenproof casserole dish. Add the onion and cook for 10 mins until really soft. Push the onion to one side of the dish and add the sausages, browning them all over (skip this step if you're using cooked leftovers).

STEP 2

Remove the sausages from the dish and set aside to cool a little. Stir the mustard powder, flour and stock cube into the oil and butter for 1-2 mins, then add the white wine. Bubble for 1 min, scraping the bottom of the dish to release any tasty bits, then add the stock. Stir to make a smooth sauce, season and bubble for 5 mins. Heat oven to 200C/180C fan/gas 6.

STEP 3

Cut the sausages and stuffing into bite-sized chunks, add to the sauce with the turkey, mustard, crème fraîche and parsley. When bubbling, remove from the heat. Crumble the potatoes in your hands over the top of the filling, so you have some larger and smaller chunks. Scatter with cheese and bake for 40 mins until the potatoes are crisp and the filling is bubbling around the edges.

Spaghetti & meatballs

Prep:30 mins **Cook:**30 mins

Makes about 10 servings

Ingredients

- 8 good-quality pork sausages
- 1 kg beef mince
- 1 onion, finely chopped
- ½ a large bunch flat-leaf parsley, finely chopped
- 85g parmesan, grated, plus extra to serve (optional)

- 100g fresh breadcrumbs
- 2 eggs, beaten with a fork
- olive oil, for roasting
- spaghetti, to serve (about 100g per portion)

For the sauce

- 3 tbsp olive oil
- 4 garlic cloves, crushed
- 4 x 400g cans chopped tomatoes
- 125ml red wine (optional)

- 3 tbsp caster sugar
- ½ a large bunch of flat-leaf parsley, finely chopped
- few basil leaves (optional)

Method

STEP 1

First, make the meatballs. Split the skins of the sausages and squeeze out the meat into a large mixing bowl.

STEP 2

Add the mince, onion, parsley, parmesan, breadcrumbs, eggs and lots of seasoning. Get your hands in and mix together really well – the more you squeeze and mash the mince, the more tender the meatballs will be.

STEP 3

Heat the oven to 220C/200C fan/gas 7. Roll the mince mixture into about 50 golf-ball-sized meatballs. Set aside any meatballs for freezing, allowing about five per portion, then spread the rest out in a large roasting tin – the meatballs will brown better if spaced out a bit.

STEP 4

Drizzle with a little oil (about 1 tsp per portion), shake to coat, then roast for 20-30 mins until browned.

STEP 5

Meanwhile, make the sauce. Heat the olive oil in a large saucepan. Add the garlic cloves and sizzle for 1 min.

STEP 6

Stir in the chopped tomatoes, red wine, if using, caster sugar, parsley and seasoning. Simmer for 15-20 mins until slightly thickened.

STEP 7

Stir in a few basil leaves, if using, spoon out any portions for freezing, then add the cooked meatballs to the pan to keep warm while you cook the spaghetti in a pan of boiling, salted water.

STEP 8

Spoon the sauce and meatballs over spaghetti, or stir them all together and serve with extra parmesan and a few basil leaves, if you like.

One-pan baked chicken with squash, sage & walnuts

Prep: 20 mins **Cook:** 1 hr

Serves 4

154

Ingredients

- 1kg mixed chicken thigh and drumstick pieces
- 3 tbsp olive oil
- 3 red onions , peeled, cut into large wedges
- 1 butternut squash , peeled, deseeded and cut into wedges
- bunch sage , leaves picked
- 100g walnut halves, very roughly chopped
- good splash sherry vinegar

Method

STEP 1

Heat oven to 220C/200C fan/gas 7. Tip the chicken pieces into a largish roasting tin and toss with the oil, onions and squash. Season with salt and pepper and arrange chicken so it's all skin-side up.

STEP 2

Roast in oven for about 25 mins, remove, toss through sage, walnuts, then drizzle over vinegar. Using tongs, again arrange chicken so it's all skin-side up. Roast for another 25-30 mins until chicken is golden brown and the veg soft and sticky. Serve straight from the tin with some mashed potato.

Rhubarb & strawberry meringue pots

Prep: 15 mins **Cook:** 1 hr

Serves 4

Ingredients

- 450g rhubarb, cut into 4cm/1½in chunks
- 100g golden caster sugar
- grated zest of 1 orange
- 1 tbsp strawberry conserve
- 2 eggs, separated

Method

STEP 1

Preheat the oven to 180C/ Gas 4/fan oven 160C. Put the rhubarb in an ovenproof dish, sprinkle over 50g/2oz of the sugar and the orange zest and stir together. Cover and bake in the oven for 35-40 minutes until tender. (Alternatively, you can cook the rhubarb with the sugar and zest in the microwave for 10 minutes on full power, stirring halfway through the cooking time, until just tender.)

STEP 2

Remove the rhubarb from the oven and allow to cool slightly. Stir in the conserve then the egg yolks. Divide the rhubarb mixture between four 175ml/6fl oz ramekins. Put on a baking sheet and cook in the oven for 10 minutes until lightly thickened.

STEP 3

While the rhubarb is cooking, whisk the egg whites until stiff. Sprinkle over half of the remaining sugar and whisk again. Gently fold in the rest of the sugar. Pile the meringue on top of the rhubarb to cover it completely and swirl the top. Return to the oven for 10 minutes until the meringue is puffy and golden. Serve immediately.

Chicken & vegetable stew with wholemeal couscous

Prep: 10 mins

Serves 2

Ingredients

- 1 tbsp olive oil
- 2 skinless chicken breasts , cut into chunks
- 1 small onion , sliced
- 1 garlic clove , crushed
- pinch each paprika and saffron

- 50g baby sweetcorn , halved
- 50g asparagus tips
- 50g peas
- 50g cherry tomatoes , halved
- 150ml chicken stock
- 140g wholemeal couscous

Method

STEP 1

Heat the oil in a pan, cook the chicken for 5-6 mins, then remove with a slotted spoon. Add onion and cook for 2-3 mins before adding the garlic, paprika, saffron, sweetcorn, asparagus, peas and tomatoes. Cook for 2-3 mins more. Return the chicken to the pan, pour in the stock, then cover and simmer for 15 mins.

STEP 2

Meanwhile, cook the couscous following pack instructions. To serve, fluff the couscous with a fork and divide between 2 bowls before spooning over the stew.

Potato & leek gratin

Cook: 1 hr and 20 mins

Serves 4

Ingredients

- 125ml stock (made with a cube - whatever you've got)
- carton double cream
- 150ml milk
- 1 garlic clove, crushed
- 1 bay leaf

- a knob of butter, for greasing
- 800g potato, peeled and thinly sliced
- 2 leeks, washed and thinly sliced
- 175g sliced ham, chopped (optional)
- 85g cheddar, grated

Method

STEP 1

Pour the stock, cream and milk into a small saucepan, add the garlic and bay leaf and bring to the boil. Remove from the heat, cover and let the flavours infuse while you get on with the rest of the dish.

STEP 2

Preheat the oven to 180C/gas 4/fan 160C. Butter a 2 litre gratin dish well. Mix the potatoes, leeks and ham (if using) together in the dish, and spread out in an even layer. Pour over the stock mixture and tuck the bay leaf in the middle. Season and sprinkle with the cheese.

STEP 3

Stand the dish on a baking tray to catch any spills. Loosely cover with foil and bake for 30 minutes. Test the potatoes with a knife – they should be just beginning to soften. Remove the foil and bake for another 35-45 minutes, spooning some of the stock mixture over every now and again until the potatoes are tender. Cool for 15 minutes before serving.

Healthy egg & chips

Prep: 10 mins **Cook:** 1 hr

Serves 4

Ingredients

- 500g potatoes , diced
- 2 shallots , sliced
- 1 tbsp olive oil

- 2 tsp dried crushed oregano or 1 tsp fresh leaves
- 200g small mushroom
- 4 eggs

Method

STEP 1

Heat oven to 200C/fan 180C/gas 6. Tip the potatoes and shallots into a large, non-stick roasting tin, drizzle with the oil, sprinkle over the oregano, then mix everything together well. Bake for 40-45 mins (or until starting to go brown), add the mushrooms, then cook for a further 10 mins until the potatoes are browned and tender.

STEP 2

Make four gaps in the vegetables and crack an egg into each space. Return to the oven for 3-4 mins or until the eggs are cooked to your liking.

Asian prawn noodles

Prep: 20 mins **Cook:** 5 mins

Serves 2

Ingredients

- 2nests wholewheat noodles
- 3 garlic cloves , finely grated
- 1 tbsp finely grated ginger
- handful coriander , leaves and stalks chopped but kept separate
- ½ - 1 red chilli , thinly sliced and deseeded if you don't like it too hot
- 1 tbsp tamari

- 4 spring onions , sliced at an angle
- 125g sugar snap peas
- 160g beansprouts , well rinsed
- 100g cooked prawns
- 1 lime , zested and juiced
- small pack mint leaves (optional)
- sesame oil , to serve (optional)

Method

STEP 1

Put the noodles in a bowl, pour over enough boiling water to cover, set aside to soak for 5 mins, then drain.

STEP 2

Meanwhile, pour 450ml water into a wok or wide pan and add the garlic, ginger, coriander stalks, chilli, tamari, spring onions and sugar snaps. Bring to the boil and simmer for 3 mins, then add the noodles and beansprouts to heat through.

STEP 3

Stir in the prawns, lime zest and juice, coriander leaves and the mint, if using. Return to the boil until steaming hot and serve in deep bowls, drizzled with a dash of sesame oil, if you like.

Sausage & squash risotto

Prep:15 mins **Cook:**25 mins

Serves 4

Ingredients

- 350g pack ready-chopped butternut squash , or half a medium squash, peeled and chopped
- 2 low-sodium chicken stock cubes
- 2 tsp olive oil
- 6 good-quality sausages , meat squeezed from the skins and rolled into mini meatballs
- 1 large onion , finely chopped
- 2 garlic cloves , crushed
- 6-8 thyme sprigs , leaves picked and chopped
- ½ tsp turmeric
- 200g risotto rice
- 25g parmesan , grated, plus a little to serve

Method

STEP 1

Boil the kettle. Put the squash in a heatproof bowl, add a splash of water and cover with cling film. Microwave on High for 8-10 mins or until the squash is tender. Meanwhile, crumble the stock cubes into a pan, add 1.2 litres hot water from the kettle and set over a low heat to simmer gently.

STEP 2

Heat the oil in a large, high-sided frying pan. Add the sausage meatballs and roll them around in the pan for 5-10 mins until browned all over and cooked through. Remove from the pan and set aside. Add the onion and sizzle gently for 5 mins, then add the garlic and cook for 1 min more, stirring to prevent it from burning. Stir in the thyme, turmeric and risotto rice for 1 min, coating the rice in the oil from the pan. Start adding the stock, a ladleful at a time, stirring well every 1-2 mins until the liquid is absorbed and the rice is cooked.

STEP 3

Mash half the squash and add to the pan along with the sausage meatballs and Parmesan. Stir, then top with the remaining squash, cover with a lid and leave for 2 mins. Serve with extra Parmesan.

Summer courgette risotto

Prep: 15 mins **Cook:** 30 mins

Serves 4

Ingredients

- 1 tbsp olive oil
- 1 onion and 2 garlic cloves, finely chopped
- 3 ripe tomatoes , roughly chopped
- 350g carnaroli or other risotto rice
- 1 tsp chopped rosemary
- 1 ½l hot vegetable stock
- 3 courgettes , finely diced
- 140g peas , fresh or frozen
- large handful basil , lightly torn

Method

STEP 1

Heat the oil in a large pan. Cook the onion and garlic for 5 mins until the onion has softened. Add the tomatoes and cook for 3-4 mins until softened and pulpy, then add the rice and rosemary.

STEP 2

Pour in half the stock and leave to cook for 10 mins or until the liquid has evaporated, stirring from time to time. Add the rest of the stock, then continue to cook for a further 5 mins.

STEP 3

Stir in the courgettes and peas, then cook for another 5 mins or so, stirring until the rice is tender, but the mixture is still a bit saucy. Can be frozen at this stage for up to 1 month. Season with plenty of black pepper, then add the basil and stir until wilted. Serve immediately.

Beetroot & butternut stew

Prep:20 mins **Cook:**35 mins

Serves 2

Ingredients

- 250g raw beetroot
- 350g butternut squash , unpeeled
- 1 garlic clove , grated
- 1 small onion , diced
- ¼ tsp cumin seeds
- ½ tsp ground coriander
- 4 cardamom pods , seeds removed and crushed
- 1 tbsp sunflower oil

- ½ tsp cinnamon
- 100g green beans , topped and cut in half
- 50g chard or spinach, stems removed and leaves roughly chopped
- small pack flat-leaf parsley , roughly chopped
- brown rice , to serve (optional)

Method

STEP 1

Peel the beetroot and chop into small pieces. Chop the butternut squash into small pieces. Put them in separate bowls until you need them.

STEP 2

In a large wide-topped saucepan, fry the garlic, onion, cumin seeds, coriander and cardamom pods in the oil for 2 mins on a medium heat. Add 125ml water along with the beetroot and leave for a further 5 mins until the water has simmered away.

STEP 3

Add 250ml water, the butternut squash and cinnamon, and leave to simmer on a medium heat for 10 mins. Add 250ml water and leave to simmer for another 10 mins.

STEP 4

Add 125ml water, the green beans and simmer for another 5 mins until the water has simmered away. Take off the heat and stir in the chard and parsley. Serve by itself or with brown rice for a fuller meal.

Lamb masala meatball curry

Prep:20 mins **Cook:**30 mins

Serves 4

Ingredients

For the meatballs

- 1 tbsp fennel seed , toasted
- 2 garlic cloves , finely grated
- thumb-sized piece ginger , finely grated
- 2 green chillies , deseeded and finely chopped

- 1 onion , finely chopped
- 60g desiccated coconut
- 400g lamb mince

For the curry sauce

- 1 tbsp olive oil
- 1 onion , finely chopped
- 1 tsp grated ginger
- 1 tbsp garam masala
- 1 tsp turmeric

- 400g can chopped tomatoes
- 1 tbsp coconut yogurt
- ½ small pack coriander , roughly chopped
- rice or naan, to serve

Method

STEP 1

Put all the meatball ingredients in a large bowl and use your hands to combine everything together. Roll into about 16 balls, cover and chill until needed.

STEP 2

162

Heat the oil in a large, deep frying pan over a gentle heat and fry the onion, ginger and spices for 10 mins until the onions are softened. Tip in the tomatoes and a splash of water, and bring to the boil over a high heat. Drop in the meatballs and reduce the heat. Cover and simmer for 15 mins or until the meatballs are cooked. Mix through the yogurt, scatter over the coriander and serve with rice or naan bread.

Pot-roast pheasant with fino & porcini

Prep: 1 hr **Cook:** 1 hr and 30 mins

Serves 4

Ingredients

- 15g dried porcini
- 2 x 800g pheasants , trussed
- 8 slices prosciutto
- 2 tbsp rapeseed oil or olive oil
- 2 bay leaves
- 30g unsalted butter
- 6 juniper berries , crushed
- 2 thyme sprigs , leaves picked

- 10 small round shallots , peeled and trimmed
- 1 tbsp plain flour
- 200ml fino sherry
- 500ml chicken stock
- 300g seedless red grapes
- 150ml double cream

Method

STEP 1

Heat oven to 180C/160C fan/gas 4. Soak the dried porcini in 100ml boiling water for 10 mins until softened and then drain, reserving the mushroom stock.

STEP 2

Cover each pheasant in four overlapping slices of prosciutto and tie them each in place with a piece of string. Heat the oil in a high-sided, heavy-bottomed skillet or frying pan over a medium heat. Season the pheasants all over and brown them one at a time in the pan, starting with the breast side for a few mins, and then turning until they are golden all over – this should take about 8 mins. Tuck the bay leaves into their cavities, then put them into one large or two medium-sized flameproof, lidded casseroles.

STEP 3

Keeping the pan on the hob, lower the heat and add the butter. When it has melted, add the juniper berries, thyme and shallots, then season. Fry gently for 5-10 mins, until the shallots are golden brown. Add the flour to the pan and cook, stirring for 1 min. Then turn up the heat and pour in the sherry, scraping the bottom of the pan to pick up any crust. Cook for 1-2 mins, stirring, then add the stock and mushroom water, and bring to the boil. Simmer for 10 mins, or until reduced by a third, then pour into the casserole with the pheasants.

STEP 4

Cover the casserole tightly with foil and put the lid on top of the foil. Roast the pheasants in the oven for 20 mins, then uncover the pot and put back in the oven for a further 15-20 mins or until cooked through (a little pinkness is okay). Lift out the pheasants onto a platter, cover with foil and rest them for at least 10 mins.

STEP 5

While the pheasants are resting add the grapes, porcini and cream to the liquor in the casserole and cook over a gentle heat for 10-15 mins (if your casserole is not flameproof, tip the cooking juices into a saucepan instead). While this is cooking, carve the breasts and legs off the birds, put in a roasting tin and cover with foil. Just before serving, return to the oven at 150C/130C fan/gas 2 for 3 mins to heat through. Serve the meat with a generous spoonful of the sauce and the side dishes.

Caponata pasta

Prep: 2 mins **Cook:** 18 mins

Serves 4

Ingredients

- 4 tbsp olive oil (or use the oil from your chargrilled veg, see below)
- 1 large onion, finely chopped
- 4 garlic cloves, finely sliced
- 250g chargrilled Mediterranean veg (peppers and aubergines, if possible) from a jar, pot or deli counter, drained if in oil (you can use this oil in place of the olive oil) and roughly chopped
- 400g can chopped tomatoes
- 1 tbsp small capers
- 2 tbsp raisins
- 350g rigatoni, penne or another short pasta shape
- bunch basil leaves, picked

- parmesan (or vegetarian alternative),   shaved, to serve

Method

STEP 1

Heat the oil in a large pan and cook the onion for 8-10 mins until starting to caramelise (or for longer if you have time – the sweeter the better). Add the garlic for the final 2 mins of cooking time.

STEP 2

Tip in the mixed veg, tomatoes, capers and raisins. Season well and simmer, uncovered, for 10 mins, or until you have a rich sauce.

STEP 3

Meanwhile, boil the kettle. Pour the kettleful of water into a large pan with a little salt and bring back to the boil. Add the pasta and cook until tender with a little bite, then drain, reserving some of the pasta water. Tip the pasta into the sauce, adding a splash of pasta water if it needs loosening. Scatter with the basil leaves and parmesan, if you like, and serve straight from the pan

Meatball & tomato soup

Prep: 5 mins **Cook:** 15 mins

Serves 4

Ingredients

- 1½ tbsp rapeseed oil
- 1 onion, finely chopped
- 2 red peppers, deseeded and sliced
- 1 garlic clove, crushed
- ½ tsp chilli flakes
- 2 x 400g cans chopped tomatoes
- 100g giant couscous
- 500ml hot vegetable stock
- 12 pork meatballs
- 150g baby spinach
- ½ small bunch of basil
- grated parmesan, to serve (optional)

Method

STEP 1

Heat the oil in a saucepan. Fry the onion and peppers for 7 mins, then stir through the garlic and chilli flakes and cook for 1 min. Add the tomatoes, giant couscous and veg stock and bring to a simmer.

STEP 2

Season to taste, then add the meatballs and spinach. Simmer for 5-7 mins or until cooked through. Ladle into bowls and top with the basil and some parmesan, if you like.

Raspberry coconut porridge

Prep:10 mins **Cook:**10 mins

Serves 4

Ingredients

- 100g rolled porridge oats (not instant)
- 25g creamed coconut , chopped
- 200g frozen raspberries
- 125g pot coconut yogurt (we used COYO)
- a few mint leaves , to serve (optional)

Method

STEP 1

Tip the oats and creamed coconut into a large bowl, pour on 800ml cold water, cover and leave to soak overnight.

STEP 2

The next day, tip the contents of the bowl into a saucepan and cook over a medium heat, stirring frequently, for 5 -10 mins until the oats are cooked. Add the raspberries to the pan with the yogurt and allow to thaw and melt into the oats off the heat. Reserve half for the next day and spoon the remainder into bowls. Top each portion with mint leaves, if you like.

Roasted summer vegetable casserole

Prep:15 mins **Cook:**1 hr

Serves 2 - 3

Ingredients

- 3 tbsp olive oil
- 1 garlic bulb , halved through the middle
- 2 large courgettes , thickly sliced
- 1 large red onion , sliced
- 1 aubergine , halved and sliced on the diagonal
- 2 large tomatoes , quartered
- 200g new potatoes , scrubbed and halved
- 1 red pepper , deseeded and cut into chunky pieces
- 400g can chopped tomatoes
- 0.5 small pack parsley , chopped

Method

STEP 1

Heat oven to 200C/180C fan/gas 6 and put the oil in a roasting tin. Tip in the garlic and all the fresh veg, then toss with your hands to coat in the oil. Season well and roast for 45 mins.

STEP 2

Remove the garlic from the roasting tin and squeeze out the softened cloves all over the veg, stirring to evenly distribute. In a medium pan, simmer the chopped tomatoes until bubbling, season well and stir through the roasted veg in the tin. Scatter over the parsley and serve.

All-in-one posh lamb balti

Prep: 35 mins **Cook:** 4 hrs and 20 mins

Serves 5 - 6

Ingredients

- 5-6 lamb shanks
- 3-4 onions , halved and sliced
- 100g fresh ginger , peeled and roughly chopped
- 6 garlic cloves
- 2 x 400g cans chopped tomatoes
- 6 tbsp balti paste
- 2 tbsp garam masala
- 4 tsp brown sugar
- handful pomegranate seeds, to serve
- handful coriander leaves, to serve
- yogurt or raita, Indian chutneys or pickles, and rice and naan or chapatis, to serve

For the curry paste marinade

- 2 tbsp balti paste (we used Patak's)
- 2 tbsp sunflower or vegetable oil
- juice 1 lemon
- 2 tsp ground cumin

- 2 tsp brown mustard seeds
- 2 tsp ground turmeric
- 2 tsp kalonji (nigella or onion) seeds
- 1 tsp ground cinnamon

Method

STEP 1

The day before, mix all the marinade ingredients together. Put the lamb shanks in a roasting tin and rub the marinade all over them. Cover and chill overnight.

STEP 2

Heat oven to 220C/200C fan/gas 7. Roast the lamb for 20 mins to brown, then reduce the oven to 160C/140C fan/gas 3. Cover the tin tightly with a couple of layers of foil, scrunching well round the sides so that no steam escapes, and return to the oven for another 3 hrs.

STEP 3

Uncover the lamb and increase the oven to 180C/160C fan/gas 4. Scatter the onions into the juices in the tin, then return to the oven for 30 mins, uncovered. Meanwhile, put the ginger, garlic, 1 can of chopped tomatoes, balti paste, garam masala and sugar into a blender or food processor. Whizz together until fairly smooth. When the onions have cooked for 30 mins, stir the tomatoey paste into the onions and juices with the second can of tomatoes, and return to the oven for a final 30 mins.

STEP 4

Scatter the lamb with pomegranate seeds and coriander, then serve straight from the tin with cooling yogurt or raita, your favourite Indian pickles, and plenty of rice and breads to mop up the tasty balti sauce.

One-pan prawn pilau

Total time30 mins Ready in 25-30 mins

Serves 4

Ingredients

- 2 tbsp korma curry paste (Patak's is good)
- 1 small onion , finely chopped
- 300g basmati rice , rinsed and drained
- 700ml chicken stock made from a cube

- 150g pack cooked peeled prawns , defrosted if frozen
- cupful frozen peas
- 1 red chilli , sliced into rings
- handful coriander leaves, chopped
- lemon wedges, to serve

Method

STEP 1

Heat a large wide pan and dry-fry the curry paste with the onions for 4-5 mins until the onion begins to soften. Add the rice to the pan and stir to coat in the curry paste. Add the stock, then bring to the boil.

STEP 2

Cover the pan and turn the heat down to low. Leave the rice to simmer slowly for 12-15 mins until all the liquid has been absorbed and the rice is cooked. Turn off the heat and stir in the prawns, peas and chilli. Cover the pan and leave to stand for 5 mins.

STEP 3

Fluff up the rice grains with a fork and season if you want. Scatter over the coriander and serve with lemon wedges.

Paprika pork

Prep:10 mins **Cook:**25 mins

Serves 4

Ingredients

- 1 tbsp olive oil
- 2 onions, finely sliced
- 400g pork fillet, trimmed of any fat, cut into thick strips
- 250g pack mushroom, sliced
- 1 ½ tbsp smoked paprika
- 1 tbsp tomato purée
- 200ml chicken stock
- 100ml soured cream
- egg noodles, tagliatelle or rice, to serve

Method

STEP 1

Heat the oil in a large pan, tip in the onions and cook for 10 mins until soft and golden. Add the pork and mushrooms and cook on a high heat for 3-4 mins until browned. Add the paprika and cook for 1 min more.

STEP 2

Stir in the tomato purée, then pour on the stock and simmer for 5-8 mins until the pork is cooked through. Finally, mix in the soured cream and some seasoning. Serve with egg noodles, tagliatelle or rice, and an extra dollop of soured cream, if you like.

French-style chicken with peas & bacon

Prep: 10 mins **Cook:** 30 mins

Serves 4

Ingredients

- 6 rashers smoked streaky bacon, chopped
- 8 skinless, boneless chicken thighs
- 2 garlic cloves, thinly sliced
- 1 bunch spring onions, roughly chopped
- 300ml hot chicken stock
- 250g frozen peas
- 1 Little Gem lettuce, roughly shredded
- 2 tbsp crème fraîche

Method

STEP 1

In a large frying pan, dry-fry the bacon over a medium heat for 3 mins until the fat is released and the bacon is golden. Transfer the bacon to a small bowl, leaving the fat in the pan. Add the chicken and brown for 4 mins each side.

STEP 2

Push the chicken to one side of the pan and tip in the garlic and spring onions, cooking for about 30 secs, just until the spring onion stalks are bright green. Pour in the chicken stock, return the bacon to the pan, cover and simmer for 15 mins.

STEP 3

Increase heat under the pan. Tip the peas and lettuce into the sauce and cook for 4 mins, covered, until the peas are tender and the lettuce has just wilted. Check chicken is cooked through. Stir in the crème fraîche just before serving.

Ham & tarragon pot pie

Prep: 20 mins **Cook:** 30 mins - 35 mins

Serves 4

Ingredients

- 50g butter
- 1 onion , chopped
- 2 celery sticks , chopped
- 50g plain flour
- 600ml milk
- 90g pack pulled ham hock

- small pack tarragon , leaves only, chopped
- 1 egg , beaten
- 320g pack ready-rolled puff pastry
- cooked peas , to serve

Method

STEP 1

Heat oven to 200C/180C fan/gas 6. In a shallow casserole dish, melt the butter over a medium heat on the hob. Add the onion and celery, and fry gently to soften. Add the flour and stir to coat the vegetables. Slowly add the milk, stirring really well after each addition, making sure there are no lumps of flour before you add the next splash of milk. Once all the milk has been added, bring to a simmer to thicken, then fold in the ham hock and the tarragon. Season to taste, then add about half the beaten egg.

STEP 2

Cut a circle of puff pastry 2cm wider than the top of the pan and pop it onto seal in the filling underneath, folding the edges to create a crust. Cut the off-cuts of pastry into rough strips and use them to decorate the top. Brush the pastry with the remaining egg and bake in the oven for 25 mins or until the pastry is golden and crisp. Serve with peas.

Blackcurrant jam

Prep: 30 mins **Cook:** 30 mins

Makes 3 x 250ml jars

Ingredients

- 600g blackcurrants , stripped off the stalks
- about 400g white caster sugar or granulated sugar
- juice of ½ a lemon

Method

STEP 1

If you don't have a cooking thermometer, put a saucer in the freezer. Sterilise the jars you want to use. Tip the blackcurrants into a heavy-based saucepan with about 100ml of water. Bring to the boil and simmer for 5 mins until the fruit has broken down to a chunky pulp. Leave to cool slightly.

STEP 2

You now have two options. For a smooth jelly-style jam, squash the fruit through a sieve into a bowl. If you prefer your jam chunky and seeded, leave the pulp as it is. Whether it's strained or unstrained, weigh the fruit pulp and then add 400g of sugar to every 500g of pulp, then tip back in the saucepan.

STEP 3

Pour in the lemon juice then heat gently, stirring, to dissolve the sugar. Turn up the heat, then boil hard for about 10 mins or until it reaches 105C (setting point) on a cooking thermometer. If you don't own a thermometer, test for setting point by spooning a little jam onto the cold saucer. After a couple of minutes gently push your finger through the jam – if the surface wrinkles, it's ready. If not, return to the boil for 2 mins, then re-test.

STEP 4

Take off the heat and skim off any froth with a slotted spoon. Cool for 10-15 minutes. Stir gently to distribute the fruit, then ladle into sterilised jars. Keeps for 6 months in a cool dry cupboard.

Succulent honey & lemon chicken

Prep:5 mins - 10 mins **Cook:**1 hr

Serves 4

Ingredients

- 3 juicy lemons
- 50g butter
- 3 tbsp clear honey
- leaves from 4 rosemary sprigs
- 1 garlic clove , finely chopped

- 8 chicken pieces, such as thighs and drumsticks, with skin
- 750g potatoes , peeled and cut into smallish chunks
- green salad , to serve

Method

STEP 1

Preheat the oven to 200C/Gas 6/fan180C. Squeeze the juice from 2 lemons into a small pan and heat with the butter, honey, rosemary, garlic and salt and pepper, until the butter melts and it smells fragrant.

STEP 2

Lay the chicken in a roasting tin – don't pile it up or it won't cook so well. Add the potatoes and drizzle with lemon butter to coat evenly. Cut the third lemon into 8 wedges and tuck them in. (Can be made up to 2 hours ahead up to this point.)

STEP 3

Roast for 50 minutes - 1 hour until the chicken is cooked and the potatoes are crisp and golden. Serve with a green salad.

Lemon-spiced chicken with chickpeas

Prep:5 mins **Cook:**15 mins

Serves 4

Ingredients

- 1 tbsp sunflower oil
- 1 onion , halved and thinly sliced
- 4 skinless chicken breasts , cut into chunks
- 1 cinnamon stick , broken in half
- 1 tsp ground coriander

- 1 tsp ground cumin
- zest and juice 1 lemon
- 400g can chickpea , drained
- 200ml chicken stock
- 250g bag spinach

Method

STEP 1

Heat the oil in a large frying pan, then fry the onion gently for 5 mins. Turn up the heat and add the chicken, frying for about 3 mins until golden.

STEP 2

Stir in the spices and lemon zest, fry for 1 more min, then tip in the chickpeas and stock. Put the lid on and simmer for 5 mins.

STEP 3

Season to taste, then tip in spinach and re-cover. Leave to wilt for 2 mins, then stir through. Squeeze over the lemon juice just before serving.

Mediterranean vegetables with lamb

Prep:15 mins **Cook:**30 mins

Serves 4

Ingredients

- 1 tbsp olive oil
- 250g lean lamb fillet, trimmed of any fat and thinly sliced
- 140g shallot , halved
- 2 large courgettes , cut into chunks
- ½ tsp each ground cumin , paprika and ground coriander

- 1 red, 1 orange and 1 green pepper , cut into chunks
- 1 garlic clove , sliced
- 150ml vegetable stock
- 250g cherry tomatoes
- handful coriander leaves, roughly chopped

Method

STEP 1

Heat the oil in a large, heavy-based frying pan. Cook the lamb and shallots over a high heat for 2-3 mins until golden. Add the courgettes and stir-fry for 3-4 mins until beginning to soften.

STEP 2

Add the spices and toss well, then add the peppers and garlic. Reduce the heat and cook over a moderate heat for 4-5 mins until they start to soften.

STEP 3

Pour in the stock and stir to coat. Add the tomatoes, season, then cover with a lid and simmer for 15 mins, stirring occasionally until the veg are tender. Stir through the coriander to serve.

Spiced bulgur pilaf with fish

Prep:10 mins **Cook:**35 mins

Serves 4

Ingredients

- 1 tbsp olive oil
- 2 onions , finely sliced
- 3 carrots , grated
- 2 tsp cumin seed
- 2 tbsp harissa
- 200g bulgur wheat

- 6 dried apricots , chopped
- 700ml weak chicken stock (we made using 1 stock cube)
- 200g baby spinach
- 4 firm white fish fillets
- 4 thin lemon slices

Method

STEP 1

Heat the oil in a lidded flameproof casserole dish. Tip in the onions and cook for 10 mins until soft and golden. Add the carrots and cumin, and cook for 2 mins more. Stir through the harissa, bulgur and apricots, pour over the stock and bring to the boil. Cover and simmer for 7 mins.

STEP 2

Add the spinach and stir through until just wilted. Arrange the fish fillets on top, pop a slice of lemon on each and season. Replace the lid and cook for 8 mins, keeping over a low-ish heat.

STEP 3

Turn heat to low and cook for 7-8 mins more until the fish is cooked through and the bulgur is tender. Season with pepper and serve.

Milk chocolate pots with citrus shortbread

Prep:20 mins **Cook:**30 mins

Serves 4

Ingredients

For the chocolate pots

- 200g good-quality milk chocolate , chopped
- 200ml double cream
- 2 large egg yolks , lightly whisked

For the shortbread

160g self-raising flour , plus extra for dusting

zest 1 orange

110g butter , cut into cubes

60g golden caster sugar , plus extra for sprinkling

1 large egg yolk

100ml whipping cream

Method

STEP 1

Put the chocolate in a heatproof bowl. Heat the cream in a saucepan until it just boils, then pour it over the chocolate. Stir until smooth, then beat in the egg yolks. Tip the mixture into a jug, then pour into four individual pots and put in the fridge to set for at least 2 hrs.

STEP 2

Meanwhile, put the flour, orange zest and butter in a large bowl and rub together until it resembles fine breadcrumbs. Add the sugar and egg yolk, mix gently and bring the biscuit dough together with your hands. Roll the shortbread out on a lightly floured surface until

1cm thick, then transfer to a baking tray lined with baking parchment. Leave to rest for 10 mins in the fridge.

STEP 3

Heat oven to 160C/140C fan/ gas 3. Bake for 23-25 mins until golden brown, then sprinkle with sugar. While still warm, cut into eight x 2cm biscuits, trimming off any excess, and leave to cool.

STEP 4

When ready to eat, whip the cream to soft peaks, then spoon on top of the chocolate pots. Serve with the shortbreads on the side.

Tomato, runner bean & coconut curry

Prep:15 mins **Cook:**30 mins

Serves 4

Ingredients

- 1 tbsp vegetable or rapeseed oil
- 1 large onion , finely chopped
- 2 tbsp mild tandoori curry paste
- small pack coriander , stalks finely chopped, leaves roughly chopped
- 2 limes , 1 zested and juiced, 1 cut into wedges

- 200g red lentils
- 400ml can coconut milk
- 300g basmati rice
- 400g cherry tomatoes , halved
- 300g stringless runner beans , thinly sliced on the diagonal

Method

STEP 1

Heat the oil in a large, heavy-based saucepan. Add the onion and cook for 5-10 mins on a medium heat until softened. Add the paste, coriander stalks and lime zest, and cook for 1-2 mins until fragrant. Tip in the red lentils, coconut milk and 400ml hot water, and bring to the boil. Turn down the heat and simmer for 15 mins. Meanwhile, put a pan of water on to boil and cook the rice following pack instructions.

STEP 2

Add the tomatoes and runner beans to the lentils and cook for a further 5 mins. Drain the rice. Add the lime juice to the curry, check the seasoning and sprinkle over the coriander leaves. Serve with the rice and lime wedges for squeezing over.

Wild mushroom, potato & pancetta gratin

Prep:30 mins **Cook:**2 hrs and 45 mins

Serves 6-8 as a side, 4 as a main course

Ingredients

- 6 garlic cloves
- 1 onion , halved
- 3 bay leaves
- 3 thyme sprigs , plus a sprinkle of leaves
- 600ml pot double cream
- 600ml whole milk
- 140g diced pancetta

- 25g butter , plus a knob
- 250g wild mushrooms , roughly chopped after cleaning
- 1 ¼kg medium potato (we used Maris Piper)
- 1 whole nutmeg
- green salad , to serve (optional)

Method

STEP 1

Put the garlic cloves, onion, bay leaves, thyme, double cream and milk in a pan. Bring slowly to the boil over a low heat, partially cover with a lid and cook for 20-30 mins until the onion is tender and the cream mixture slightly thickened. Turn off and leave everything to infuse for 1 hr.

STEP 2

Strain the cream mixture into a jug (or bowl) and discard the herbs. Put the garlic cloves and onion in a food processor or blender and whizz until smooth – add a drop of the cream if it helps. Stir the paste back into the rest of the cream and season with 2 tsp salt.

STEP 3

Put the pancetta in a cold frying pan and cook gently, over a low-medium heat so the fat melts into the pan, until the pancetta is really crispy. Lift out with a slotted spoon, add the butter and mushrooms and turn up the heat, frying the mushrooms, until golden and dry.

STEP 4

Leave the skins on the potatoes and slice as thinly as possible. Grease a large baking dish with a little more butter. Layer up the potato slices, scattering over some of the cooked pancetta, the mushrooms and a little freshly grated nutmeg and pepper as you go. Finish by slowly pouring over the cream so that it settles among all the layers, then scatter over a few more thyme leaves. Cover with foil.

STEP 5

Heat oven to 180C/160C fan/gas 4. Bake the gratin for 1 hr, then remove the foil and bake for 35-45 mins more until golden and crispy on top. Poke a knife in to check the potatoes are tender, then leave for 10-15 mins to settle, before serving with a salad, if you like.

Spring chicken paella

Prep: 20 mins **Cook:** 55 mins

Serves 4 - 5

Ingredients

- 6 chicken thighs , skin-on
- 2 tbsp plain flour
- 3 tbsp olive oil
- 2 onions , finely chopped
- 3 garlic cloves , finely sliced
- 400g paella rice
- 1 tsp sweet paprika
- 2 good pinches of saffron

- zest and juice 2 lemons
- 1 ½l chicken stock
- 200g fresh or frozen peas and broad bean (weight after podding and skinning)
- ½ small bunch dill , chopped
- ½ small bunch mint , chopped
- ½ small bunch parsley , chopped

Method

STEP 1

Heat oven to 180C/160C fan/gas 4. Season the chicken thighs well and then dust all over with the flour. Heat 1 tbsp of the oil in a paella pan or large, deep frying pan. Fry the thighs until golden brown all over, then transfer to a shallow roasting tin and finish in the oven for 30-40 mins.

STEP 2

Add the remaining oil, onions and garlic, and fry very gently until soft, about 10-15 mins. Stir in the rice, paprika, saffron and lemon zest, then add the stock and simmer, stirring occasionally, for about 20 mins on a medium heat until the rice is nearly cooked.

STEP 3

Add the peas, broad beans and juice of 1 lemon until the rice is just cooked through, along with the veg. Stir through the herbs and as much of the remaining lemon juice as it needs, along with some seasoning. Tuck the chicken thighs back in and cover for 5 mins to let everything settle before serving.

Squash & chorizo pot pies

Prep:15 mins **Cook:**50 mins

Serves 4

Ingredients

- 1 tsp olive oil
- 2 red onions , chopped
- 175g chorizo , skin removed, sliced
- 300g butternut squash , peeled and cut into cubes
- 400g can chickpeas
- 200g bag spinach
- 140g crème fraîche
- 320g puff pastry sheet
- 1 egg , beaten

Method

STEP 1

Heat the oil in a large pan, add the onions and cook for a few mins until soft, then add the chorizo. Stir around the pan for a few more mins until the chorizo leaks some of its oils, then add the squash and 100ml water. Cover with a lid and leave to cook for 10-15 mins until the squash is just cooked through.

STEP 2

Add the chickpeas with any liquid from the can, the spinach and some seasoning. Stir, then cover with a lid and simmer for 1-2 mins until the spinach has wilted. Stir in the crème fraîche and bubble for 3-4 mins, adding a splash of water if the sauce looks too thick.

STEP 3

Heat oven to 200C/180C fan/gas 6. Divide the filling between 4 pie dishes. Unroll the pastry and cut out 4 lids, large enough to cover the pies. Brush the edge of each dish with a little beaten egg, then put a pastry lid on top and brush this with egg too. Poke a hole in the top of each pie. Bake on a tray for 25 mins until the lids are puffed and golden.

Rhubarb & custard sandwich biscuits

Prep:30 mins **Cook:**35 mins

MAKES 16

Ingredients

- 175g unsalted butter , cubed
- 50g caster sugar
- 50g icing sugar
- ¼ tsp fine sea salt

- 250g plain flour , plus extra for dusting
- 50g custard powder
- 2 egg yolks
- 1 tbsp vanilla bean paste

For the rhubarb jam filling

- 200g rhubarb , trimmed and chopped
- 200g caster sugar

- ¼ lemon , juiced

Method

STEP 1

To make the jam, put the rhubarb, sugar and lemon juice in a pan over a medium heat. Bring to a simmer and cook for 15 mins, or until the rhubarb has broken down and released its liquid. Blitz using a hand blender until smooth, then simmer for another 5-10 mins until thick and jammy. To test it's ready, run a wooden spoon over the base of the pan – it should leave a trail rather than filling in straightaway. Leave to cool (it will set more as it does), then chill until ready to use. Will keep in a sealed container or jar in the fridge for up to one week.

STEP 2

To make the biscuit dough, put the butter, both sugars and salt in a food processor and pulse a few times to a coarse paste. Scrape down the sides, then add the flour and custard powder and pulse again to a damp, sandy consistency. Add the egg yolks and vanilla and pulse again until the dough comes together into a ball. Add ½-1 tbsp water to bring it together, if needed. Tip the dough out, then wrap and put in the fridge to chill for at least 30 mins.

STEP 3

Roll the dough out on a floured surface to a 5mm thickness. Stamp out as many biscuits as you can using a 6mm round cutter – you should get about 32 in total.

STEP 4

Cut circles or hearts out of the centres of half the biscuits using the wide end of a plain piping nozzle (about 1.5cm), or a small heart cutter. Transfer all the biscuits to lined baking sheets, then transfer to the fridge and chill for 15 mins. You can also cook the cut-out shapes to make mini biscuits – if doing so, put these on their own baking sheet.

STEP 5

Heat the oven to 200C/180C fan/ gas 6, then bake the biscuits for 8-10 mins until golden (5-6 mins for the mini biscuits). Put on a wire rack and leave to cool completely.

STEP 6

Transfer the jam to a piping bag, snip off the end, and pipe a small layer of jam onto the plain biscuits (those without the centres cut out). Or, use a teaspoon. Spread the jam out – it may squidge out of the sides when sandwiching the biscuits, so don't go too far to the edge.

STEP 7

Sandwich the remaining biscuits over the jam (don't press down too firmly), then transfer to an airtight container in a single layer and leave to set overnight. This ensures the jam won't leak when you bite into them, but they can be eaten straightaway if you can't resist. Will keep in an airtight container for up to three days, but the biscuits will start to soften over time.

Chocolate honeycomb

Prep:5 mins **Cook:**10 mins

Makes a 20cm sheet of honeycomb

Ingredients

- butter , for the tin
- 200g golden caster sugar
- 5 tbsp golden syrup
- 2 tsp bicarbonate of soda

- 150g dark or milk chocolate , broken   into chunks

Method

STEP 1

Butter a 20cm square tin. Mix the sugar and golden syrup in a deep saucepan over a gentle heat until the sugar has melted. Try not to let the mixture bubble until the sugar has completely dissolved.

STEP 2

Turn up the heat a little and simmer until you have an amber coloured caramel (this won't take long). To test if it's ready, turn off the heat and drop a little into a glass of very cold water. If it forms a hard ball, it's ready. If not, turn the heat back on and cook a little more. Then, as quickly as you can, turn off the heat, tip in the bicarb and beat with a wooden spoon until it's disappeared and the mixture is foaming. Scrape into the tin immediately – be careful, the mixture will be very hot.

STEP 3

Leave the honeycomb in the tin for 1 hr-1 hr 30 mins until hard (it will continue to bubble).

STEP 4

Line a baking sheet with parchment paper. Melt the chocolate in a small heatproof bowl over a pan of just simmering water.

STEP 5

Snap the honeycomb into chunks and dip half of each piece into the chocolate. Drizzle with any remaining chocolate and a pinch of sea salt, if you like. Leave to set in the fridge for 1 hr.

Chilli beef with black beans and avocado salad

Prep:20 mins **Cook:**35 mins

Serves 6

Ingredients

- 1 tbsp cumin seed
- 1 tbsp ground coriander
- 2 tbsp hot chilli powder
- 2 tbsp sweet paprika
- 500g pack extra lean steak mince
- 4 garlic cloves , sliced
- 400g can chopped tomato
- 1 reduced-salt beef stock cube
- 2 tbsp tomato purée
- pack of 3 peppers , deseeded and diced
- large pack coriander , stalks and leaves chopped and separated
- 2 x 400g cans black beans

For the salad and rice (to serve 2, easily doubled)

- 250g pack wholegrain cooked rice
- 1 small avocado , chopped
- small bag baby leaf salad
- 1 small red onion , halved and thinly sliced
- handful cherry tomatoes , halved

Method

STEP 1

Tip the spices into a large pan and warm for a few seconds to toast them. Add the mince and garlic, and stir, breaking down the beef as it browns. Pour in the tomatoes and a can of water, crumble in the stock cube, then stir in the tomato purée, peppers and coriander stalks.

STEP 2

Cover the pan and cook for 15 mins. Stir in the black beans and their juice, and cook for 10 mins more until everything is tender. Meanwhile, heat the rice following pack instructions and toss the salad ingredients together. Stir the coriander leaves into the chilli and serve.

One-pan salmon with roast asparagus

Prep:20 mins **Cook:**50 mins

Serves 2

Ingredients

- 400g new potato, halved if large
- 2 tbsp olive oil
- 8 asparagus spears, trimmed and halved
- 2 handfuls cherry tomatoes
- 1 tbsp balsamic vinegar
- 2 salmon fillets, about 140g/5oz each
- handful basil leaves

Method

STEP 1

Heat oven to 220C/fan 200C/gas 7. Tip the potatoes and 1 tbsp of olive oil into an ovenproof dish, then roast the potatoes for 20 mins until starting to brown. Toss the asparagus in with the potatoes, then return to the oven for 15 mins.

STEP 2

Throw in the cherry tomatoes and vinegar and nestle the salmon amongst the vegetables. Drizzle with the remaining oil and return to the oven for a final 10-15 mins until the salmon is cooked. Scatter over the basil leaves and serve everything scooped straight from the dish.

Turkey tortilla pie

Prep:5 mins **Cook:**25 mins

Serves 4

Ingredients

- 2 onions , finely chopped
- 1 tbsp olive oil , plus a little extra if needed
- 2 tsp ground cumin
- 500g pack turkey mince
- 1 ½ tbsp chipotle paste
- 400g can chopped tomato

- 400g can kidney bean , drained and rinsed
- 198g can sweetcorn , drained
- 2 corn tortillas , snipped into triangles
- small handful grated cheddar
- 2 spring onions , finely sliced

Method

STEP 1

In a deep flameproof casserole dish, cook the onions in the oil for 8 mins until soft. Add the cumin and cook for 1 min more. Stir in the mince and add a bit more oil, if needed. Turn up the heat and cook for 4-6 mins, stirring occasionally, until the mince is browned.

STEP 2

Stir in the chipotle paste, tomatoes and half a can of water, and simmer for 5 mins. Mix in the beans and sweetcorn, and cook for a few mins more until thick, piping hot and the mince is cooked.

STEP 3

Heat the grill. Take the pan off the heat and put the tortilla triangles randomly on top. Scatter over the cheese and grill for a few mins until the topping is crisp, taking care that it doesn't burn. Sprinkle with the spring onions and serve.

Chilli con carne recipe

Prep: 10 mins **Cook:** 1 hr

Serves 4

Ingredients

- 1 large onion
- 1 red pepper
- 2 garlic cloves
- 1 tbsp oil
- 1 heaped tsp hot chilli powder (or 1 level tbsp if you only have mild)
- 1 tsp paprika
- 1 tsp ground cumin
- 500g lean minced beef
- 1 beef stock cube

- 400g can chopped tomatoes
- ½ tsp dried marjoram
- 1 tsp sugar (or add a thumbnail-sized piece of dark chocolate along with the beans instead, see tip)
- 2 tbsp tomato purée
- 410g can red kidney beans
- plain boiled long grain rice , to serve
- soured cream , to serve

Method

STEP 1

Prepare your vegetables. Chop 1 large onion into small dice, about 5mm square. The easiest way to do this is to cut the onion in half from root to tip, peel it and slice each half into thick matchsticks lengthways, not quite cutting all the way to the root end so they are still held together. Slice across the matchsticks into neat dice.

STEP 2

Cut 1 red pepper in half lengthways, remove stalk and wash the seeds away, then chop. Peel and finely chop 2 garlic cloves.

STEP 3

Start cooking. Put your pan on the hob over a medium heat. Add 1 tbsp oil and leave it for 1-2 minutes until hot (a little longer for an electric hob).

186

STEP 4

Add the onion and cook, stirring fairly frequently, for about 5 minutes, or until the onion is soft, squidgy and slightly translucent.

STEP 5

Tip in the garlic, red pepper, 1 heaped tsp hot chilli powder or 1 level tbsp mild chilli powder, 1 tsp paprika and 1 tsp ground cumin.

STEP 6

Give it a good stir, then leave it to cook for another 5 minutes, stirring occasionally.

STEP 7

Brown 500g lean minced beef. Turn the heat up a bit, add the meat to the pan and break it up with your spoon or spatula. The mix should sizzle a bit when you add the mince.

STEP 8

Keep stirring and prodding for at least 5 minutes, until all the mince is in uniform, mince-sized lumps and there are no more pink bits. Make sure you keep the heat hot enough for the meat to fry and become brown, rather than just stew.

STEP 9

Make the sauce. Crumble 1 beef stock cube into 300ml hot water. Pour this into the pan with the mince mixture.

STEP 10

Add a 400g can of chopped tomatoes. Tip in ½ tsp dried marjoram, 1 tsp sugar and add a good shake of salt and pepper. Squirt in about 2 tbsp tomato purée and stir the sauce well.

STEP 11

Simmer it gently. Bring the whole thing to the boil, give it a good stir and put a lid on the pan. Turn down the heat until it is gently bubbling and leave it for 20 minutes.

STEP 12

Check on the pan occasionally to stir it and make sure the sauce doesn't catch on the bottom of the pan or isn't drying out. If it is, add a couple of tablespoons of water and make sure that the heat really is low enough. After simmering gently, the saucy mince mixture should look thick, moist and juicy.

STEP 13

Drain and rinse a 410g can of red kidney beans in a sieve and stir them into the chilli pot. Bring to the boil again, and gently bubble without the lid for another 10 minutes, adding a little more water if it looks too dry.

STEP 14

Taste a bit of the chilli and season. It will probably take a lot more seasoning than you think.

STEP 15

Now replace the lid, turn off the heat and leave your chilli to stand for 10 minutes before serving. This is really important as it allows the flavours to mingle.

STEP 16

Serve with soured cream and plain boiled long grain rice.

Beef & bean hotpot

Prep: 15 mins **Cook:** 45 mins

Serves 8

Ingredients

- 750g lean minced beef
- 1 beef stock cube
- 2 large onions , roughly chopped
- 450g carrots , peeled and thickly sliced
- 1.25kg/2lb 12oz potato , peeled and cut into large chunks

- 2g cans baked beans
- Worcestershire sauce or Tabasco sauce , to taste
- large handful of parsley , roughly chopped

Method

STEP 1

Heat a large non-stick pan, add the beef then fry over a medium-high heat until browned, stirring often and breaking up any lumps with a spoon. Crumble in the stock cube and mix well.

STEP 2

Add the vegetables, stir to mix with the beef and pour in enough boiling water (about 1.3 litres) to cover. Bring to the boil, then lower the heat and stir well. Cover the pan and simmer gently for about 30 mins or until the vegetables are tender.

STEP 3

Tip in the baked beans, sprinkle with Worcestershire sauce or Tabasco to taste, stir well and heat through. Taste for seasoning and sprinkle with parsley. Serve with extra Worcestershire sauce or Tabasco, for those who like a peppery hot taste.

Pastrami & sweet potato hash

Prep:15 mins **Cook:**35 mins

Serves 4

Ingredients

- 800g sweet potatoes , peeled and cut into 1.5cm chunks
- 2 tbsp olive oil
- 1 tbsp smoked paprika
- 1 large red onion , halved and thinly sliced
- 2 garlic cloves , finely chopped
- 6 thyme sprigs , leaves picked
- 4 slices pastrami , cut into strips
- 4 eggs
- small pack flat-leaf parsley , chopped

Method

STEP 1

Heat oven to 200C/180C fan/gas 6. Toss the sweet potatoes with 1 tbsp oil, the paprika and seasoning. Spread over a shallow roasting tin and cook in the oven for 30 mins. Meanwhile, heat the remaining oil in a large non-stick frying pan and add the onion, garlic and thyme. Cover with a lid and cook over a low heat for 15-20 mins until softened and starting to caramelise. Stir occasionally; if it starts to catch, add a splash of water. Remove the lid, add the pastrami and fry for another 5 mins until the pastrami is hot and starting to crisp.

STEP 2

Bring a large pan of water to a simmer on a medium heat. Take the sweet potatoes out of the oven, add to the onion pan and stir. Add the eggs, one at a time, to the water and simmer for 2-3 mins until the whites are cooked and the yolks are still soft. Stir the parsley through the hash, divide between 4 bowls and top with the poached eggs.

Creamy cod chowder stew

Prep: 10 mins **Cook:** 20 mins

Serves 2

Ingredients

- 200g floury potatoes , cubed
- 200g parsnips , cubed
- 140g skinless cod fillet
- 140g skinless undyed smoked haddock fillets
- 500ml semi-skimmed milk
- ¼ small pack parsley , leaves finely chopped, stalks reserved

- 6 spring onions , whites and greens separated, both finely chopped
- 2 tbsp plain flour
- zest and juice 1 lemon
- 2 tbsp chopped parsley
- crusty wholemeal bread , to serve

Method

STEP 1

Bring a saucepan of salted water to the boil, add the potato and parsnips, and boil until almost tender – about 4 mins. Drain well.

STEP 2

Meanwhile, put the fish in a pan where they will fit snugly but not on top of each other. Cover with the milk, poke in the parsley stalks and bring the milk to a gentle simmer. Cover the pan, turn off the heat and leave to sit in the milk for 5 mins. Lift the fish out and break into large chunks. Discard the parsley stalks but keep the milk.

STEP 3

Put the spring onion whites, milk and flour in a saucepan together. Bring to a simmer, whisking continuously, until the sauce has thickened and become smooth. Turn the heat down, add the drained potatoes and parsnips, the lemon zest and half the juice, and cook gently for 5 mins, stirring occasionally. Stir in the spring onion greens, fish and parsley, and taste for seasoning – it will need plenty of pepper, some salt and maybe more lemon juice from the leftover half. Divide between two shallow bowls, serve with chunks of crusty bread and enjoy.

Lentil & sweet potato curry

Prep: 10 mins **Cook:** 25 mins

Serves 2

Ingredients

- 2 tbsp vegetable or olive oil
- 1 red onion, chopped
- 1 tsp cumin seeds
- 1 tsp mustard seeds (any colour)
- 1 tbsp medium curry powder
- 100g red or green lentil, or a mixture

- 2 medium sweet potatoes, peeled and cut into chunks
- 500ml vegetable stock
- 400g can chopped tomato
- 400g can chickpea, drained
- ¼ small pack coriander (optional)
- natural yogurt and naan bread, to serve

Method

STEP 1

Heat 2 tbsp vegetable or olive oil in a large pan, add 1 chopped red onion and cook for a few mins until softened.

STEP 2

Add 1 tsp cumin seeds, 1 tsp mustard seeds and 1 tbsp medium curry powder and cook for 1 min more, then stir in 100g red or green lentils (or a mixture), 2 medium sweet potatoes, cut into chunks, 500ml vegetable stock and a 400g can chopped tomatoes.

STEP 3

Bring to the boil, then cover and simmer for 20 mins until the lentils and sweet potatoes are tender. Add a drained 400g can chickpeas, then heat through.

STEP 4

Season, sprinkle with ¼ small pack coriander, if you like, and serve with seasoned yogurt and naan bread.

Smoked haddock & bacon gratin

Prep: 15 mins **Cook:** 1 hr and 35 mins

Serves 6

Ingredients

- small knob of butter
- 4 rashers smoked streaky bacon
- 1 onion , finely sliced
- ½ small pack thyme , leaves only
- 1kg baking potatoes , washed and sliced

- 350g skinless smoked haddock , cut into large chunks
- 300ml half-fat crème fraîche
- crisp green salad , to serve

Method

STEP 1

Heat oven to 200C/180C fan/gas 6. Heat the butter in a shallow flameproof casserole dish and sizzle the bacon until it changes colour. Add the onion and thyme and fry with the bacon for 5 mins until the onion is starting to soften. Lower the heat, add the potatoes to the onion and cover the pan. Steam-fry the potatoes for 25-35 mins until they soften, stirring occasionally to stop them sticking to the bottom of the pan.

STEP 2

When the potatoes are ready, stir through the haddock, crème fraîche and a good grinding of black pepper, and mix until everything is combined. Flatten down with a fish slice and bake in the oven for 40 mins until golden. Serve with a green salad.

All-in-one-baked mushrooms

Prep: 5 mins **Cook:** 25 mins

Serves 2

Ingredients

- 2 tbsp olive oil
- 4 very large field mushrooms
- 4 slices good-quality cooked ham
- 4 eggs

Method

STEP 1

Heat oven to 220C/fan 200C/gas 7. Drizzle a little olive oil over the base of a ceramic baking dish, then pop in the mushrooms.

STEP 2

Drizzle with the remaining oil and seasoning. Bake for 15 mins until soft, then remove from the oven.

STEP 3

Tuck the ham slices around the mushrooms to create little pockets. Crack the eggs into the pockets, then return to the oven for 10 mins until the egg white is set and the yolk is still a little runny. Serve scooped straight from the dish. Great with baked beans and chips.

Sausage & white bean casserole

Prep:20 mins **Cook:**1 hr and 5 mins

Serves 4

Ingredients

- 1 red or yellow pepper, deseeded and cut into chunks
- 2 carrots, cut into thick slices
- 2 red onions, cut into wedges
- 8 chipolatas, cut into thirds
- 400g can peeled cherry tomatoes
- 400g can white beans, drained
- 200ml low-salt chicken stock
- 2 tsp Dijon mustard
- 100g frozen peas
- potatoes, pasta or rice, to serve

Method

STEP 1

Heat oven to 220C/200C fan/gas 7. Roast the pepper, carrots and onion in a deep baking dish for 15 mins. Add the sausages and roast for a further 10 mins.

STEP 2

Reduce oven to 200C/180C fan/gas 6, tip in the tomatoes and beans, then stir in the stock. Cook for another 35 mins. Stir in the mustard and peas and return to the oven for 5 mins. Rest for 10 mins, then serve with potatoes, pasta or rice.

Next level steak & ale pie

Prep:1 hr **Cook:**3 hrs

Serves 6-8

Ingredients

- 1 tbsp vegetable oil
- 100g smoked bacon lardons or smoked bacon, chopped
- 1kg beef shin, cut into large chunks
- 2 onions, roughly chopped
- 3 carrots, peeled and cut into large chunks
- 3 tbsp plain flour
- 1 tbsp tomato purée

- 1 tbsp tomato purée
- 1 tsp malt or red wine vinegar
- 1 tsp brown miso paste (optional)
- 400ml sweet brown ale
- 600ml beef stock made from 2 stock cubes
- few thyme sprigs, stalks and leaves separated
- 2 bay leaves

For the pastry

- 700g plain flour, plus extra for dusting
- 2 tsp English mustard powder
- 150g lard

- 150g butter, plus extra for the dish
- 2 egg yolks, beaten

Method

STEP 1

Heat the oven to 160C/140C fan/gas 3. Heat the vegetable oil in a large casserole dish and gently fry the bacon for 5 mins until lightly browned. Remove with a slotted spoon and set aside. In the same pan, brown the beef well in batches for 5-8 mins, adding a drizzle more oil if you need to, then set aside.

STEP 2

Add the onions and carrots to the pan and cook on a low heat for 5 mins. Stir in the flour, then add the tomato purée, vinegar and miso, if using. Tip the beef and bacon, along with any juices, back into the pan and give it all a good stir. Pour in the ale and stock, and nestle in the thyme stalks and bay. Season generously and bring to a simmer. Cover with a lid and cook in the oven for about 2 hrs or until the meat is really tender. Leave everything to cool slightly, then strain off about half the braising liquid into another container. Leave to cool completely. Can be made up to two days ahead and kept chilled in the fridge – the pie will be better if the filling is fridge-cold when added. Can also be frozen for up to three months.

STEP 3

To make the pastry, mix the flour, mustard powder, lard and butter with a generous pinch of sea salt until completely combined, then gradually add up to 250ml ice-cold water to make a soft dough. This can be done in a food processor if you prefer. Knead the thyme leaves into the pastry, then cover and leave to rest in the fridge for at least 1 hr. Can be made up to two days ahead and kept chilled, or frozen for up to a month.

STEP 4

Heat the oven to 220C/200C fan/gas 7 and put a baking tray in the oven. Heavily butter a 26-28cm pie dish and dust well with flour. Cut off a third of the pastry and set aside. Roll out the remaining pastry to a thick round that will easily line the pie dish with an overhang, then line the tin. Tip in the beef mixture. You want the filling to be slightly higher than the rim of the dish. Brush the edges with egg yolk. Roll out the remaining pastry to a thick round, big enough to cover the pie, then lift onto the pie dish. Trim the edges, crimp together, then re-roll the trimmings and cut into decorative shapes, such as leaves. Brush the top with more yolk. Make a hole in the centre of the pie with a knife, and put it on the hot baking tray.

STEP 5

Bake for 20 mins, remove, brush again with yolk, scatter with sea salt and bake for 20-25 mins until golden. Leave to rest for 10 mins while you heat up the extra gravy.

Braised pork belly with borlotti beans

Prep:20 mins **Cook:**1 hr and 40 mins

Serves 4

Ingredients

- 800g skinless, boneless pork belly, cut into large chunks, or 800g pork belly slices
- 1 tbsp plain flour
- 2 tbsp olive oil
- 1 large onion, finely chopped
- 2 carrots, finely chopped
- 2 celery sticks, finely chopped, any leaves reserved and chopped, to serve
- 1 rosemary sprig
- 2 bay leaves
- 2 garlic cloves, roughly chopped
- 1 tbsp tomato purée
- 200ml white wine
- 500ml chicken stock
- 2 x 400g cans borlotti beans, drained
- large handful of parsley, leaves picked and finely chopped, to serve
- 1 lemon, zested, to serve

Method

STEP 1

Heat the oven to 160C/140C fan/gas 3. Toss the pork in the flour with some seasoning. Heat the oil in an ovenproof casserole dish and fry the pork for 10 mins until golden, then transfer to a plate. Tip all the veg into the pan with the rosemary, bay leaves and garlic, and cook on a low heat for 10 mins until softened. Stir in the tomato purée and cook for a minute, then add the wine. Pour over the stock, then bring to a simmer and stir in the fried pork.

STEP 2

Cover, then cook in the oven for 1 hr. Remove from the oven, stir through the beans, cover again and return to the oven for 30 mins, or until the pork is very tender. Leave to cool a little, then scatter over the parsley, lemon zest and reserved celery leaves.

Egg fried rice with prawns & peas

Prep:5 mins **Cook:**20 mins

Serves 4

Ingredients

- 250g basmati rice
- 2 tbsp vegetable oil
- 2 garlic cloves , finely chopped
- 1 red chilli , deseeded and shredded
- 2 eggs , beaten
- 200g frozen pea
- 1 bunch spring onions , finely sliced
- 285g pack cooked small prawns
- 1 tbsp soy sauce , plus extra for serving, if you like

Method

STEP 1

Put the rice in a saucepan with 600ml water. Bring to boil, cover, then simmer for 10 mins or until almost all the water has gone. Leave off the heat, covered, for 5 mins more.

STEP 2

Heat the oil in wok or large frying pan. Add the garlic and chilli, then cook for 10 secs – making sure not to let it burn. Throw in the cooked rice, stir fry for 1 min, then push to the side of the pan. Pour the eggs into the empty side of the pan, then scramble them, stirring. Once just set, stir the peas and spring onions into the rice and egg, then cook for 2 mins until the peas are tender. Add the prawns and soy sauce, heat through, then serve with extra soy sauce on the side, if you like.

Summer pork, fennel & beans

Prep:15 mins **Cook:**45 mins

Serves 4

Ingredients

- 2 tbsp extra virgin olive oil
- 1 tbsp butter
- 4 large on-the-bone pork chops (about 250g each), rind removed
- 2 banana shallots , 1 sliced, 1 finely chopped
- 2 large fennel bulbs , each cut into 8 wedges

- 100ml white wine
- 1 lemon 0.5 cut into wedges, 0.5 juiced
- 100g cherry tomatoes
- 2 x 400g cans cannellini beans , rinsed and drained
- 1 tsp fennel seeds , lightly crushed
- handful basil leaves

Method

STEP 1

Heat oven to 200C/180C fan/gas 6. Heat 1 tbsp oil and the butter in a large ovenproof frying pan or wide flameproof casserole dish. Season the chops generously and fry over a medium-high heat for 3 mins each side until lightly golden – brown the edges of the fat for 30 secs or so too. Remove to a plate.

STEP 2

Add the sliced shallot and fennel to the pan and cook for 2 mins, stirring now and then. Splash in the wine and simmer for a few secs to reduce a little. Add the lemon wedges, drizzle with the remaining oil and put in the oven to roast for 10 mins.

STEP 3

Toss the veg gently, sit the pork chops on top and roast for another 20 mins. Add the tomatoes to the pan and cook for 5 mins more or until the chops are cooked through, the fennel is tender and turning golden, and the tomatoes are soft.

STEP 4

Meanwhile, mix the chopped shallot, the lemon juice, beans and fennel seeds. Remove the meat to a plate to rest for a few mins while you fold the dressed beans and basil leaves into the pan. Add the resting juices, season to taste, then serve with the pork.

Spicy seafood stew with tomatoes & lime

Prep: 15 mins **Cook:** 30 mins

Serves 4 - 6

Ingredients

- 2 dried ancho or guajillo chillies
- 1 tbsp olive oil
- 1 large onion , chopped
- 4 garlic cloves , chopped
- 1 tsp chipotle paste or 1 tsp smoked hot paprika (pimentón)
- 1 tsp ground cumin
- 700ml chicken stock
- 250g chopped tomato , from a can
- 200g large peeled raw prawn
- 300g halibut or other firm white fish fillets, cut into 2.5cm pieces
- 300g clam
- 500g small new potato , halved and boiled
- juice 2 limes

To serve

- lime wedges
- 1 avocado , chopped
- handful coriander leaves
- 1 small red onion , finely diced
- corn tortillas , sliced and baked

Method

STEP 1

Toast the chillies in a hot dry frying pan for a few moments (they will puff up a bit), then remove. Deseed and stem chillies, and soak in boiling water for 15 mins.

STEP 2

Heat the olive oil in a large saucepan over a medium heat. Add the onion and garlic, season and cook for about 5 mins or until softened. Add the chipotle paste, reconstituted chillies, cumin, stock and tomatoes. Sauté for 5 mins, then purée until very fine in a blender. Pour back into the pan and bring to the boil. Reduce the heat and simmer for 10 mins. When close to eating, add the prawns, fish fillets, clams and potatoes. Place a lid on top and cook for 5 mins over a medium-high heat. Add the lime juice and serve with lime wedges, avocado, coriander, red onion and tortilla chips for sprinkling over.

Panzanella

Prep:30 mins **Cook:**15 mins

Serves 4-6

Ingredients

- 1kg ripe mixed tomatoes , halved if small, quartered if large
- 300g day-old sourdough or ciabatta, torn into large chunks
- 100ml extra virgin olive oil
- 50ml red wine vinegar

- 1 small shallot , finely chopped
- 50g tin anchovies , drained and roughly chopped
- 100g black olives , pitted
- large handful of basil leaves, torn

Method

STEP 1

Heat the oven to 180C/160C fan/gas 4. Put the tomatoes in a colander and sprinkle over 1 tsp sea salt, then leave to sit for 15 mins.

STEP 2

Spread the chunks of bread out on a baking tray and toss with 1 tbsp of the oil. Bake for 10-15 mins, or until lightly toasted.

STEP 3

In a bowl, whisk together the remaining oil, the vinegar and shallot. Season to taste. Toss the anchovies with the tomatoes, croutons, olive oil dressing, the olives and half the basil in a large bowl. Spoon the panzanella onto a serving plate and top with the remaining basil.

One-pan roast dinner

Prep: 20 mins **Cook:** 1 hr and 20 mins

Serves 4

Ingredients

- 1 ½kg chicken
- 1 lemon , halved
- 50g softened butter
- 2 tsp dried mixed herbs
- 750g potatoes , chopped into roastie size
- about 7 carrots , roughly 500g, each chopped into 2-3 chunks
- 2 tbsp olive oil
- 100g frozen peas
- 300ml chicken stock
- 1 tsp Marmite

Method

STEP 1

Heat oven to 220C/200C fan/gas 7. Snip the string or elastic off the chicken if it's tied up, then place in a big roasting tin. Shove the lemon halves into the cavity. Rub the butter, herbs and seasoning all over the chicken. Put the potatoes and carrots around it, drizzle everything with oil, season and toss together.

STEP 2

Roast for 20 mins, then turn the oven down to 200C/180C fan/gas 6 and roast for 50 mins more. Stir the peas, stock and Marmite into the veg in the tin, then return to the oven for 10 mins more.

Winter warmer hearty risotto

Prep: 10 mins **Cook:** 50 mins

Serves 4

Ingredients

- 1 medium butternut squash
- 2 tbsp olive oil
- pinch of nutmeg , or pinch of cinnamon
- 1 red onion , finely chopped
- 1 vegetable stock cube
- 2 garlic cloves , crushed
- 500g risotto rice (we used arborio)
- 100g frozen peas
- 320g sweetcorn , drained
- 2 tbsp grated parmesan (or vegetarian alternative)
- handful chopped mixed herbs of your choice

Method

STEP 1

Heat oven to 200C/180C fan/gas 6. Peel the butternut squash, slice it in half, then scoop out and discard the seeds.

STEP 2

Cut the flesh of the butternut squash into small cubes and put in a mixing bowl. Drizzle 1 tbsp olive oil over the squash, and season with black pepper, and nutmeg or cinnamon. Transfer the squash to a roasting tin and roast in the oven for about 25 mins until cooked through, then set aside.

STEP 3

Heat the remaining oil in a large saucepan over a low heat. Add the onion and cover the pan with a tight-fitting lid. Allow the onion to cook without colouring for 5-10 mins, stirring occasionally.

STEP 4

In a measuring jug, make up 1.5 litres of stock from boiling water and the stock cube. Stir well until the stock cube has dissolved. When the onion is soft, remove the lid and add the garlic to the onion pan. Leave it to cook for 1 min more.

STEP 5

Rinse the rice under cold water. Turn up the heat on the pan and add the rice to the onion and garlic, stirring well for 1 min. Pour a little of the hot stock into the pan and stir in until the liquid is absorbed by the rice.

STEP 6

Gradually add the rest of the stock to the pan, a little at a time, stirring constantly, waiting until each addition of stock is absorbed before adding more. Do this until the rice is cooked through and creamy – you may not need all the stock. This should take 15-20 mins. Take the roasting tin out of the oven – the squash should be soft and cooked.

STEP 7

Add the squash, peas and sweetcorn to the risotto and gently stir it in. Season to taste. Take the risotto pan off the heat and stir in the Parmesan and herbs. Put the lid back on the pan and let the risotto stand for 2-3 mins before serving.

Family meals: Chicken & veg casserole

Prep: 15 mins **Cook:** 1 hr

Serves a family of 3-4

Ingredients

- knob of butter
- 1 onion , finely chopped
- 3 medium carrots , finely chopped
- 2 medium sticks celery , finely chopped
- 500g approx chicken thigh
- 2 fat garlic cloves , crushed
- 1 tsp sweet smoked paprika
- ½ tsp ground cumin
- 1 tsp dried thyme
- 2 x 400g cans chopped tomatoes
- 1 chicken stock cube
- 1 red or orange pepper , diced
- 1 x 400g can chickpeas , drained (optional)

Method

STEP 1

Heat the butter in a large heavy-based pan. Add the onion, carrot and celery and cook gently until softened.

STEP 2

Add the chicken thighs, garlic, spices and thyme. Cook stirring until the chicken is opaque.

STEP 3

Pour in the tomatoes, plus one extra can of water or enough to cover the chicken and vegetables. Add the stock and pepper. Bring to a simmer and cook uncovered for 50 mins.

STEP 4

If using, add the chickpeas and cook for a further five mins. Serve with rice. For young children, break the chicken into smaller pieces and serve.

Swede, lamb & feta bake

Prep: 20 mins **Cook:** 1 hr and 15 mins

Serves 4

Ingredients

- 2 tbsp olive oil , plus extra for greasing
- 1 large onion , finely chopped
- 2 garlic cloves , finely chopped
- ¼ tsp cinnamon
- 1 tsp dried oregano
- pinch of chilli flakes

- 500g lamb mince
- 1 tbsp tomato purée
- 400g can chopped tomatoes
- 600g swede , peeled and sliced as thinly as possible

For the topping

- 25g butter
- 25g plain flour
- 300ml milk

- 1 large egg
- 100g feta , crumbled

Method

STEP 1

Heat the oil in a large saucepan and fry the onion until softened. Add the garlic and cook for a further few mins. Stir in the cinnamon, oregano and chilli flakes. Add the lamb and brown all over for a few mins, breaking it up with a wooden spoon. Drain the fat from the mince and return the pan to the heat. Stir in the tomato purée and cook for 1 min, then tip in the tomatoes. Half-fill the can with water and add to the pan. Stir well, season and simmer for 15 mins.

STEP 2

Preheat the oven to 180C/160C fan/gas 4. Lightly oil the bottom of a 1.5-litre ovenproof dish and arrange a third of the swede on the bottom. Ladle over half the mince mixture, top with another layer of swede, followed by another layer of lamb. Finish with a layer of swede.

STEP 3

For the topping, heat the butter in a small saucepan and add the flour. Stir briskly until you have a smooth paste. Remove from the heat and slowly add the milk until you have a smooth sauce. Return to the heat and cook for 4-5 mins until the sauce thickens. Remove from the heat and whisk in the egg and half the feta.

STEP 4

Pour the sauce over the top of the swede and sprinkle the surface with the remaining feta. Cover with foil and bake in the oven for 35-45 mins. Remove the foil and cook for a further 25-30 mins or until the top is golden and the swede is tender - be sure to test that the swede is fully cooked before serving. Leave to sit for a few mins before serving.

Pork & parsnip cobbler

Prep:45 mins - 1 hr **Cook:**2 hrs and 15 mins

Serves 8

Ingredients

- 6 tbsp vegetable oil
- 900g diced pork
- 2 small onions , finely sliced
- 1 tbsp plain flour
- 2 celery sticks, finely chopped
- 225g ready-to-eat dried apricot
- finely grated zest 1 lemon
- finely grated zest 1 orange
- 2 Cox's apples , peeled and chopped

- 3 garlic cloves , crushed
- 2 tsp each finely chopped fresh thyme , rosemary and sage
- good pinch of curry powder
- ½ tsp ground fennel seed
- ½ bottle red wine
- 600ml vegetable stock
- 650g parsnip

For the cobbler crust

- 200g self-raising flour
- 85g shredded suet
- 50g chilled butter , grated

- 3 tbsp chopped fresh parsley
- finely grated zest and juice of 1 lemon
- beaten egg , to glaze

Method

STEP 1

For the filling, heat 2 tablespoons of oil in a large pan and fry the pork in small batches for 4-5 minutes until just browned, then remove with a slotted spoon and set aside. Add the onions to the pan and fry for 5-6 minutes until soft and golden. Return the pork to the pan and sprinkle in the flour. Cook for 1 minute, stirring well.

STEP 2

Add the celery, apricots, lemon and orange zest, apples, garlic, herbs and spices. Pour in the wine and stock and bring to simmering point, then cover and gently cook for 1 1/4 hours or until the pork is tender. Remove from the heat.

STEP 3

Meanwhile, preheat the oven to 200C/Gas 6/fan oven 180C. Peel and cut the parsnips into 2.5cm/1in dice. Put the remaining oil in a roasting tin and put in the oven for 5 minutes until hot. Tip the parsnip chunks into the roasting tin and coat in the hot oil. Roast in the oven for 30 minutes until cooked through and golden brown. Drain and set aside. When the pork is tender, stir in the parsnips. Spoon into a 2 litre/3 1/2 pint ovenproof dish and leave to cool completely.

STEP 4

For the cobbler crust, sift the flour and season. Add the suet, butter and parsley and lightly mix in with a fork. Make a well in the centre, then add the lemon zest and juice and gently bring together to make a soft and pliable dough. If it is too dry, add a little cold water, but don't knead the dough or it will become tough. Reduce the temperature to 180C/Gas 4/fan oven 160C.

STEP 5

Roll out the dough on a lightly floured surface to about 5mm/1/4in thick. Cut the dough into rounds using a 7.5cm/3in pastry cutter. Re-roll the trimmings and cut out more rounds until all the dough is used up. Arrange the circles of dough so that they slightly overlap on top.

STEP 6

Brush the dough with beaten egg and bake in the oven for 45 minutes until the crust is golden.

Melon & crunchy bran pots

Prep: 10 mins **Serves 1**

Ingredients

- ½ x 200g pack melon medley
- 150g pot fat-free yogurt
- 2 tbsp fruit & fibre cereal

- 1 tbsp mixed seed
- 1 tsp clear honey

Method

STEP 1

Top melon medley with yogurt, then sprinkle over cereal mixed with seeds. Drizzle over honey and eat immediately.

Spicy merguez & couscous pot

Prep: 15 mins **Cook:** 30 mins

Serves 2

Ingredients

- drizzle of olive oil
- 4 merguez sausages (about 250g/9oz)
- ½ preserved lemon , peel only, chopped
- 1 red onion , chopped
- 1 fat red chilli , deseeded and finely chopped

- 1 red pepper , deseeded and chopped
- 1 tbsp ras el hanout
- 400g can chopped tomatoes with olives
- 1 chicken stock cube
- handful of coriander , finely chopped
- 100g couscous

Method

STEP 1

Heat the oil in a pan. Squeeze the sausagemeat from the skins and shape into 8 meatballs. Add them to the pan and sizzle on a medium-high heat for 5-10 mins, rolling around the pan, until they are cooked. Set aside.

STEP 2

Drain the fat from the pan, leaving 1 tbsp behind. Reduce the heat and add the lemon, onion, chilli and pepper. Stir for 5 mins. Add the ras el hanout and stir for 1 min more.

STEP 3

Add the tomatoes and 300ml water, and crumble in the stock cube. Return the meatballs to the pan and simmer, covered with a lid, for 10-15 mins, until the sauce is rich and the veg are tender. Season and stir in the coriander. Transfer to 2 microwavable containers with tight-fitting lids, and chill until you're ready to eat. Weigh 50g couscous into 2 sandwich bags to take to work too.

STEP 4

When you're ready to eat, add the couscous to the cold sauce. Stir well and microwave for 3 mins, until the couscous is cooked through.

Orange & rhubarb amaretti pots

Prep:10 mins **Cook:**30 mins

Serves 8

Ingredients

- 400g double cream
- 360g thick full-fat Greek yogurt

- 150g amaretti biscuits , broken into small pieces

For the rhubarb & orange curd

- 500g rhubarb , chopped into 2.5cm lengths
- 150g golden caster sugar , plus a large pinch

- 150ml orange juice , plus zest 1 orange
- 4 medium eggs , plus 2 medium yolks
- 150g unsalted butter

Method

STEP 1

First, make the curd. Put the rhubarb, a pinch of sugar and the orange juice in a pan over a medium heat and cover with a lid. Cook for 10-15 mins until the rhubarb is very tender. Remove from the heat.

STEP 2

Pass the rhubarb through a fine sieve, pushing it to squeeze out as much pulp as possible. Keep the flesh in the sieve to incorporate later.

STEP 3

Whisk the eggs, egg yolks and sugar together until pale and frothy. Melt the butter steadily in a pan on a low heat. Once melted, slowly pour in the egg mix and orange zest, stirring continuously. Add in the strained rhubarb pulp and mix to combine, continuing to cook gently until the curd has thickened like custard. This could take 10-12 mins, but be patient and do not turn up the heat, as you might scramble the eggs.

STEP 4

Once the curd has thickened, transfer it to a bowl and whisk until smooth. At this point I like to add back in the rhubarb flesh from the sieve, to give more body to the dessert – but if you want a smooth curd, don't do this.

STEP 5

Whip the cream, stopping just before soft peaks start to form. Fold in the yogurt, 300g of the curd and most of the amaretti biscuits.

STEP 6

Spoon the mix into eight glasses and sprinkle on the reserved amaretti. Save the remaining curd to use on pancakes, granola or to make little tartlets. Store it in a sterilised jar (wash a jar in hot soapy water, rinse, then put in the oven upside down at 120C/100C fan/gas 1 /2 for 15 mins to dry).

Lighter Lancashire hotpot

Prep: 40 mins **Cook:** 2 hrs and 30 mins

Serves 4

Ingredients

- 650g boned lamb shoulder , excess fat trimmed
- 4 tsp plain flour
- 1 tbsp rapeseed oil
- 2 medium onions , halved lengthways and thinly sliced
- 3 carrots (350g total weight), halved lengthways and cut into bite-sized chunks
- 225g swede , cut into bite-sized chunks
- 3 thyme sprigs , plus extra leaves to garnish
- 2 bay leaves
- 200ml chicken stock , made with 1/2 chicken stock cube
- 1 ½ tsp Worcestershire sauce
- 750g potato , such as Maris Piper or Desirée, very thinly sliced

Method

STEP 1

Heat oven to 190C/170C fan/gas 5. Cut the lamb into chunky 5-6cm pieces. Tip the flour onto a large plate, season with pepper and a little salt, and toss the lamb in the flour to coat evenly and completely. Set aside.

STEP 2

Heat 2 tsp of the oil in a large, deep frying or sauté pan. Put the onions, carrots, swede, thyme sprigs and bay leaves in the pan and season with pepper. Cook on a medium-high heat for 6-8 mins, stirring occasionally so it doesn't stick, until the vegetables start to go brown around the edges – the bottom of the pan should be slightly brown and caramelised too. Pour in the stock; it should sizzle then bubble in the pan. Immediately remove the pan from the heat so the stock does not reduce in volume. Stir in the Worcestershire sauce.

STEP 3

Overlap a single layer of the potato slices in the bottom of a 2-litre casserole dish (about 20cm diameter x 10cm deep). Lay half the lamb over the potatoes, then spoon half the vegetable mix over the meat. Season with pepper. Sit the rest of the lamb on top, then tip the rest of the vegetables, herbs and all the liquid over the lamb. Press down with the back of a spoon, if necessary, to make room for the remaining potatoes. Start to layer up the potato slices in 3 tightly overlapping layers, seasoning each layer with pepper and brushing with oil as you go – save a bit of oil for the top layer. Cover the dish with a tight-fitting lid and bake for 10 mins.

STEP 4

Reduce the oven to 160C/140C fan/gas 3. Cook for a further 2 hrs until the lamb is really tender and the potatoes are cooked. Take the lid off and pop under the grill for 8-10 mins until the potatoes are golden and crisp around the edges. Remove and let the hotpot settle for 5-10 mins, then serve scattered with thyme leaves.

Turkish lamb pilau

Cook:30 mins **Serves 4**

Ingredients

- small handful pine nuts or flaked almonds
- 1 tbsp olive oil
- 1 large onion , halved and sliced
- 2 cinnamon sticks, broken in half
- 500g lean lamb neck fillet, cubed
- 250g basmati rice
- 1 lamb or vegetable stock cube
- 12 ready-to-eat dried apricots
- handful fresh mint leaves, roughly chopped

Method

STEP 1

Dry-fry the pine nuts or almonds in a large pan until lightly toasted, then tip onto a plate. Add the oil to the pan, then fry the onion and cinnamon together until starting to turn golden. Turn up the heat, stir in the lamb, fry until the meat changes colour, then tip in the rice and cook for 1 min, stirring all the time.

STEP 2

Pour in 500ml boiling water, crumble in the stock cube, add the apricots, then season to taste. Turn the heat down, cover and simmer for 12 mins until the rice is tender and the stock has been absorbed. Toss in the pine nuts and mint and serve.

Red braised ginger pork belly with pickled chillies

Prep:10 mins **Cook:**2 hrs and 15 mins

Serves 6-8 as part of a buffet

Ingredients

- 2 ½kg pork belly , rind removed, cut into 5cm pieces
- 1 tbsp dark soy sauce
- 200ml Shaohsing rice wine
- 2 tbsp vegetable oil
- 2 garlic cloves , thinly sliced
- thumb-sized piece ginger , cut into matchsticks
- pinch of chilli flakes
- 100ml Chinese black vinegar (available from Waitrose)
- 140g soft brown sugar
- 700ml vegetable stock

To serve

- toasted sesame seeds
- sliced spring onions
- 2 red chillies , sliced and soaked in rice wine vinegar for 1 hr, then drained
- steamed white rice

Method

STEP 1

Toss the pork with the soy and 1 tbsp of the rice wine. Leave for 1 hr or, even better, overnight in the fridge.

STEP 2

Heat some of the oil in a medium heavy-based saucepan. Brown the meat, in batches, on both sides and set aside. Add a little more oil and cook the garlic, ginger and chilli for 2-3 mins until golden.

STEP 3

Pour the vinegar, remaining rice wine, sugar and stock into the pan and bring to the boil. Add the pork, then turn down the heat, cover and simmer for 2 hrs or until the meat is tender. For the final 30 mins, remove the lid, increase the heat and let the liquid reduce until thick and syrupy. Serve scattered with the sesame seeds, spring onions and sliced chillies, with rice.

Spinach & ricotta pancake bake

Prep:10 mins **Cook:**35 mins

Serves 4

Ingredients

- 1 tbsp olive oil , plus a drizzle
- 3 garlic cloves , crushed
- 400g can chopped tomatoes
- 200g bag baby spinach
- 250g tub ricotta
- grating of nutmeg
- 4 large pancakes or crêpes (see recipe, below)
- 225g ball mozzarella , drained and torn into small pieces
- 50g parmesan or vegetarian alternative, grated

Method

STEP 1

Heat the oil in a pan, add 2 garlic cloves and sizzle for a few seconds, then tip in the tomatoes. Season, and bubble for 10-15 mins until reduced to a thick sauce. Microwave the spinach for 2 mins to wilt, or by tipping into a colander and pouring over a kettle full of hot water. When cool enough to handle, squeeze out as much liquid as you can, then roughly chop.

STEP 2

Heat the oven to 220C/200C fan/gas 7. Mix together the ricotta, spinach, a generous grating of nutmeg, the remaining crushed garlic and some salt and pepper. Spread the tomato sauce over the base of a shallow baking dish about 20cm x 30cm. Divide the spinach mixture between the pancakes, spreading it over half the surface. Fold each pancake in half, then in half again to make a triangle. Lay the pancakes on top of the sauce, scatter with the mozzarella and parmesan. Drizzle with a little more oil and bake for 15-20 mins until bubbling.

One-pan lamb & couscous

Prep: 5 mins **Cook:** 20 mins

Serves 2

Ingredients

- 2 lamb steaks, approx 140g/5oz each, or 4 lamb chops trimmed of excess fat
- 1-2 tsp harissa paste
- 1 tbsp olive oil
- handful dried fruit and nuts
- 85g couscous
- 400g can chickpeas , rinsed and drained
- 100ml/3½ fl oz hot chicken stock or lamb stock (from a cube is fine)
- handful mint leaves, torn

Method

STEP 1

Rub the lamb with half the harissa paste. Heat the oil in a frying pan and fry the lamb for 3 mins on each side for medium-rare, or a little longer for well-done. Lift the meat out of the pan and tip in the remaining harissa, the dried fruit and nuts, couscous and chickpeas, then stir to coat in the paste. Take the pan off the heat and pour in the stock. Stir briefly, return the lamb to the pan and cover with a lid or tightly-fitting foil for 10 mins until the couscous has absorbed all the liquid.

STEP 2

Fluff up the couscous with a fork, season to taste and fold the mint leaves through to serve.

Curried mango & chickpea pot

Prep: 15 mins

Serves 1

Ingredients

- 200g chickpeas , drained and rinsed
- 2 tbsp fat-free Greek yogurt
- ½ lemon , juiced
- 1 heaped tbsp korma curry paste
- ½ carrot , julienned or grated
- 70g red cabbage , shredded

- 50g baby spinach , shredded
- 40g mango , finely diced
- ½ tsp nigella seeds
- ½ small red chilli , finely sliced (deseeded if you want less heat)

Method

STEP 1

Combine the chickpeas, yogurt, lemon and korma paste in a bowl, then toss with the carrot, cabbage, spinach and mango. Tip into your lunchbox or an airtight container and scatter with the nigella seeds and red chilli.

Slow-cooker chicken curry

Prep: 10 mins **Cook:** 6 hrs

Serves 2

Ingredients

- 1 large onion, roughly chopped
- 3 tbsp mild curry paste
- 400g can chopped tomatoes

- 2 tsp vegetable bouillon powder
- 1 tbsp finely chopped ginger
- 1 yellow pepper, deseeded and chopped

- 2 skinless chicken legs, fat removed
- 30g pack fresh coriander, leaves chopped
- cooked brown rice, to serve

Method

STEP 1

Put 1 roughly chopped large onion, 3 tbsp mild curry paste, a 400g can chopped tomatoes, 2 tsp vegetable bouillon powder, 1 tbsp finely chopped ginger and 1 chopped yellow pepper into the slow cooker pot with a third of a can of water and stir well.

STEP 2

Add 2 skinless chicken legs, fat removed, and push them under all the other ingredients so that they are completely submerged. Cover with the lid and chill in the fridge overnight.

STEP 3

The next day, cook on Low for 6 hrs until the chicken and vegetables are really tender.

STEP 4

Stir in the the chopped leaves of 30g coriander just before serving over brown rice.

Vegetarian bean pot with herby breadcrumbs

Prep:10 mins **Cook:**35 mins

Serves 2

Ingredients

- 1 slice crusty bread
- ½ small pack parsley leaves
- ½ lemon , zested
- 2 tbsp olive oil
- pinch chilli flakes (optional)
- 2 leeks , rinsed and chopped into half-moons
- 2 carrots , thinly sliced
- 2 celery sticks , thinly sliced
- 1 fennel bulb , thinly sliced
- 2 large garlic cloves , chopped
- 1 tbsp tomato purée
- few thyme sprigs
- 150ml white wine
- 400g can cannellini beans , drained

Method

STEP 1

Toast the bread, then tear into pieces and put in a food processor with the parsley, lemon zest, ½ tbsp olive oil, a good pinch of salt and pepper and the chilli flakes, if using. Blitz to breadcrumbs. Set aside.

STEP 2

Heat the remaining oil in a pan and add the leeks, carrots, celery and fennel along with a splash of water and a pinch of salt. Cook over a medium heat for 10 mins until soft, then add the garlic and tomato purée. Cook for 1 min more, then add the thyme and white wine. Leave to bubble for a minute, then add the beans. Fill the can halfway with water and pour into the pot.

STEP 3

Bring the cassoulet to the boil, then turn down the heat and leave to simmer for 15 mins before removing the thyme sprigs. Mash half the beans to thicken the stew. Season to taste, then divide between bowls and top with the herby breadcrumbs to serve.

Roast chicken traybake

Prep: 10 mins **Cook:** 1 hr and 5 mins

Serves 2

Ingredients

- 2 red onions (320g), sliced across into rings
- 1 large red pepper , deseeded and chopped into 3cm pieces
- 300g potatoes , peeled and cut into 3cm chunks
- 2 tbsp rapeseed oil
- 4 bone-in chicken thighs , skin and any fat removed
- 1 lime , zested and juiced
- 3 large garlic cloves , finely grated
- 1 tsp smoked paprika
- 1 tsp thyme leaves
- 2 tsp vegetable bouillon powder
- 200g long stem broccoli , stem cut into lengths if very thick

Method

STEP 1

Heat the oven to 200C/180C fan/gas 6. Put the onion, pepper, potatoes and oil in a non-stick roasting tin and toss everything together. Roast for 15 mins while you rub the chicken with the lime zest, garlic, paprika and thyme. Take the veg from the oven, stir, then snuggle the chicken thighs among the veg, covering them with some of the onions so they don't dry out as it roasts for 40 mins.

STEP 2

As you approach the end of the cooking time, mix 200ml boiling water with the bouillon powder. Take the roasting tin from the oven, add the broccoli to the tin, and pour over the hot stock followed by the lime juice, then quickly cover with the foil and put back in the oven for 10 more mins until the broccoli is just tender.

Courgette & lemon risotto

Prep: 10 mins **Cook:** 40 mins

Serves 2

Ingredients

- 50g butter
- 1 onion, finely chopped
- 1 large garlic clove, crushed
- 180g risotto rice
- 1 vegetable stock cube
- zest and juice 1 lemon

- 2 lemon thyme sprigs
- 250g courgette, diced
- 50g parmesan (or vegetarian alternative), grated
- 2 tbsp crème fraîche

Method

STEP 1

Melt the butter in a deep frying pan. Add the onion and fry gently until softened for about 8 mins, then add the garlic and stir for 1 min. Stir in the rice to coat it in the buttery onions and garlic for 1-2 mins.

STEP 2

Dissolve the stock cube in 1 litre of boiling water, then add a ladle of the stock to the rice, along with the lemon juice and thyme. Bubble over a medium heat, stirring constantly. When almost all the liquid has been absorbed, add another ladle of stock and keep stirring. Tip in the courgette and keep adding the stock, stirring every now and then until the rice is just tender and creamy.

STEP 3

To serve, stir in some seasoning, the lemon zest, Parmesan and crème fraîche.

Pot-roast chicken with stock

Prep: 10 mins **Cook:** 2 hrs and 10 mins

Serves 4 with leftovers

Ingredients

- 2 tbsp olive oil
- 2.4kg chicken – buy the best you can afford
- 4 onions , peeled and cut into large wedges

- ½ bunch thyme
- 3 garlic cloves
- 6 peppercorns
- 175ml white wine
- 1.2l chicken stock

Method

STEP 1

Heat oven to 170C/150C fan/gas 5. Heat the oil in a large flameproof casserole dish and brown the chicken well on all sides, then sit it breast-side up. Pack in the onions, thyme, garlic and peppercorns, pour over the wine and stock, and bring to the boil. Pop on the lid and transfer to the oven for 2 hrs.

STEP 2

Remove and rest for 20 mins. Carefully lift the chicken onto a chopping board and carve as much as you need. Serve the carved chicken in a shallow bowl with the onions and some of the stock poured over. Serve with some usual Sunday veg and roast potatoes.

STEP 3

Strain the leftover stock into a bowl and strip the carcass of all the chicken. Chill both for up to three days or freeze for up to a month to use for other recipes like our one-pot chicken noodle soup.

Vegan jambalaya

Prep: 10 mins **Cook:** 35 mins

Serves 2

Ingredients

- 2 tbsp cold-pressed rapeseed oil
- 1 large onion (180g), finely chopped
- 4 celery sticks , finely chopped
- 1 yellow pepper , chopped
- 2 tsp smoked paprika
- ½ tsp chilli flakes
- ½ tsp dried oregano

- 115g brown basmati rice
- 400g can chopped tomatoes
- 2 garlic cloves , finely grated
- 400g butter beans , drained and rinsed
- 2 tsp vegetable bouillon powder
- large handful of parsley , chopped

Method

STEP 1

Heat the oil in a large pan set over a high heat and fry the onion, celery and pepper, stirring occasionally, for 5 mins until starting to soften and colour.

STEP 2

Stir in the spices and rice, then tip in the tomatoes and a can of water. Stir in the garlic, beans and bouillon. Bring to a simmer, then cover and cook for 25 mins until the rice is tender and has absorbed most of the liquid. Keep an eye on the pan towards the end of the cooking time to make sure it doesn't boil dry – if it starts to catch, add a little more water. Stir in the parsley and serve hot.

Chicken tagine with lemons, olives & pomegranate

Prep: 10 mins **Cook:** 1 hr and 30 mins

Serves 4-5

Ingredients

- 2 tbsp olive oil
- 8 chicken thighs

- 1 onion , chopped
- 2 garlic cloves

- 2 tbsp Moroccan spice mix (see below)
- 1 large or 2 small preserved lemons , skin only, finely chopped
- 2 large tomatoes , chopped
- 1 chicken stock cube
- 1 tbsp honey
- couscous , to serve

- 1 tbsp red wine vinegar
- handful olives
- 1 small lemon , 1/2 very thinly sliced
- ½ pomegranate , seeds only
- 100g feta , crumbled
- small bunch mint , leaves only

For the Moroccan spice mix

- 2 tbsp coriander seeds
- 1 tbsp cumin seeds
- 1½ tsp fennel seeds
- ½ tsp black pepper

- ¼ tsp ground ginger
- 1 tsp ground cinnamon
- good pinch saffron

Method

STEP 1

Heat 1 tbsp oil in a wide, shallow casserole dish or ovenproof pan. Season the chicken and cook, skin-side down, for 8-10 mins, until crispy. Flip over and cook for another 5 mins. Transfer to a plate. Heat oven to 170C/150C fan/gas 3.

STEP 2

Add the rest of the oil and the onion to the pan. Stir for a few mins, then add the garlic and Moroccan spice mix. Stir, scraping any bits of onions and chicken from the bottom, until the spices smell fragrant. Add the preserved lemon, tomatoes, stock cube, honey, vinegar and 750ml water. Bring to the boil, then place the chicken on top. Cover with a lid or foil and transfer to the oven for 1 hr.

STEP 3

Uncover, place the olives and lemon slices on top and drizzle the lemons with a little oil. Return to the oven for 20 mins, or until the sauce has reduced a little (you can do this on the hob if you're short on time). Check the seasoning, adding a squeeze of lemon, more honey or salt if you think it needs it. Scatter over the pomegranate seeds, feta and mint, and serve with couscous.

Smoky bacon pot noodle for one

Prep: 2 mins **Cook:** 5 mins

Serves 1

Ingredients

- 1 rasher smoked back bacon , trimmed and chopped
- 2 spring onions , white and green separated and finely sliced
- 50g frozen pea
- quarter tsp paprika

- 2 tsp cornflour
- 200ml vegetable stock
- 150g block straight-to-wok wheat noodle , or equivalent of dried, cooked
- splash Worcestershire sauce

Method

STEP 1

In a small non-stick pan, fry the bacon for a few mins, add the white parts of the spring onions, peas and paprika, then cook for 1 min more. Mix the cornflour with a little of the stock to get a paste, then stir this into the pan with the rest of the stock, noodles and a good splash of Worcestershire sauce. Simmer for a couple of mins until thick and saucy, then scatter with the green parts of spring onion.

Potted cheddar with ale & mustard

Prep: 10 mins **Cook:** 5 mins

6-8 (1 x 400ml jar)

Ingredients

- 250g extra mature cheddar cheese , chopped
- 140g butter

- 1 tbsp ale
- 1 tbsp wholegrain mustard
- 1 thyme sprig (optional)

Method

STEP 1

Put the cheese, 100g butter and ale in a food processor. Blitz until creamy and well combined. Stir in the mustard, then pack into a large sterilised jar, ramekin or ceramic pot, making sure to eliminate any air pockets.

STEP 2

Melt the remaining butter and leave to sit for a minute to let the fat separate from the milk solids (these will form a milky puddle at the bottom). Pour the clear fat over the cheese, leaving the milk solids in the pan. Place a thyme sprig on top, if using, and chill for a few hours. The sealed cheese will keep for a couple of months in the fridge. Once you've cracked the buttery crust, use up within a week.

Peanut butter & date oat pots

Prep: 10 mins

Serves 6

Ingredients

- 180g porridge oats
- 75g 100% crunchy peanut butter
- 40g stoned medjool dates , chopped
- 2 tsp vanilla extract

- 5 x 120g pots plain bio yogurt (or 600g from a large pot)
- ground cinnamon , for dusting

Method

STEP 1

Tip the oats into a large bowl and pour over 600ml boiling water. Add the peanut butter, dates and vanilla and stir well. Cool, then stir through 240g of the yogurt. Dilute with a small amount of water if the consistency is a little stiff.

STEP 2

Spoon into six glasses, then top with the remaining yogurt and dust with cinnamon. Cover each glass and keep in the fridge until ready to eat. Will keep well for up to five days.

One-pan lamb with hasselback potatoes

Prep: 30 mins **Cook:** 2 hrs

Serves 6-8

Ingredients

- 1 leg of lamb , about 2kg
- 2 garlic bulbs
- 15 sprigs rosemary
- 15 sprigs thyme

- 1.7kg medium-sized potatoes (Maris Piper work well), unpeeled
- 14 bay leaves
- 4 tbsp olive oil
- 1 lemon , juiced

Method

STEP 1

Use a small, sharp knife to make at least 30 small, deep, incisions all over the lamb. Halve the garlic bulbs, so at the top the cloves fall away and at the bottom, they remain attached. Peel and slice the tops that have fallen away and keep the other halves for later. Use your fingers to push the slices into each slit. Next, pull off small sprigs of rosemary and thyme, keeping the stalks on, and poke them into the slits, too. Can be done a day ahead, then cover the lamb and chill. Remove from the fridge 1 hr before roasting.

STEP 2

Heat oven to 210C/190C fan/gas 7. Sit each potato between the handles of two wooden spoons and cut widthways at 3mm intervals – the spoon handles will stop you slicing all the way through. Slot a bay leaf into the middle slit of each potato. Tip the potatoes into a large roasting tin with the halved garlic bulb and the rest of the rosemary and thyme. Drizzle with half the oil and season, then toss to coat and turn the potatoes so they're all cut-side up. Nestle the lamb in the middle of the tin, pushing the potatoes to the outside, then rub the lamb with the rest of the oil and the lemon juice and season generously.

STEP 3

Roast for 1 hr 30 mins, basting the potatoes and shaking the tin occasionally, until the lamb is dark brown and the potatoes are crisp and golden. The lamb will be pink in the middle but cooked. For rare, cook for 10 mins less, and for well done, 15 mins more. Remove the lamb from the tin and leave to rest for 15 mins, putting the potatoes back in the oven if you need to. Serve drizzled with our green olive & herb dressing.

One-pan seafood roast with smoky garlic butter

Prep:20 mins **Cook:**40 mins

Serves 4

Ingredients

- 400g baby new potatoes
- 1 tbsp olive or rapeseed oil
- 2 corn cobs
- 8-12 large prawns , heads and shells on
- 8-12 mussels or large clams (or a mixture)
- 2 medium squids with tentacles, cleaned
- 150g butter
- small bunch parsley , chopped, plus a little to serve
- 1 tsp smoked paprika
- 3 garlic cloves , crushed
- 1 lemon , zested then cut into wedges
- 200g ring chorizo , peeled and sliced

Method

STEP 1

Heat oven to 200C/180C fan/gas 6. Use a large knife to hasselback the potatoes; cut incisions in each potato making sure you don't cut through to the base, and keep the cuts as close together as possible. Toss the potatoes in oil and some seasoning in your largest roasting tin (an oven tray is ideal – line with parchment first if it's old). Roast for 20 mins.

STEP 2

Butterfly the prawns by cutting a line down the back of each one, through the shell from the base of the head to the top of the tail. Pull out the black line of intestine from each one. Clean the mussels under cold water, pulling off any hairy or stringy bits. Hasselback the squid in the same way you did the potatoes.

STEP 3

Cut each corn cob into four pieces – the easiest way to do this is by positioning your knife, covering it with a tea towel and hitting it with a rolling pin. Add the corn to the tray, toss in the oil and return to the oven for 5 mins.

STEP 4

Mash together the butter, parsley, paprika, garlic and lemon zest. Stuff some of the butter into the back of each prawn and inside the squids. Turn the oven up to 220C/200C fan/gas 6. Add the seafood, lemon wedges and chorizo to the pan and toss everything together. Dot the remaining butter over the top, season well and return to the oven for 10 mins. If any of the prawns haven't turned pink or any mussels haven't opened, move them around the pan to the hot spots, then return to the oven for another 2-3 mins. Remove and discard any mussels which haven't opened. Scatter some parsley over and serve.

Christmas dinner for one

Prep:35 mins **Cook:**45 mins

Serves 1

Ingredients

- 3 pork chipolatas
- 1 small apple , cored, ½ grated, ½ cut into wedges
- 3 pecans , chopped
- 2 slices white bread , chopped into small pieces
- pinch of dried sage
- 1 skinless chicken breast
- 4 rashers streaky bacon
- 5 Brussels sprouts , trimmed
- 2 small potatoes , quartered
- 1 medium parsnip , trimmed

To serve

- 1-2 tbsp pickled red cabbage

- 1 garlic clove , sliced
- 3 bay leaves
- 2 tbsp vegetable or sunflower oil
- 250ml milk
- 2 cloves
- 1 shallot
- 2 tsp butter
- 1 tbsp balsamic vinegar
- 250ml red wine
- 250ml beef or chicken stock (can be made with 1/2 stock cube)

- 1 tsp cranberry sauce

Method

STEP 1

Heat the oven to 200C/180C fan/gas 6. Squeeze the meat from one of the chipolatas into a bowl, discarding the skin. Put the grated apple in a clean tea towel and squeeze out any excess liquid, then add to the sausagemeat with the pecans, a quarter of the bread and the sage. Season, then combine using your hands and form into a fat sausage shape. Cut a long slit in the chicken breast lengthways on one side, being careful not to cut it in half (you should be able to open it up like a book). Stuff the chicken breast with the stuffing sausage, then wrap two of the bacon rashers around it so it's fully enclosed, securing it with a couple of cocktail sticks.

STEP 2

Put the stuffed chicken breast in a large roasting tin. Wrap the remaining bacon rashers around the remaining chipolatas and add to the tin around the chicken.

STEP 3

Add the apple wedges, sprouts and potatoes to the roasting tin. Cut the parsnip in half lengthways and put it, cut-side down, on a chopping board. Make very thin, close cuts into the parsnip halves that go almost but not fully through – put a wooden spoon on either side of the parsnip halves to stop the knife going through, if you like. Transfer to the roasting tin with the garlic and two of the bay leaves. Drizzle over the oil and season everything with salt and pepper. Roast for 40-45 mins, or until everything is cooked through. Brush the vegetables in the oil and meat juices once or twice near the end of the cooking time.

STEP 4

Meanwhile, pour the milk into a small saucepan with the remaining bay leaf, the cloves and shallot. Heat gently for 5-6 mins, stirring occasionally, or until the shallot is starting to soften. Strain the milk into a heatproof jug, reserving the shallot and discarding the bay leaf and cloves. Return the milk to the pan with the remaining bread and cook, stirring, until you have a thick, porridge-like sauce. Add half the butter and stir until melted, then season, remove from the heat and set aside.

STEP 5

Slice the reserved shallot, then add to a deep frying pan with the rest of the butter. Fry until just golden, then pour in the balsamic vinegar. Continue to cook until the vinegar has reduced and is thick and sticky, then add the wine. Cook until the wine has reduced by half, then stir in the stock and bubble until the sauce is glossy and slightly thickened.

STEP 6

Gently reheat the bread sauce. Slice half the chicken (reserving the rest for leftovers) and put on a plate with the pigs in blankets and the roast apple, sprouts, potatoes and parsnip. Drizzle over the red wine gravy and serve with the pickled red cabbage and cranberry and bread sauces on the side.

Potted crab

Prep:10 mins **Cook:**2 mins

Serves 2

Ingredients

- 150g picked white crabmeat , the freshest you can buy
- 2 tbsp mayonnaise
- 1 shallot , peeled and finely chopped

For the paprika butter

- 60g butter

- small handful chives , chopped
- ½ orange , zested
- 2 large slices sourdough , grilled or griddled, to serve

- ¼ tsp smoked paprika

Method

STEP 1

Tip the crabmeat into a bowl and mix with the mayonnaise, shallot, chives, orange zest and some seasoning. Spoon the mixture into a shallow serving dish. Smooth the top over, then pop in the fridge to chill.

STEP 2

Gently melt the butter and smoked paprika together. Leave the butter to cool a little, but don't let it solidify. Carefully pour the clear butter fat over the crab, leaving the milky butter residue still in the saucepan. Return to the fridge for 20-25 mins or up to a day to firm the butter up. Serve with some grilled sourdough for spreading everything over.

Ultimate apple pie

Total time 2 hrs and 30 mins Ready in 2½ hours

Serves 8

Ingredients

For the filling

- 1kg Bramley apples
- 140g golden caster sugar

- ½ tsp cinnamon
- 3 tbsp flour

For the pastry

- 225g butter, room temperature
- 50g golden caster sugar, plus extra
- 2 eggs

- 350g plain flour, preferably organic
- softly whipped cream, to serve

Method

STEP 1

Put a layer of paper towels on a large baking sheet. Quarter, core, peel and slice the apples about 5mm thick and lay evenly on the baking sheet. Put paper towels on top and set aside while you make and chill the pastry.

STEP 2

For the pastry, beat the butter and sugar in a large bowl until just mixed. Break in a whole egg and a yolk (keep the white for glazing later). Beat together for just under 1 min – it will look a bit like scrambled egg. Now work in the flour with a wooden spoon, a third at a time, until it's beginning to clump up, then finish gathering it together with your hands. Gently work the dough into a ball, wrap in cling film, and chill for 45 mins. Now mix the 140g/5oz sugar, the cinnamon and flour for the filling in a bowl that is large enough to take the apples later.

STEP 3

After the pastry has chilled, heat the oven to 190C/fan 170C/gas 5. Lightly beat the egg white with a fork. Cut off a third of the pastry and keep it wrapped while you roll out the rest, and use this to line a pie tin – 20-22cm round and 4cm deep – leaving a slight overhang. Roll the remaining third to a circle about 28cm in diameter. Pat the apples dry with kitchen paper, and tip them into the bowl with the cinnamon-sugar mix. Give a quick mix with your hands and immediately pile high into the pastry-lined tin.

STEP 4

Brush a little water around the pastry rim and lay the pastry lid over the apples pressing the edges together to seal. Trim the edge with a sharp knife and make 5 little slashes on top of the lid for the steam to escape. (Can be frozen at this stage.) Brush it all with the egg white and sprinkle with caster sugar. Bake for 40-45 mins, until golden, then remove and let it sit for 5-10 mins. Sprinkle with more sugar and serve while still warm from the oven with softly whipped cream.

One-pan roast butter chicken

Prep: 30 mins **Cook:** 1 hr and 10 mins

Serves 4

Ingredients

- 1 lemon , halved
- 1 medium chicken

For the curry butter

- 100g soft unsalted butter
- 2 garlic cloves , crushed
- small piece ginger , finely grated
- 1 tsp garam masala

- 1 tsp turmeric
- 1 tsp ground cloves
- handful coriander leaves , chopped

For the sauce

- 3 garlic cloves , finely grated
- small piece ginger , finely grated
- 4 cardamom pods
- 4 cloves
- 1 tsp fennel seeds

- 2 tsp garam masala
- 1 tsp hot chilli powder
- 2 tsp turmeric
- 500ml passata
- 200ml double cream

Method

STEP 1

Heat oven to 220C/200C fan/gas 7. Put the lemon halves in the chicken cavity. Stir all the ingredients for the curry butter together and season with salt and lots of pepper. Use your fingers to stuff the curry butter under the skin and smear it all over the meat.

STEP 2

Place the chicken in a flameproof roasting tin, on a trivet, if you have one. Roast for 20 mins, then turn the oven down to 180C/160C/gas 4. Continue to roast for 40 mins, or until the chicken is cooked through. Remove the chicken from the tin and leave to rest while you make the sauce.

STEP 3

If your roasting tin is flameproof, place it directly on the heat, if not, scrape all the buttery goodness from the tin into a saucepan and set over a low heat to make the sauce. Gently sweat the garlic and ginger in the curry butter. Scatter in the cardamom, cloves and fennel seeds and cook for 2 mins, then add the ground spices and cook for another 2 mins. Pour in the passata and gently reduce by half before adding the cream and reducing by a third. To finish the sauce, pour in the resting juices, season and add a squeeze of the roasted lemon from the cavity of the chicken. Carve the chicken and serve with the sauce.

Smoky sausage casserole

Prep: 15 mins **Cook:** 1 hr

Serves 4

Ingredients

- 1 tbsp olive oil
- 1 onion, finely chopped
- 1 garlic clove, crushed
- 1 large celery stick, finely chopped
- 2 peppers (any colour), cut into chunks
- pack 6 pork sausage (about 400g/14oz)
- 1 tsp sweet smoked paprika
- ½ tsp ground cumin

- ½ tsp chilli flakes
- 2 x 400g cans chopped tomatoes
- 400g can cannellini beans, drained
- 250g bag spinach (or use the same quantity as frozen)
- 2 tbsp fresh breadcrumbs (or frozen with herbs)

Method

STEP 1

Put the oil in a large, heatproof casserole dish over a medium heat and add the onion, cooking for 5 mins until starting to soften. Tip in the garlic, celery and peppers, and give everything a good stir. Cook for 5 mins more.

STEP 2

Turn the heat to high and add the sausages. Cook for a few mins until browned all over, then reduce the heat to medium, sprinkle in the spices and season well. Pour over the tomatoes and bring to a simmer. Cover and continue simmering gently for 40 mins, stirring every now and then.

STEP 3

Heat the grill to high and uncover the casserole. Add the beans and spinach, and stir to warm through. Scatter over the breadcrumbs and grill for 2-3 mins until golden and crisp.

Slow-cooker beef pot roast

Prep: 15 mins **Cook:** 7 hrs and 30 mins

Serves 6 - 8

Ingredients

- 2 tbsp sunflower oil
- 1½ kg rolled beef brisket
- 2 tbsp plain flour
- 3 carrots, chopped
- 3 sticks of celery, chopped
- 2 parsnips, chopped
- 1 onion, chopped

- 80g button mushrooms
- 2 bay leaves
- 2 garlic cloves, crushed
- 2 tsp English mustard
- 500ml red wine
- 250ml beef stock

Method

STEP 1

Heat 2 tbsp sunflower oil in a large pan. Dust 1½ kg rolled beef brisket with 2 tbsp plain flour and season well with salt and pepper.

STEP 2

Put 3 chopped carrots, 3 chopped celery sticks, 2 chopped parsnips, 1 chopped onion and 80g button mushrooms in the bottom of your slow cooker and turn it to Low.

STEP 3

Sear the beef all over in the hot pan then place it on top of the vegetables in the slow cooker.

STEP 4

Add the 2 bay leaves, 2 crushed garlic cloves and 2 tsp English mustard then pour over 500ml red wine and 250ml beef stock. Cover with the lid and cook for 7 hours.

STEP 5

Heat oven to 200C/180C fan/gas 6. Carefully take the beef out of the slow cooker and place it on a baking tray then roast it in the oven for 20 mins.

STEP 6

While the beef is in the oven, carefully ladle the cooking liquid out of the slow cooker into a shallow pan. Boil rapidly on a high heat to reduce to a rich gravy.

STEP 7

Serve the beef sliced with roast potatoes, the softened vegetables, gravy and wilted greens, if you like.

Honey mustard chicken pot with parsnips

Prep:5 mins **Cook:**40 mins

Serves 4

Ingredients

- 1 tbsp olive oil
- 8 bone-in chicken thighs, skin removed
- 2 onions, finely chopped
- 350g parsnip, cut into sticks
- 300ml vegetable stock
- 2 tbsp wholegrain mustard
- 2 tbsp clear honey
- few thyme sprigs
- flat-leaf parsley, to serve (optional)

Method

STEP 1

Heat half the oil in a large frying pan or shallow casserole with a lid. Brown the chicken until golden, then set aside. Heat the remaining oil, then cook the onions for 5 mins until softened.

STEP 2

Nestle the thighs back amongst the onions and add the parnips. Mix the stock with the mustard and honey, then pour in. Scatter over the thyme, then bring to a simmer. Cover, then cook for 30 mins (or longer, see tip) until the chicken is tender, then season. Serve with steamed greens.

Home-style chicken curry

Prep:15 mins **Cook:**30 mins

Serves 4

Ingredients

- 1 large onion
- 6 garlic cloves, roughly chopped
- 50g ginger, roughly chopped
- 4 tbsp vegetable oil
- 2 tsp cumin seeds
- 1 tsp fennel seeds
- 5cm cinnamon stick
- 1 tsp chilli flakes
- 1 tsp garam masala
- 1 tsp turmeric
- 1 tsp caster sugar
- 400g can chopped tomatoes
- 8 chicken thighs, skinned, boneless (about 800g)
- 250ml hot chicken stock
- 2 tbsp chopped coriander

Method

STEP 1

Roughly chop 1 large onion, transfer to a small food processor, and add 3 tbsp of water - process to a slack paste. You could use a stick blender for this or coarsely grate the onion into a bowl – there's no need to add any water if you are grating the onion. Tip into a small bowl and leave on one side.

STEP 2

Put 6 roughly chopped garlic cloves and 50g roughly chopped ginger into the same food processor and add 4 tbsp water – process until smooth and spoon into another small bowl. Alternatively, crush the garlic to a paste with a knife or garlic press and finely grate the ginger.

STEP 3

Heat 4 tbsp vegetable oil in a wok or sturdy pan set over a medium heat.

STEP 4

Combine 2 tsp cumin seeds and 1 tsp fennel seeds with a 5cm cinnamon stick and 1 tsp chilli flakes and add to the pan in one go. Swirl everything around for about 30 secs until the spices release a fragrant aroma.

STEP 5

Add the onion paste – it will splutter in the beginning. Fry until the water evaporates and the onions turn a lovely dark golden - this should take about 7-8 mins.

STEP 6

Add the garlic and ginger paste and cook for another 2 mins – stirring all the time.

STEP 7

Stir in 1 tsp garam masala, 1 tsp turmeric, and 1 tsp caster sugar and continue cooking for 20 secs before tipping in a 400g can chopped tomatoes.

STEP 8

Continue cooking on a medium heat for about 10 mins without a lid until the tomatoes reduce and darken.

STEP 9

Cut 8 skinless, boneless chicken thighs into 3cm chunks and add to the pan once the tomatoes have thickened to a paste.

STEP 10

Cook for 5 mins to coat the chicken in the masala and seal in the juices, and then pour over 250ml hot chicken stock.

STEP 11

Simmer for 8-10 mins without a lid until the chicken is tender and the masala lightly thickened – you might need to add an extra ladleful of stock or water if the curry needs it.

STEP 12

Sprinkle with 2 tbsp chopped coriander and serve with Indian flatbreads or fluffy basmati rice and a pot of yogurt on the side.

Spiced chicken, spinach & sweet potato stew

Prep:15 mins **Cook:**40 mins

Serves 4

Ingredients

- 3 sweet potatoes, cut into chunks
- 190g bag spinach
- 1 tbsp sunflower oil

For the spice paste

- 2 onions, chopped
- 1 red chilli, chopped
- 1 tsp paprika
- thumb-sized piece ginger, grated

To serve

- pumpkin seeds, toasted
- 2-3 preserved lemons, deseeded and chopped

- 8 chicken thighs, skinless and boneless
- 500ml chicken stock

- 400g can tomatoes
- 2 preserved lemons, deseeded and chopped

- 4 naan bread, warmed

Method

STEP 1

Put the sweet potato in a large, deep saucepan over a high heat. Cover with boiling water and boil for 10 mins. Meanwhile, put all the paste ingredients in a food processor and blend until very finely chopped. Set aside until needed.

STEP 2

Put the spinach in a large colander in the sink and pour the sweet potatoes and their cooking water over it to drain the potatoes and wilt the spinach at the same time. Leave to steam-dry.

STEP 3

Return the saucepan to the heat (no need to wash it first), then add the oil, followed by the spice paste. Fry the paste for about 5 mins until thickened, then add the chicken. Fry for 8-10 mins until the chicken starts to colour. Pour over the stock, bring to the boil and leave to simmer for 10 mins, stirring occasionally.

STEP 4

Check the chicken is cooked by cutting into one of the thighs and making sure it's white throughout with no signs of pink. Season with black pepper, then add the sweet potato. Leave to simmer for a further 5 mins. Meanwhile, roughly chop the spinach and add to the stew. *At this point you can leave the stew to cool and freeze for up to 3 months, if you like.*

STEP 5

Scatter over the pumpkin seeds and preserved lemons, and serve with warm naan bread on the side.

Spanish meatball & butter bean stew

Prep: 15 mins **Cook:** 35 mins

Serves 3

Ingredients

- 350g lean pork mince
- 2 tsp olive oil
- 1 large red onion, chopped
- 2 peppers, sliced, any colour will do
- 3 garlic cloves, crushed
- 1 tbsp sweet smoked paprika
- 2 x 400g cans chopped tomatoes
- 400g can butter beans, drained
- 2 tsp golden caster sugar
- small bunch parsley, chopped

- crusty bread, to serve (optional)

Method

STEP 1

Season the pork, working the seasoning in with your hands, then shape into small meatballs. Heat the oil in a large pan, add the meatballs and cook for 5 mins, until golden brown all over. Push to one side of the pan and add the onion and peppers. Cook for a further 5 mins, stirring now and then, until the veg has softened, then stir in the garlic and paprika. Stir everything around in the pan for 1 min, then add the tomatoes. Cover with a lid and simmer for 10 mins.

STEP 2

Uncover, stir in the beans, the sugar and some seasoning, then simmer for a further 10 mins, uncovered. Just before serving, stir in the parsley. Serve with crusty bread for dunking, if you like.

Coconut fish curry

Prep:15 mins **Cook:**15 mins

Serves 4

Ingredients

- 1 tbsp vegetable oil
- 1 onion, finely chopped
- thumb-sized piece ginger, finely grated
- 3 garlic cloves, crushed
- 1 tsp shrimp paste
- 1 small red chilli, shredded (deseeded if you don't like it too hot)
- 2 lemongrass stalks, split, then bruised with a rolling pin
- 1 heaped tbsp medium curry powder
- cooked rice, to serve

- 1 heaped tbsp light muscovado sugar
- small bunch coriander, stems finely chopped
- 400g can coconut milk
- 450g skinless hake fillets, cut into rectangles, roughly credit card size
- 220g pack frozen raw whole prawns (we used Big & Juicy Tiger Prawns, which are sustainably fished)
- 1 lime, halved

Method

STEP 1

Heat the oil in a wide, lidded frying pan, then soften the onion for 5 mins. Increase the heat a little, stir in the ginger, garlic, shrimp paste, chilli and lemongrass, and cook for 2 mins. Add the curry powder and sugar, and keep stirring. When the sugar starts to melt and everything starts to clump together, add the coriander stems, coconut milk and 2 tbsp water, then bring to a simmer.

STEP 2

Add the fish to the sauce, tuck the prawns in here and there, then squeeze over half the lime. Pop on the lid and simmer for 5 mins more or until the hake is just cooked and flaking, and the prawns are pink through. Taste for seasoning, adding a squeeze more lime to the sauce if you like. Scatter over the coriander leaves and serve with rice.

Chicken & chorizo rice pot

Prep: 20 mins **Cook:** 1 hr and 20 mins

Serves 4

Ingredients

- 1 tbsp oil
- 8 chicken pieces or 1 whole chicken, jointed
- 1 large onion, chopped
- 1 red pepper, deseeded and chopped into large chunks
- 3 garlic cloves, crushed

- 225g chorizo, skinned and sliced
- 1 tbsp tomato purée
- 1 tbsp thyme leaf, chopped
- 150ml white wine
- 850ml chicken stock
- 400g long grain rice
- 2 tbsp chopped parsley

Method

STEP 1

Heat the oil in a large flameproof casserole dish and brown the chicken pieces on all sides – you may have to do this in batches. Remove from the dish and put to one side.

STEP 2

Lower the heat, add the onion and pepper, and gently cook for 10 mins until softened. Add the garlic and chorizo, and cook for a further 2 mins until the chorizo has released some of its oils into the dish. Stir in the tomato purée and cook for 1 min more.

STEP 3

Return the chicken pieces to the dish along with the thyme, white wine and stock. Bring the liquid to a boil, cover the dish with a tight-fitting lid and lower the heat. Cook for 30 mins.

STEP 4

Tip in the rice and stir everything together. Cover, set over a low heat and cook for a further 15 mins, or until the rice is cooked and has absorbed most of the cooking liquid. Remove from the heat and leave the dish to sit for 10 mins to absorb any remaining liquid. Season to taste and scatter with parsley to serve.

Spring chicken in a pot

Prep:20 mins **Cook:**45 mins

Serves 4

Ingredients

- 1 tbsp olive oil
- 1 onion , chopped
- 500g boneless, skinless chicken thigh
- 300g small new potato
- 425ml low-salt vegetable stock (such as Kallo low-salt vegetable stock cubes)

- 350g broccoli , cut into small florets
- 350g spring green , shredded
- 140g petits pois
- bunch spring onion , sliced
- 2 tbsp pesto

Method

STEP 1

Heat the oil in a large, heavy pan. Add the onion, gently fry for 5 mins until softened, add the chicken, then fry until lightly coloured. Add the potatoes, stock and plenty of freshly ground black pepper, then bring to the boil. Cover, then simmer for 30 mins until the potatoes are tender and the chicken is cooked. Can be frozen at this point.

STEP 2

Add the broccoli, spring greens, petit pois and spring onions, stir well, then return to the boil. Cover, then cook for 5 mins more, stir in the pesto and heat through.

Easter chocolate pots with pick 'n' mix toppings

Prep: 10 mins **Cook:** 5 mins

plus 2-3 hrs chilling

Serves 6

Ingredients

- 500g fresh custard
- ½ tsp ground cinnamon
- 200g dark chocolate , chopped into small pieces

- 100g crème fraîche
- mixture of crushed chocolate mini eggs, chopped toasted hazelnuts and sprinkles, to serve

Method

STEP 1

Heat the custard with the cinnamon in a saucepan until just simmering. Remove from the heat, add the chocolate, stir until melted, then fold in the crème fraîche.

STEP 2

Divide the mixture between six ramekins or teacups, or tip into one large dish. Transfer to the fridge to chill for 2-3 hrs, or until set. Put the mini eggs, hazelnuts and sprinkles in separate small bowls and serve with the chocolate pots for everyone to top as they like.

Lamb shank Madras

Prep: 40 mins **Cook:** 4 hrs

Serves 4

Ingredients

- 4 tbsp natural yogurt
- 1 tbsp ground cumin
- 1 tsp turmeric
- 4 lamb shanks
- 2 tbsp sunflower oil
- 4 onions , sliced
- 4 tbsp Madras curry powder
- 8 garlic cloves , grated or crushed
- thumb-sized piece ginger , grated
- 220g tin chopped tomatoes
- 3 whole dried red chillies
- 5 curry leaves
- 4 cardamom pods , split
- 3 tbsp lime pickle
- 300ml chicken stock
- chopped mint leaves, naan bread and rice, to serve

Method

STEP 1

Tip the yogurt, cumin, turmeric, 1 tsp sea salt and the lamb shanks into a large mixing bowl, then mix to coat the lamb. Cover and pop in the fridge for a couple of hrs, or overnight if you have time.

STEP 2

Heat oven to 160C/140C fan/gas 4. Heat the oil in a large flameproof casserole dish over a medium heat, add the shanks and brown all over for 10 mins, then remove from the dish. Scatter the onions into the dish and fry for 10 mins until golden brown. Stir in the curry powder, garlic and ginger and cook for 3 mins until aromatic. Add the lamb shanks back to the dish along with the tomatoes, chillies, curry leaves, cardamom pods and lime pickle. Give everything a good stir and pour over the stock. Bring up to a simmer, cover, then transfer to the oven and cook for 3 hrs.

STEP 3

Remove the lid and cook for 1 hr more – this will help reduce some of the liquid and char any exposed meat. When the lamb is very tender, leave to rest for 30 mins or leave to cool completely and reheat the next day for the best flavour. (Can be made up to two days in advance.) Scatter with chopped mint and serve with naan bread and rice on the side.

All-in-one chicken with wilted spinach

Prep: 20 mins **Cook:** 1 hr

Serves 2

Ingredients

- 2 beetroot , peeled and cut into small chunks
- 300g celeriac , cut into small chunks
- 2 red onions , quartered
- 8 garlic cloves , 4 crushed, the rest left whole, but peeled
- 1 tbsp rapeseed oil
- 1½ tbsp fresh thyme leaves , plus extra to serve
- 1 lemon , zested and juiced
- 1 tsp fennel seeds
- 1 tsp English mustard powder
- 1 tsp smoked paprika
- 4 tbsp bio yogurt
- 4 bone-in chicken thighs , skin removed
- 260g bag spinach

Method

STEP 1

Heat oven to 200C/180C fan/gas 6. Tip the beetroot, celeriac, onions and whole garlic cloves into a shallow roasting tin. Add the oil, 1 tbsp thyme, half the lemon zest, fennel seeds and a squeeze of lemon juice, then toss together. Roast for 20 mins while you prepare the chicken.

STEP 2

Stir the mustard powder and paprika into 2 tbsp yogurt in a bowl. Add half the crushed garlic, the remaining lemon zest and thyme, and juice from half the lemon. Add the chicken and toss well until it's coated all over. Put the chicken in the tin with the veg and roast for 40 mins until the chicken is cooked through and the vegetables are tender.

STEP 3

About 5 mins before the chicken is ready, wash and drain the spinach and put it in a pan with the remaining crushed garlic. Cook until wilted, then turn off the heat and stir in the remaining yogurt. Scatter some extra thyme over the chicken and vegetables, then serve.

Prawn laksa curry bowl

Prep: 5 mins **Cook:** 10 mins

Serves 2

Ingredients

- 1 tbsp olive oil
- 1 red chilli , finely sliced
- 2 ½ tbsp Thai red curry paste
- 1 vegetable stock cube
- 400ml can reduced fat coconut milk
- 2 tsp fish sauce
- 100g rice noodles
- 2 limes , juice of 1, the other halved
- 150g cooked king prawns
- ½ small pack coriander , roughly chopped

Method

STEP 1

Heat the oil in a medium saucepan and add the chilli. Cook for 1 min, then add the curry paste, stir and cook for 1 min more. Dissolve the stock cube in a large jug in 700ml boiling water, then pour into the pan and stir to combine. Tip in the coconut milk and bring to the boil.

STEP 2

Add the fish sauce and a little seasoning. Toss in the noodles and cook for a further 3-4 mins until softening. Squeeze in the lime juice, add the prawns and cook through until warm, about 2-3 mins. Scatter over some of the coriander.

STEP 3

Serve in bowls with the remaining coriander and lime wedges on top for squeezing over.

One-pan egg & veg brunch

Prep: 5 mins **Cook:** 25 mins

Serves 2 adults + 2 children

Ingredients

- 300g baby new potatoes , halved
- ½ tbsp rapeseed oil
- 1 knob of butter
- 1 courgette , cut into small chunks
- 1 yellow pepper , cut into small chunks
- toast , to serve
- 1 red pepper , cut into small chunks
- 2 spring onions , finely sliced
- 1 garlic clove , crushed
- 1 sprig thyme , leaves picked
- 4 eggs

Method

STEP 1

Boil the new potatoes for 8 mins, then drain.

STEP 2

Heat the oil and butter in a large non-stick frying pan, then add the courgette, peppers, potatoes and a little salt and pepper. Cook for 10 mins, stirring from time to time until everything is starting to brown. Add the spring onions, garlic and thyme and cook for 2 mins more.

STEP 3

Make four spaces in the pan and crack in the eggs. Cover with foil or a lid and cook for around 4 mins, or until the eggs are cooked (with the yolks soft for dipping into). Sprinkle with more thyme leaves and ground black pepper if you like. Serve with toast.

Beer-braised brisket pot roast

Prep:5 mins **Cook:**3 hrs - 5 hrs

Serves 6

Ingredients

- 1 beef stock cube , crushed
- 1 tsp dried tarragon
- 2 tsp cracked black pepper
- 2kg rolled beef brisket
- 1 tbsp sunflower oil
- 500-550ml bottle of dark ale
- 2 tbsp beef extract
- 1 tbsp muscovado sugar
- 2 tbsp dried onion flakes
- 500ml beef stock
- long-stem broccoli , to serve (optional)

Method

STEP 1

Heat the oven to 150C/130C fan/gas 2. Mix the stock cube with the tarragon and pepper in a small bowl. Rub over the brisket and season. Heat the oil in a large flameproof casserole dish or roasting tin over a medium-high heat, add the brisket and brown well on all sides.

STEP 2

Stir in the ale and beef extract, then tip in the sugar and onion flakes and add enough of the beef stock to come two-thirds of the way up the sides of the brisket. Bring to the boil, cover and roast in the oven for 3 hrs, checking every 30 mins to see if the brisket is tender (but you may need to roast it for up to 5 hrs). Transfer the brisket to a board and leave to rest for 15 mins. Slice and serve with the stock spooned over and some steamed long stem broccoli on the side, if you like.

Simple fish stew

Prep: 10 mins **Cook:** 20 mins - 25 mins

Serves 2

Ingredients

- 1 tbsp olive oil
- 1 tsp fennel seeds
- 2 carrots, diced
- 2 celery sticks, diced
- 2 garlic cloves, finely chopped
- 2 leeks, thinly sliced

- 400g can chopped tomatoes
- 500ml hot fish stock, heated to a simmer
- 2 skinless pollock fillets (about 200g), thawed if frozen, and cut into chunks
- 85g raw shelled king prawns

Method

STEP 1

Heat the oil in a large pan, add the fennel seeds, carrots, celery and garlic, and cook for 5 mins until starting to soften. Tip in the leeks, tomatoes and stock, season and bring to the boil, then cover and simmer for 15-20 mins until the vegetables are tender and the sauce has thickened and reduced slightly.

STEP 2

Add the fish, scatter over the prawns and cook for 2 mins more until lightly cooked. Ladle into bowls and serve with a spoon.

Butter bean, mushroom & bacon pot pies

Prep: 15 mins **Cook:** 50 mins

Serves 4

Ingredients

- 3 tbsp rapeseed oil
- 2 red onions , thinly sliced
- 500g mushrooms , thickly sliced
- 70g smoked streaky bacon , sliced into thin strips
- 2 tbsp plain flour
- 500ml low-salt vegetable stock

- 250g kale , roughly sliced
- 3 tsp wholegrain mustard
- 2 tbsp reduced-fat crème fraîche
- 1 tbsp finely chopped tarragon
- 1 lemon , zested and juiced
- 2 x 400g cans butter beans , drained and rinsed

Method

STEP 1

Heat 2 tbsp of the oil in a saucepan or large flameproof casserole dish. Fry the onions for 10 mins until soft, then add the mushrooms and bacon and fry for another 5 mins until golden. Stir in the flour and cook for 2 mins more. Gradually pour in the stock, then bring to the boil and bubble for 2 mins. Add the kale and cook for another 5 mins, then stir in the mustard, crème fraîche, half the tarragon and the lemon juice. Spoon the mushroom mixture into four small baking dishes.

STEP 2

Heat the oven to 180C/160C fan/gas 4. Put the butter beans in a food processor with the remaining oil and tarragon and the lemon zest. Blitz until chunky, adding 2-3 tbsp water to loosen if needed.

STEP 3

Spoon the butter bean mixture over the filling, smoothing with the back of a spoon. Bake for 20-25 mins until golden. Leave to cool slightly, then serve.

Sausage & bean casserole

Prep: 15 mins **Cook:** 1 hr

Serves 4 - 6

Ingredients

- 2 tbsp olive or rapeseed oil
- 1 onion, finely chopped
- 2 medium sticks celery, finely chopped
- 1 yellow pepper, chopped
- 1 red pepper, chopped
- 6 cooking chorizo sausages (about 400g)
- 6 pork sausages (about 400g)
- 3 fat garlic cloves, chopped
- 1 ½ tsp sweet smoked paprika

- ½ tsp ground cumin
- 1 tbsp dried thyme
- 125ml white wine
- 2 x 400g cans cherry tomatoes or chopped tomatoes
- 2 sprigs fresh thyme
- 1 chicken stock cube
- 1 x 400g can aduki beans, drained and rinsed
- 1 bunch chives, snipped (optional)

Method

STEP 1

Heat 2 tbsp olive or rapeseed oil in a large heavy-based pan.

STEP 2

Add 1 finely chopped onion and cook gently for 5 minutes.

STEP 3

Add 2 finely chopped medium celery sticks, 1 chopped yellow pepper and 1 chopped red pepper and cook for a further 5 mins.

STEP 4

Add 6 chorizo sausages and 6 pork sausages and fry for 5 minutes.

STEP 5

Stir in 3 chopped garlic cloves, 1 ½ tsp sweet smoked paprika, ½ tsp ground cumin and 1 tbsp dried thyme and continue cooking for 1 – 2 mins or until the aromas are released.

STEP 6

Pour in 125ml white wine and use a wooden spoon to remove any residue stuck to the pan.

STEP 7

Add two 400g cans of tomatoes, and 2 sprigs of fresh thyme and bring to a simmer. Crumble in the chicken stock cube and stir.

STEP 8

Cook for 40 minutes. Stir in a 400g drained and rinsed can of aduki beans and cook for a further five minutes.

STEP 9

Remove the thyme sprigs, season with black pepper and stir through some snipped chives, if using. Serve.

Peri-peri chicken pilaf

Prep:20 mins **Cook:**40 mins

Serves 4

Ingredients

- 1 tbsp olive oil
- pack of 6 skinless boneless chicken thighs , cut into large chunks
- 2 tbsp peri-peri seasoning
- 1 onion , finely chopped
- 2 garlic cloves , crushed
- 350g basmati rice
- 500ml hot chicken stock
- 3 peppers (any colour you like), sliced into strips
- 3 large tomatoes , deseeded and roughly chopped
- small pack parsley , roughly chopped
- 2 red chillies , sliced (optional)
- ½ lemon , cut into wedges, to serve

Method

STEP 1

Heat the oil in a large pan over a medium heat. Rub the chicken with 1 tbsp of the peri-peri and brown in the pan for 1 min each side until golden. Transfer to a plate and set aside.

STEP 2

Add the onion to the pan and cook on a gentle heat for 8-10 mins until soft. Add the garlic and remaining peri-peri, and give everything a stir. Tip in the rice and stir to coat.

STEP 3

Add the stock and return the chicken to the pan. Add the peppers and cover with a lid, then simmer gently for 25 mins until cooked. About 5 mins before the end of cooking, add the tomatoes.

STEP 4

Stir through the parsley, scatter over the chillies (if you like it spicy) and serve with lemon wedges.

Penang prawn & pineapple curry

Prep: 25 mins **Cook:** 40 mins

Serves 8, with other dishes

Ingredients

For the toasted coconut

- 100g fresh coconut flesh
- 2 tsp sunflower oil

For the curry

- thumb-sized piece ginger , peeled
- 6 garlic cloves , peeled
- 1 ½ tbsp mild curry powder
- 100ml sunflower oil
- 7 curry leaves
- 1 cinnamon stick
- 1 star anise
- 3 cardamom pods
- 6 cloves
- 6 shallots , thinly sliced lengthways
- 3 tbsp tamarind paste
- 1 pineapple , peeled, cored and cut into chunks
- 1 tbsp palm sugar or soft brown sugar
- 400ml can full-fat thick coconut milk
- 24 large raw king prawns , peeled
- handful coriander leaves and cooked white or brown rice, to serve

Method

STEP 1

Finely grate the coconut, then toast slowly in a wok, stirring until evenly dark brown (it will start to smell very strong, but it will work a treat). While it's still warm, pound to a paste with the sunflower oil using a pestle and mortar. Set aside.

STEP 2

Finely grate or pound the ginger and garlic together using a pestle and mortar. Make a loose curry paste by adding 75ml water to the curry powder. Heat the oil in the wok until it's just starting to smoke, then throw in the curry leaves, cinnamon stick, star anise, cardamom pods and cloves and cook for 1 min until fragrant.

STEP 3

Add the shallots and ginger and garlic paste, cook for around 7 mins until softened and starting to brown, then add the curry powder paste. This is the most important part of making the curry. Ideally, cook over a very low heat and wait until the oil separates and bubbles over the paste, around 10-12 mins. Scrape the bottom of the pan occasionally to remove the crust.

STEP 4

When the oil has come to the top, add the tamarind paste, pineapple and sugar. Pour in the coconut milk. When the mixture starts boiling, add the prawns and return to the boil, then stir through the toasted coconut. Season the curry with salt, scatter over the coriander and serve with rice.

One-pan spaghetti with nduja, fennel & olives

Prep: 15 mins **Cook:** 15 mins

Serves 4

Ingredients

- 400g spaghetti
- 3 garlic cloves , very thinly sliced
- ½ fennel , halved and very thinly sliced
- 75g nduja or sobrasada paste (see tip)
- 200g tomatoes (the best you can get), chopped into chunks
- 75g black olives , pitted and sliced
- 2 tsp tomato purée
- 3 tbsp olive oil , plus a drizzle
- 2 tsp red wine vinegar
- 40g pecorino , plus extra to serve
- handful basil , torn

Method

STEP 1

Boil the kettle. Put all the ingredients except the pecorino and basil in a wide saucepan or deep frying pan and season well. Pour over 800ml kettle-hot water and bring to a simmer, using your tongs to ease the spaghetti under the liquid as it starts to soften.

STEP 2

Simmer, uncovered, for 10-12 mins, tossing the spaghetti through the liquid every so often until it is cooked and the sauce is reduced and clinging to it. Add a splash more hot water if the sauce is too thick or does not cover the pasta while it cooks. Turn up the heat for the final few mins to drive off the excess liquid, leaving you with a rich sauce. Stir through the pecorino and basil, and serve with an extra drizzle of oil and pecorino on the side.

Fruity lamb tagine

Prep: 15 mins **Cook:** 1 hr and 30 mins

Serves 4

Ingredients

- 2 tbsp olive oil
- 500g lean diced lamb
- 1 large onion, roughly chopped
- 2 large carrots, quartered lengthways and cut into chunks
- 2 garlic cloves, finely chopped

To serve

- 120g pack pomegranate seeds

- 2 tbsp ras-el-hanout spice mix
- 400g can chopped tomato
- 400g can chickpea, rinsed and drained
- 200g dried apricot
- 600ml chicken stock

- 2 large handfuls coriander, roughly chopped

Method

STEP 1

Heat oven to 180C/160C fan/gas 4. Heat the oil in a casserole and brown the lamb on all sides. Scoop the lamb out onto a plate, then add the onion and carrots and cook for 2-3 mins until golden. Add the garlic and cook for 1 min more. Stir in the spices and tomatoes, and season. Tip the lamb back in with the chickpeas and apricots. Pour over the stock, stir and bring to a simmer. Cover the dish and place in the oven for 1 hr.

STEP 2

If the lamb is still a little tough, give it 20 mins more until tender. When ready, leave it to rest so it's not piping hot, then serve scattered with pomegranate and herbs, with couscous or rice alongside.

Pea & ham pot pie

Prep:10 mins **Cook:**30 mins

Serves 1

Ingredients

- 100g fresh or frozen soffritto mix (or any ready chopped onions, carrots and celery)
- 2 tsp rapeseed oil
- 2 button mushrooms , quartered
- 2 tbsp frozen peas
- 1 slice of ham , cut into pieces

- 2-3 tbsp cream (of any sort)
- 1 tsp Dijon mustard or other French mustard
- ¼ pack puff pastry (freeze the rest for another time)
- flour (any kind), for rolling

Method

STEP 1

Heat oven to 200C/180C fan/gas 6. Fry the soffrito mix in the oil until it softens and starts to turn golden, add the mushrooms and cook for a couple of mins. Add the peas and ham and cook until the peas are heated through. Stir in the cream and mustard, then turn off the heat. Season well and tip into a pie dish, ovenproof bowl or large shallow mug.

STEP 2

Roll out the pastry using a little of the flour until it is larger than the top of your dish. Lightly score a criss-cross pattern into the pastry. Wet the rim of the dish with water and lift the pastry on top, pressing the pastry on to the edges of the dish.

STEP 3

Cook for 20-25 mins or until the pastry is risen and golden.

One-pan nachos with black beans

Prep: 15 mins **Cook:** 15 mins

Serves 4-6

Ingredients

- 175g yellow or blue tortilla chips
- 200g fresh tomato salsa
- 150g medium cheddar , grated
- 1 red pepper , quartered, cored and finely chopped
- 400g can black beans , drained
- 1 avocado , diced
- soured cream , to serve

Method

STEP 1

Heat oven to 200C/180C fan/gas 6. Arrange the tortilla chips over two-thirds of the tray, spoon most of the salsa on top and scatter over half of the cheese.

STEP 2

Mix the remaining salsa with the red pepper and beans, and tip onto the empty third of the tray. Scatter over the rest of the cheese. Bake for 10-15 mins or until the cheese has melted. Scatter the avocado over the beans and add dollops of the soured cream to serve.

Layered rainbow salad pots

Prep: 25 mins **Cook:** 12 mins

Serves 4

Ingredients

- 350g pasta shapes (De Cecco is a good brand that stays nice and firm)
- 200g green beans , trimmed and chopped into short lengths
- 160g can tuna in olive oil, drained
- 4 tbsp mayonnaise
- 4 tbsp natural yogurt

252

- ½ small pack chives , snipped (optional)
- 200g cherry tomatoes , quartered
- 1 orange pepper , cut into little cubes 195g can sweetcorn, drained

Method

STEP 1

Cook the pasta until it is still a little al dente (2 mins less than the pack instructions) and drain well. Cook the green beans in simmering water for 2 mins, then rinse in cold water and drain well. Mix the tuna with the mayonnaise and yogurt. Add the chives, if using.

STEP 2

Tip the pasta into a large glass bowl or four small ones, or four wide-necked jars (useful for taking on picnics). Spoon the tuna dressing over the top of the pasta. Add a layer of green beans, followed by a layer of cherry tomatoes, then the pepper and sweetcorn. Cover and chill until you're ready to eat.

Slow-cooked Greek lamb

Prep: 15 mins **Cook:** 5 hrs - 6 hrs

Serves 6

Ingredients

- shoulder of lamb , about 2kg
- 1 garlic bulb , cloves separated but the skin left on
- about 30g anchovies
- 2 tbsp olive oil
- 10 tomatoes , left whole
- 6 carrots , peeled but left whole
- handful fresh sage
- handful fresh rosemary
- handful fresh thyme
- tzatziki , chickpea salad and flatbreads, to serve

Method

STEP 1

Heat oven to 160C/140C fan/gas 3 and sit a shelf as low as possible. Pierce the lamb all over with a small knife, then fill each slit with a garlic clove and half an anchovy fillet. Rub all over with the oil, then season.

STEP 2

Heat a flameproof casserole dish and sear the lamb all over until well browned. Take off the heat, remove the lamb from the dish and tip in the tomatoes, carrots, sage and rosemary. Sit the lamb on top and scatter over the thyme.

STEP 3

Cover the dish, slip it onto the bottom shelf of the oven and cook for 4-5 hrs until pull-apart tender. Carefully lift the lamb from the dish, discard the herbs and roughly squash the tomatoes into the juices. Sit the lamb back in the dish and serve in big shredded chunks with tzatziki, chickpea salad and flatbreads for mopping up the juices.

All-in-one leek & pork pot roast

Prep:15 mins **Cook:**2 hrs

Serves 6

Ingredients

- 1kg boned and rolled shoulder joint of pork
- 6 bay leaves
- 2 garlic cloves , sliced
- bunch of thyme
- 25g butter
- sunflower oil

- 2 onions , peeled and cut into wedges
- 5 juniper berries , crushed
- 1 tsp golden caster sugar
- 1 tbsp white wine vinegar
- 4 whole leeks , trimmed then each cut into 3
- 250ml white wine

Method

STEP 1

Heat oven to 180C/fan 160C/gas 4. I like to untie and unroll the joint then lay 4 bay leaves, the sliced garlic and half the thyme sprigs through it, then retie it. If you're not confident doing this then stab the meat all over and stuff the garlic, bay and thyme into the slits.

STEP 2

Heat the butter and 1 tbsp oil in a casserole, then spend about 10 mins browning the pork on all sides. Add the onions, then continue to cook for about 5 mins until they start to soften. Add the juniper berries, scatter with sugar and add the vinegar. Simmer for a sec, then tuck the leeks and the rest of the bay and thyme in among the pork. Pour over the wine, cover, then cook in the oven for 1½-1¾ hrs until the meat is tender. The dish may now be cooled, then frozen for up to 1 month. Lift the meat from the pan to a board.

STEP 3

Season the veg, then use a slotted spoon to lift it into a bowl. Taste the sauce and, if you think it needs it, reduce to intensify the flavour. Serves slices of meat with a bowl of vegetables and the sauce on the side.

Baked cauliflower pizzaiola

Prep: 15 mins **Cook:** 40 mins

Serves 4

Ingredients

- 1 large cauliflower, cut into 8 wedges
- 2 tbsp olive oil, plus 1 tbsp for roasting
- 600g ripe tomatoes (we used a mixture of red and yellow cherry tomatoes), halved or quartered depending on their size
- 6 unpeeled garlic cloves, bashed
- small pack basil
- ½ small pack fresh oregano, or 1/2 tsp dried

- pinch of chilli flakes
- 4 tbsp dry white wine
- 2 tbsp grated parmesan, or vegetarian alternative
- 3 tbsp breadcrumbs
- 125g mozzarella (check the pack for a vegetarian brand), torn
- crusty bread, to serve
- green salad, to serve

Method

STEP 1

Heat oven to 200C/180C fan/gas 6. Brush the cauliflower wedges with the 1 tbsp oil, then put them in a large roasting dish. Season and roast for 10 mins or until beginning to soften. Carefully turn the wedges over.

STEP 2

Tuck the tomatoes, garlic and most of the basil and oregano around the cauliflower, then sprinkle with the chilli flakes, wine and 2 tbsp more oil. Season and return to the oven for 25 mins or until the tomatoes are soft and starting to catch here and there. Squish the tomatoes slightly to help the juices flow.

STEP 3

Mix the Parmesan and breadcrumbs together. Tear the mozzarella over the cauliflower and tomatoes, scatter over the cheesy crumbs and bake for 10 mins more or until the topping is crisp and the cauliflower is tender. Top with the rest of the herbs and serve with crusty bread and a green salad.

One-pan coriander-crusted duck, roasted plums & greens

Prep: 5 mins **Cook:** 15 mins

Serves 2

Ingredients

- 2 tbsp coriander seeds , lightly crushed
- 2 small duck breasts
- 2 plums , stoned, halved and cut into wedges
- 2 pak choi , halved lengthways

- 100ml chicken stock
- 2 tbsp honey
- 1 tbsp soy sauce
- 1 tbsp red wine vinegar
- ¼ tsp chilli flakes , to serve

Method

STEP 1

Heat the oven to 200C/180C fan/gas 6 and put the coriander seeds on a plate. Score the skin of the duck breasts as many times as you can with a small sharp knife, then season with salt and press the skin into the coriander seeds. Heat an ovenproof frying pan and add the breasts, skin-side down. Put a heavy pan on top to weigh them down, and cook for 7-8 mins to render the fat, occasionally draining off the excess.

STEP 2

Add the plums and pak choi to the pan, flip the breasts over and add half the stock. Transfer to the oven and cook for 4-5 mins. Remove the duck breasts from the pan and transfer to a plate to rest along with the pak choi.

STEP 3

Return the pan with the plums to the heat and add the honey, soy, vinegar and remaining stock. Bring to the boil and continue to cook until syrupy. Carve each duck breast into four chunks. Arrange two halves of pak choi over each plate, and nestle the chunks of duck breast and the plums among the greens. Drizzle with the sauce, then sprinkle over the chilli flakes.

Smoky BBQ pork buns with crushed avocado

Prep:5 mins **Cook:**1 hr and 15 mins

Serves 4-6

Ingredients

- 1 tbsp olive or rapeseed oil
- 2 tsp fennel seeds
- 500g pork mince
- 2 tsp sweet paprika
- 2 x 390g cartons passata with onion and garlic

- 100g good-quality barbecue sauce (we used Stokes)
- 400g can pinto or black beans , drained
- 2 ripe avocados
- 1 lime , juiced
- 4-6 rolls or a French stick and grated cheddar, to serve

Method

STEP 1

Heat the oil and fennel in a pan for about 1-2 mins until sizzling. Add the pork and fry until starting to brown in places, breaking it up with your spoon as it cooks. Add the paprika, passata and some seasoning. Cover the pan with a lid and simmer gently for 30 mins, then cook with the lid off for another 15 mins until the mince has broken down and the sauce is thick. Stir through the barbecue sauce and add the beans, then cook for 1 min until warmed through. Turn the heat off but leave on the hob for up to 3 hrs. *Can be chilled for up to two days, or frozen for up to two months. Reheat individual portions in the microwave or in a smaller pan.*

STEP 2

Halve the avocados and scoop the flesh into a bowl. Add the lime juice and some salt. Squash the avocados in your palms through your fingers to make a chunky, crushed guacamole consistency – this is a great job for kids. If you don't want to use your hands, use a fork instead. Cover the surface directly with cling film to prevent it from browning. *Can be chilled in the fridge for up to a day.* Serve the pork mince piled into buns or with a French stick, with the avocado and some grated cheese.

Chicken & mushroom hot-pot

Prep:35 mins **Cook:**25 mins

Serves 4

Ingredients

50g butter or margarine, plus extra for greasing

1 onion, chopped

100g button mushrooms, sliced

40g plain flour

1 chicken stock cube or 500ml fresh chicken stock

pinch of nutmeg

pinch of mustard powder

250g cooked chicken, chopped

2 handfuls of a mixed pack of sweetcorn, peas, broccoli and carrots, or pick your favourites

For the topping

2 large potatoes, sliced into rounds

knob of butter, melted

Method

STEP 1

Heat oven to 200C/180C fan/gas 6. Put the butter in a medium-size saucepan and place over a medium heat. Add the onion and leave to cook for 5 mins, stirring occasionally. Add the mushrooms to the saucepan with the onions.

STEP 2

Once the onion and mushrooms are almost cooked, stir in the flour – this will make a thick paste called a roux. If you are using a stock cube, crumble the cube into the roux now and stir well. Put the roux over a low heat and stir continuously for 2 mins – this will cook the flour and stop the sauce from having a floury taste.

STEP 3

Take the roux off the heat. Slowly add the fresh stock, if using, or pour in 500ml water if you've used a stock cube, stirring all the time. Once all the liquid has been added, season with pepper, a pinch of nutmeg and mustard powder. Put the saucepan back onto a medium heat and slowly bring it to the boil, stirring all the time. Once the sauce has thickened, place on a very low heat. Add the cooked chicken and vegetables to the sauce and stir well. Grease a medium-size ovenproof pie dish with a little butter and pour in the chicken and mushroom filling.

STEP 4

Carefully lay the potatoes on top of the hot-pot filling, overlapping them slightly, almost like a pie top.

STEP 5

Brush the potatoes with a little melted butter and cook in the oven for about 35 mins. The hot-pot is ready once the potatoes are cooked and golden brown.

Easy chicken & chickpea tagine

Prep: 10 mins **Cook:** 1 hr and 15 mins

Serves 4

Ingredients

- 800g skinless boneless chicken thighs , cut into large chunks
- 1 tbsp harissa
- 1 tbsp vegetable oil
- 1 large onion , finely sliced
- 1 tsp ground cinnamon

- 1 tsp ground cumin
- 1 tsp ground turmeric
- 500ml chicken stock
- 400g can chopped tomatoes
- 100g raisins
- 400g can chickpeas , drained and rinsed

259

- 250g couscous , to serve
- small handful mint , leaves only, to serve

Method

STEP 1

Mix the chicken thighs with the harissa in a large bowl and chill, covered, for 20-30 mins.

STEP 2

Heat the oil in a large flameproof casserole or tagine dish and fry the chicken for 2-3 mins until browned. Remove from the dish and set aside.

STEP 3

Fry the onion for 8-10 mins until soft, then stir in the spices. Return the chicken to the dish, together with the stock, tomatoes and raisins. Season, bring to the boil, then reduce the heat to low. Simmer, covered, for 45 mins.

STEP 4

Add the chickpeas to the dish, and simmer, uncovered, for 15 mins until the sauce reduces slightly and thickens. Serve with couscous and a handful of mint leaves on top.

Berry yogurt pots

Prep:5 mins

Serves 2

Ingredients

- 150g bio yogurt
- 160g blueberries , raspberries or cherries (or a combination)
- 1 tbsp pumpkin seeds , sunflower seeds or flaked almonds
- a little chopped mint (optional)

Method

Spoon the yogurt into two tumblers. Mix the fruit, seeds or nuts of your choice with the mint, if using, and pile into the tumblers.

Chicken, morel mushroom & asparagus one-pan pie

Prep:30 mins **Cook:**35 mins

Serves 5

Ingredients

- 100g fresh morel or 30g dried morels
- 200ml chicken stock (if using fresh morels)
- 50g butter
- 2 shallots , finely sliced
- 3 thyme sprigs , leaves picked
- 2 bay leaves
- 1 tbsp plain flour , plus extra for dusting
- 100ml dry sherry or white wine
- 200ml crème fraîche
- 6 skinless boneless chicken thighs , cut into large chunks
- bunch asparagus , woody ends removed, stalks cut into 4cm pieces
- ½ pack tarragon , leaves roughly chopped, plus a sprig to decorate
- 1 block puff pastry (375g), all-butter is best
- 1 egg , beaten, to glaze

Method

STEP 1

If you are using dried mushrooms, heat the stock and soak them for 10 mins, then remove them, strain the liquid and set it aside. If you're using fresh mushrooms, clean them thoroughly before using. Set a couple of the nicest-looking morels aside to decorate the top of the pie, and halve the rest.

STEP 2

Heat half the butter in a skillet and fry the halved morels for 3-4 mins or until wilted. Scoop them onto a plate and set aside. Heat the remaining butter and gently cook the shallots in the pan with the thyme and bay. Once softened, stir in the flour and cook for 1 min or until you have a sandy paste.

STEP 3

Pour in the sherry and sizzle, then carefully stir in the strained soaking liquid (or 200ml chicken stock if you've used fresh morels), followed by the crème fraîche. Season well and bring the sauce to a gentle simmer. Add the chicken and poach in the sauce for 10 mins or until the chicken is just cooked through. Remove the bay, stir through the asparagus, tarragon and fried morels, then remove from the heat.

STEP 4

Heat oven to 220C/200C fan/gas 8. The pastry needs to sit on top of the ingredients, so if your pan is too deep, use a pie dish instead. Roll out the pastry on a floured surface to the thickness of a £1 coin, then cut the pastry to fit the pan or dish, and drape it over the pie mixture using a rolling pin to help you. Liberally brush with egg, season the pastry with flaky sea salt, and pop your reserved morels on the top. Bake for 20 mins or until the pastry has puffed and is a deep golden brown. Leave tor rest for 5 mins before serving straight from the pan.

One-pan Easter lamb

Prep: 20 mins **Cook:** 2 hrs and 15 mins

Serves 6

Ingredients

- 1.6kg bone-in leg of lamb
- 50ml olive oil , plus a splash
- 3 oregano sprigs, leaves picked and roughly chopped
- 4 rosemary sprigs, leaves of 2 picked and roughly chopped
- 1 lemon , zested (save the juice for the spring greens, see goes well with)
- 1 garlic bulb , cloves lightly smashed

- 1 red chilli , pierced
- 1kg potatoes , skins on, cut into thick wedges
- 3 fennel bulbs , cut into quarters lengthways, tops removed, green fronds reserved
- 250ml white wine
- 250ml good-quality chicken stock

Method

STEP 1

Take the lamb out of the fridge 1 hr before cooking it and use a sharp knife to make small incisions all over the meat. Mix the oil with the oregano, chopped rosemary and lemon zest. Rub the marinade all over the lamb, massaging it well into the cuts.

STEP 2

Heat oven to 200C/180C fan/gas 6. Put the garlic, chilli, potatoes, fennel and remaining rosemary into a large roasting tin, pour over some olive oil and toss together. Season the lamb generously, then lay it on top of the veg. Roast for 45 mins until the lamb is starting to brown, then pour in the wine and stock. Continue cooking for 30 mins for rare (55C on a cooking thermometer), 35-40 mins for medium rare (60C) or 45 mins for cooked through (70C).

STEP 3

Remove the lamb and rest for up to 30 mins. Turn oven down to 160C/140C fan/gas 3, cover the veg with foil and, while the lamb rests, put back in the oven until braised in the roasting juices. Scatter the fennel fronds over the veg, place the lamb back on top and bring the whole tin to the table to serve.

Coconut fish curry traybake

Prep: 15 mins **Cook:** 25 mins

Serves 4

Ingredients

- 2 x 250g pouches cooked brown rice
- 160ml can coconut milk
- 4 tbsp Thai red curry paste
- 1 tbsp fish sauce
- 4 fillets white fish (around 120g each)
- 200g pack Tenderstem broccoli

- 235g pack pak choi
- ½ small bunch spring onions , sliced on the diagonal
- small pack coriander , leaves picked
- 2 limes , cut into wedges, to serve

Method

STEP 1

Heat oven to 200C/180C fan/gas 6. Tip the rice into a roasting tin. Whisk the coconut milk with the curry paste and fish sauce. Nestle the fish into the rice, put the broccoli, pak choi and half the spring onions on top, and season. Drizzle the coconut mixture over everything, cover with foil and cook in the oven for 25 mins or until the veg is cooked through and the fish is flaking apart.

STEP 2

Serve in bowls, topped with coriander leaves and the remaining spring onions, with lime wedges on the side.

Lemony chicken stew with giant couscous

Prep: 25 mins **Cook:** 1 hr

Serves 4

Ingredients

- 1 tbsp olive oil
- 2 onions, chopped
- 500g skinless boneless chicken thighs, each cut into 2-3 chunks
- 3 tbsp tagine paste or 2 tbsp ras el hanout
- 2 x 400g cans tomato with chopped mixed olives

- small handful fresh oregano, leaves picked and chopped
- 2 preserved lemons, flesh removed, skin rinsed and finely chopped
- 2 tbsp clear honey
- 1 chicken stock cube
- 200g giant couscous
- handful parsley, chopped

Method

STEP 1

Heat the oil in a large flameproof casserole dish with a lid. Add the onions and cook for 10 mins until starting to caramelise. Push the onions to one side of the dish and add the chicken. Cook over a high heat for 5 mins or so until the chicken is browning.

STEP 2

Add the tagine paste, tomatoes, oregano, preserved lemons and honey, and crumble in the stock cube. Fill one of the tomato cans halfway with water and pour this into the dish. Season with a little salt and plenty of black pepper. Give everything a good stir, then cover with a lid and simmer for 40 mins, on a gentle bubble, or for up to 4 hrs over a very low heat if you're eating at different times.

STEP 3

Add the couscous 10 mins before you're ready to serve, cover and simmer for 10 mins or until cooked. If you're eating at different times, scoop your portion into a pan, add 50g couscous and cook in the same way. Stir in some parsley just before serving.

Smoked chicken, pot barley & cranberry salad

Prep:25 mins **Cook:**20 mins

Serves 4-6

Ingredients

- 200g pot barley , soaked overnight, or pearl barley
- 50g dried cranberries
- 200g green beans , halved
- 1 red-skinned pear
- 1/2 lemon , juiced

For the dressing

- 1½ tbsp cider vinegar
- 3 tsp Dijon mustard
- 1 tbsp maple syrup

- 50g pecans , lightly toasted
- 50g lamb's lettuce
- small bunch of flat-leaf parsley , roughly chopped
- 250g smoked chicken , sliced or torn into chunks

- 4 tbsp extra virgin olive oil
- 4 tbsp hazelnut or walnut oil

Method

STEP 1

Put the soaked pot barley in a pan, cover with water and bring to the boil, or cook the pearl barley following pack instructions. Turn the heat down to a simmer and cook until the barley is tender but retains a little firmness, about 10-15 mins. Drain and leave to cool completely. Meanwhile, put the cranberries in a small bowl, cover with boiling water and leave to plump up for 20 mins.

STEP 2

Make the dressing by whisking all the ingredients together with a fork. Taste for balance – it should be slightly sweet. Add more vinegar or maple syrup, if you like.

STEP 3

Cook the beans in boiling water for 1-2 mins or until they're tender but still have a little bite. Drain and run cold water over them to help them keep their bright colour. Drain the cranberries and pat them dry with a tea towel. Core, quarter and slice the pear, then toss the slices with the lemon juice.

STEP 4

Put the drained barley, beans, cranberries, pear, pecans, lamb's lettuce, parsley and chicken into a broad, shallow serving bowl with the dressing. Gently toss everything together and serve.

Chicken & new potato traybake

Prep:15 mins **Cook:**1 hr and 15 mins

Serves 2 - 4

Ingredients

- 3 tbsp olive oil
- 500g new potatoes
- 140g large pitted green olives
- 1 lemon, quartered

- 8 fresh bay leaves
- 6 garlic cloves, unpeeled
- 4 large chicken thighs
- bag watercress or salad leaves, to serve

Method

STEP 1

Heat oven to 200C/180C fan/gas 6. Pour the olive oil into a large roasting tin and add the potatoes, olives, lemon quarters, bay leaves and garlic. Toss everything together so it's coated in oil and evenly distributed. Add the chicken thighs, skin-side up, and season.

STEP 2

Put the roasting tin in the oven and roast for 1 hr, basting with the pan juices halfway through cooking. After 1 hr, check that the potatoes are soft and the chicken is cooked through, then return to the oven for a final 15 mins to crisp the chicken skin.

STEP 3

Remove the roasting tin from the oven. Press down on the roasted garlic cloves with the back of a spoon, discard the skins, and mix the mashed garlic with the meat juices. Serve with watercress or your favourite salad leaves on the side.

Red berry granola yogurt pots

Prep:20 mins

Makes 4

Ingredients

- 150g strawberries
- 4 tbsp Greek yogurt
For the coulis

- ½ lemon
- 150g raspberries
For the quick granola

- 1 tbsp coconut oil
- 1 tsp cinnamon
- 150g oats

- 4 tbsp quick granola (see below)

- ½ tbsp honey

- 50g sunflower seeds
- 50g pumpkin seeds
- 2 tbsp honey

Method

STEP 1

To make the coulis, juice the half lemon, then put in a pan with the raspberries and honey. Cook over a gentle heat for a few moments, breaking down with the back of a wooden spoon. Blend to a purée, then push through a sieve and discard the raspberry seeds. Divide between the bottom of four little pots or jars.

STEP 2

To make the quick granola, melt the coconut oil, cinnamon and pinch of salt in a medium pan over a gentle heat. Pour in the oats, seeds and honey and stir well to combine. Continue to move around the pan until evenly browned, about 5 mins. Spread out on a baking sheet to cool.

STEP 3

While it's cooking, slice up the strawberries and divide between the pots, layering up over the coulis. Spoon 1 tbsp of yogurt on top of each pot. Finish each pot with 1 tbsp of granola sprinkled over (the remaining granola will keep in a jar for a week).

One-pan pigs-in-blanket beans

Prep:20 mins **Cook:**40 mins

Serves 8-10

Ingredients

- 1 tbsp sunflower oil
- 6 chipolatas or 12 cocktail sausages
- 200g diced pancetta or bacon lardons
- 2 onions , chopped
- 2 garlic cloves , finely chopped
- 1 tbsp tomato purée

- 75g dark brown soft sugar
- 150ml red wine vinegar
- 2 x 400g cans chopped tomatoes
- 2 x 400g cans cooked white bean , drained
- 6 sage leaves, finely chopped

Method

STEP 1

Heat the oil in a flameproof casserole dish. Sizzle the sausages in the pan until brown on all sides, then lift onto a plate and leave to cool. If you're using chipolatas, cut them into shorter pieces. In the same pan, sizzle the pancetta for 5-8 mins until starting to brown. Scatter the onions over the pancetta and cook until soft, then add the garlic and cook for 1 min longer.

STEP 2

Add the tomato purée and sugar, then pour over the vinegar and chopped tomatoes and use about 100ml of water to rinse out the cans and add that as well. Stir through the beans and sausages, then simmer everything for 20 mins. When the sauce is nice and thick, stir through the sage, simmer for a few minutes more and serve. *The beans can be made up to three days ahead, chilled and reheated.*

One-cup pancakes

Prep: 5 mins **Cook:** 10 mins

Serves 6

Ingredients

- 1 cup plain flour
- 1½ cups milk
- 1 large egg or 2 medium eggs
- 20g butter

- 2 tbsp vegetable or sunflower oil
- caster sugar and lemon wedges, to serve (optional)

Method

STEP 1

Tip the flour and a pinch of salt into a bowl. Make a well in the centre and pour in the milk and egg. Whisk together, starting in the middle, to create a smooth batter. It should be the thickness of double cream.

STEP 2

Heat a little of the butter and oil in a non-stick frying pan. Add a sixth of the batter to the pan, quickly swirling it so there are no holes. Fry on one side for 1-2 mins then flip over and cook for a further 1 min. Keep on a plate, covered, in a warm oven. Repeat with the remaining batter to make six pancakes in total. Serve with sugar and lemon, if you like.

Brazilian pork stew with corn dumplings

Prep: 25 mins **Cook:** 2 hrs and 35 mins

Serves 6

Ingredients

- 900g pork shoulder , cut into 4cm chunks
- 2 tbsp sunflower oil
- 2 onions , finely chopped
- 2 celery sticks, finely chopped

- 3 bay leaves
- 1 tbsp oregano leaves (or 2 tsp dried), plus extra, to serve
- 1 tbsp ground cumin
- 1 tbsp ground coriander

- 1 tbsp allspice
- 1 stock cube (beef, pork or chicken)
- 2 x 400g cans chopped tomatoes
- 1 tbsp cocoa powder
- 2 tbsp soft dark brown or muscovado sugar
- 3 tbsp red wine vinegar
- zest and juice 2 oranges

- 2 red chillies , halved lengthways - seeds in or out, depending on whether you like it spicy
- bunch spring onions , finely sliced
- 400g sweet potatoes , peeled and cut into 3-4cm/1.25in - 1.5in chunks
- 2 red peppers , deseeded and cut into chunks
- 2 x 400g cans black beans , drained and rinsed

For the dumplings

- 100g cold butter , diced
- 200g self-raising flour
- 140g cornmeal or finely ground polenta, plus extra for dusting
- ½ tsp bicarbonate of soda

- 140g sweetcorn , from a can, drained, or freshly cut from a cob (just boil for 3 mins first)
- 75ml buttermilk
- 1 medium egg , beaten

Method

STEP 1

Start by getting your biggest flameproof casserole dish and sealing the pork chunks in the oil – they don't have to be very well browned. Do in batches, then transfer to a plate and tip three-quarters of the onions, the celery, bay and oregano into the dish. Add a splash more oil, if you need, and fry gently until softened.

STEP 2

Tip in the spices, stir for 1 min to toast, then return the pork to the dish. Crumble in the stock cube and stir in the tomatoes, cocoa, sugar, 2 tbsp of the vinegar, the zest and juice from 1 orange, and 3 of the chilli halves. Bring to a simmer, then cover and leave to bubble for 1 hr.

STEP 3

Meanwhile, finely chop the reserved chilli half and mix with the remaining onions, the spring onions, and red wine vinegar and the zest and juice from the last orange. Keep cold in the fridge.

STEP 4

After 1 hr, stir the sweet potatoes and red peppers into the stew, then re-cover and simmer for another 30 mins.

STEP 5

When the stew has about 15 mins to go, make the dumplings. Rub the butter into the flour until it resembles fine crumbs, then stir in the cornmeal, bicarb and sweetcorn. Finally, mix in the buttermilk and all but 1 tbsp of the egg to make a soft dough. Season with some salt and roll the mixture into 12 soft dumplings, then roll in a little more cornmeal to coat the tops. Brush the tops with the reserved beaten egg.

STEP 6

Heat oven to 200C/180C fan/gas 6. Stir the beans into the stew, then taste for seasoning. Sit 6 of the dumplings on top of the stew and the rest on a baking tray lined with baking parchment. Put both in the oven – the stew without its lid – and cook for 25 mins until the dumplings are golden and risen.

STEP 7

Carry the stew straight to the table, and sprinkle over a little more oregano before spooning into bowls. Serve the extra dumplings alongside for those who fancy another one, and the onion relish.

Indian chicken protein pots

Prep: 10 mins **Cook:** 1 min

Serves 2

Ingredients

- 90g pack Indian spiced lentils (we used Men's Health from Tesco)
- 160g cherry tomatoes , quartered
- 150g cooked, skinless chicken breast, chopped
- handful fresh coriander , chopped
- 4 tbsp tzatziki

Method

STEP 1

Tear the corner from the lentil pack and microwave on High for 1 min. Leave to cool then tip into 2 large packed lunch pots. Top with the cherry tomatoes and chicken, add the fresh coriander then spoon on the tzatziki. Seal until ready to eat (see tip below).

Chicken biryani

Prep: 10 mins **Cook:** 30 mins

Serves 4

Ingredients

- 300g basmati rice
- 25g butter
- 1 large onion, finely sliced
- 1 bay leaf
- 3 cardamom pods
- small cinnamon stick
- 1 tsp turmeric
- 30g coriander, ½ chopped, ½ leaves picked and 2 tbsp toasted flaked almonds, to serve
- 4 skinless chicken breasts, cut into large chunks
- 4 tbsp curry paste (we used Patak's balti paste)
- 85g raisins
- 850ml chicken stock

Method

STEP 1

Soak 300g basmati rice in warm water, then wash in cold until the water runs clear.

STEP 2

Heat 25g butter in a saucepan and cook 1 finely sliced large onion with 1 bay leaf, 3 cardamom pods and 1 small cinnamon stick for 10 mins.

STEP 3

Sprinkle in 1 tsp turmeric, then add 4 chicken breasts, cut into large chunks, and 4 tbsp curry paste. Cook until aromatic.

STEP 4

Stir the rice into the pan with 85g raisins, then pour over 850ml chicken stock.

STEP 5

Place a tight-fitting lid on the pan and bring to a hard boil, then lower the heat to a minimum and cook the rice for another 5 mins.

STEP 6

Turn off the heat and leave for 10 mins. Stir well, mixing through 15g chopped coriander. To serve, scatter over the leaves of the remaining 15g coriander and 2 tbsp toasted almonds.

One-pan tikka salmon with jewelled rice

Prep: 10 mins **Cook:** 45 mins

Serves 3

Ingredients

- 3 tbsp tikka curry paste
- 150ml pot natural low-fat yogurt
- 3 salmon fillets , skinned
- 2 tsp olive oil
- 1 large red onion , chopped

- 1 tsp turmeric
- 50g soft dried apricots , chopped
- 200g brown basmati rice
- 100g pack pomegranate seeds
- small pack coriander , leaves picked

Method

STEP 1

Combine 1 tbsp of the curry paste with 2 tbsp yogurt. Season the salmon and smear the yogurt paste all over the fillets, then set aside.

STEP 2

Heat the oil in a large pan (with a lid) and add the onion. Boil the kettle. Cook the onion for 5 mins to soften, and stir in the remaining curry paste then cook for 1 min more. Add the turmeric, apricots and rice, season well and give everything a good stir. Pour in 800ml water from the kettle. Bring to a boil, and simmer for 15 mins. Cover with a lid, lower the heat to a gentle simmer and cook for 15 mins more.

STEP 3

Uncover the rice and give it a good stir. Put the salmon fillets on top of the rice and re-cover the pan. Turn the heat to its lowest setting and leave undisturbed for 15-20 mins more until the salmon and rice are perfectly cooked. Scatter over the pomegranate seeds and coriander, and serve with the yogurt.

Spicy chicken & bean stew

Prep: 15 mins **Cook:** 1 hr and 20 mins

Serves 6

Ingredients

- 1 ¼kg chicken thighs and drumsticks (approx. weight, we used a 1.23kg mixed pack)
- 1 tbsp olive oil
- 2 onions , sliced
- 1 garlic clove , crushed
- 2 red chillies , deseeded and chopped
- 250g frozen peppers , defrosted

- 400g can chopped tomatoes
- 420g can kidney beans in chilli sauce
- 2 x 400g cans butter beans , drained
- 400ml hot chicken stock
- small bunch coriander , chopped
- 150ml pot soured cream and crusty bread, to serve

Method

STEP 1

Pull the skin off the chicken and discard. Heat the oil in a large casserole dish, brown the chicken all over, then remove with a slotted spoon. Tip in the onions, garlic and chillies, then fry for 5 mins until starting to soften and turn golden.

STEP 2

Add the peppers, tomatoes, beans and hot stock. Put the chicken back on top, half-cover with a pan lid and cook for 50 mins, until the chicken is cooked through and tender.

STEP 3

Stir through the coriander and serve with soured cream and crusty bread.

Chicken & chorizo jambalaya

Prep: 10 mins **Cook:** 45 mins

Serves 4

Ingredients

- 1 tbsp olive oil
- 2 chicken breasts, chopped
- 1 onion, diced
- 1 red pepper, thinly sliced
- 2 garlic cloves, crushed
- 75g chorizo, sliced
- 1 tbsp Cajun seasoning
- 250g long grain rice
- 400g can plum tomato
- 350ml chicken stock

Method

STEP 1

Heat 1 tbsp olive oil in a large frying pan with a lid and brown 2 chopped chicken breasts for 5-8 mins until golden.

STEP 2

Remove and set aside. Tip in the 1 diced onion and cook for 3-4 mins until soft.

STEP 3

Add 1 thinly sliced red pepper, 2 crushed garlic cloves, 75g sliced chorizo and 1 tbsp Cajun seasoning, and cook for 5 mins more.

STEP 4

Stir the chicken back in with 250g long grain rice, add the 400g can of tomatoes and 350ml chicken stock. Cover and simmer for 20-25 mins until the rice is tender.

Summer chicken stew

Prep: 10 mins **Cook:** 55 mins

Serves 4

Ingredients

- 2 tbsp olive oil
- 500g leeks , finely sliced
- 2 plump garlic cloves , finely sliced
- 2 thyme sprigs , leaves picked
- 8 chicken thighs , skinless and boneless

- 500g new potatoes , larger ones quartered, smaller ones halved
- 350ml chicken stock
- 200g green beans
- 350g frozen petit pois
- lemon wedges, to serve

Method

STEP 1

Heat the oil in a large casserole dish over a medium heat. Add the leeks, garlic and thyme, cover and cook gently for 10 mins, stirring occasionally. Season the chicken and tip into the dish with the potatoes.

STEP 2

Turn up the heat, pour in the stock and bring to a simmer. Reduce the heat and allow to gently bubble with the lid on for 35 mins. Add the green beans and peas for the final 10 mins of cooking. Season to taste, then ladle into bowls or lipped plates with a squeeze of lemon.

Moroccan vegetable stew

Prep:30 mins **Cook:**35 mins

Serves 4

Ingredients

- 1 tbsp cold-pressed rapeseed oil
- 1 medium onion , peeled and finely sliced
- 2 thin leeks , trimmed and cut into thick slices
- 2 large garlic cloves , peeled and finely sliced
- 2 tsp ground coriander
- 2 tsp ground cumin
- 1/2 tsp dried chilli flakes
- 1/4 tsp ground cinnamon

- 400g can of chopped tomatoes
- 1 red pepper , deseeded and cut into chunks
- 1 yellow pepper , deseeded and cut into chunks
- 400g can of chickpeas , drained and rinsed
- 100g dried split red lentils
- 375g sweet potatoes , peeled and cut into chunks

- juice 1 large orange plus peel, thickly sliced with a vegetable peeler
- 50g mixed nuts, such as brazils, hazelnuts, pecans and walnuts, toasted and roughly chopped

- 1/2 small pack coriander , roughly chopped, to serve
- full-fat natural bio-yogurt , to serve (optional)

Method

STEP 1

Heat the oil in a large flameproof casserole or saucepan and gently fry the onion and leeks for 10-15 mins until well softened, stirring occasionally. Add the garlic and cook for 2 mins more.

STEP 2

Stir in the ground coriander, cumin, chilli and cinnamon. Cook for 2 mins, stirring occasionally. Season with plenty of ground black pepper. Add the chopped tomatoes, peppers, chickpeas, lentils, sweet potatoes, orange peel and juice, half the nuts and 400ml/14fl oz water and bring to a simmer. Cook for 15 mins, adding a splash of water if the stew looks too dry, and stir occasionally until the potatoes are softened but not breaking apart.

STEP 3

Remove the pan from the heat and ladle the stew into bowls. Scatter with coriander and the remaining nuts and top with yogurt, if using.

Bean & pepper chilli

Prep:15 mins **Cook:**30 mins

Serves 4

Ingredients

- 1 tbsp olive oil
- 1 onion , chopped
- 350g pepper , deseeded and sliced
- 1 tbsp ground cumin

- 1-3 tsp chilli powder , depending on how hot you want your chilli to be
- 1 tbsp sweet smoked paprika
- 400g can kidney bean in chilli sauce
- 400g can mixed bean , drained

- 400g can chopped tomato
- rice , to serve (optional)

Method

STEP 1

Heat the oil in a large pan. Add the onion and peppers, and cook for 8 mins until softened. Tip in the spices and cook for 1 min.

STEP 2

Tip in the beans and tomatoes, bring to the boil and simmer for 15 mins or until the chilli is thickened. Season and serve with rice, if you like.

Greek-style roast chicken

Prep: 10 mins **Cook:** 1 hr

Serves 4

Ingredients

- 750g new potatoes, thickly sliced lengthways
- 2 tbsp olive oil
- 8 chicken thighs, skin on and bone in
- 300g cherry tomatoes
- 100g black olives
- ½ small pack oregano, leaves picked
- 200g pack feta, crumbled into chunks
- 2 tbsp red wine vinegar

Method

STEP 1

Heat oven to 200C/180C fan/gas 6. Put the potatoes in a roasting tin and drizzle with half the oil. Sit the chicken thighs on top, drizzle over the remaining oil and season. Roast in the oven for 30 mins.

STEP 2

Add the cherry tomatoes, olives, oregano leaves and feta, then drizzle with the red wine vinegar. Return to the oven for another 25-30 mins until the chicken is cooked through and golden.

Spicy harissa chicken with lentils

Prep: 10 mins **Cook:** 45 mins

Serves 4

Ingredients

- 1 tbsp olive oil
- 1 red onion , chopped
- 1 garlic clove , crushed
- 50g harissa
- 500g chicken thigh , skin removed, boned and diced
- 1 medium carrot , grated
- 200g dried puy lentils
- 2 x 400g cans chopped tomatoes
- 1.2l stock , made from 1 chicken or vegetable stock cube
- flat-leaf parsley , to serve (optional)

Method

STEP 1

Heat the oil in a large frying pan. Fry the onion on a low heat for 5-6 mins until softened and translucent. Add the garlic and cook for 1 min more.

STEP 2

Stir in the harissa, add the chicken and cook until well browned all over. Stir in the carrot, lentils and tomatoes, then add the stock so the chicken is fully immersed.

STEP 3

Reduce the heat and cook, uncovered, for 30-35 mins until the chicken is thoroughly cooked, and the lentils are tender and have absorbed the liquid. Season well, scatter with parsley (if using) and serve.

Andalusian-style chicken

Prep: 10 mins **Cook:** 25 mins - 30 mins

Serves 4 as part of a tapas spread

Ingredients

- large pinch of saffron
- ½ chicken stock cube , crumbled into 100ml boiling water
- 2 tbsp olive oil
- 1 small onion , thinly sliced
- 2 large chicken breasts or 6 boneless, skinless thighs, cut into bite-sized pieces
- large pinch of ground cinnamon
- 1 red chilli , deseeded and chopped
- 2 tbsp sherry vinegar
- 1 tbsp clear honey
- 6 cherry tomatoes , quartered
- 1 tbsp raisins
- handful of coriander , roughly chopped
- 25g toasted pine nuts or almonds
- crusty bread , to serve

Method

STEP 1

Add the saffron to the hot stock to soak. Heat the oil in a medium pan and cook the onion until it is soft and just beginning to turn golden. Push to the side of the pan and add the chicken. Cook for a few mins until the chicken is browned all over.

STEP 2

Add the cinnamon and chilli, and cook for a couple of mins. Add the stock, vinegar, honey, tomatoes and raisins. Bring to the boil, turn down the heat and simmer for 10 mins until the sauce is reduced and the chicken is cooked through. When ready to serve, scatter with the coriander and nuts, and serve with bread on the side.

Spicy asparagus & chorizo baked egg

Prep: 5 mins **Cook:** 20 mins

Serves 1

Ingredients

- 125g asparagus , cut into 3cm pieces
- 20g diced chorizo
- ½ tsp hot smoked paprika
- 75g frozen spinach
- 1 tbsp half-fat crème fraîche
- 1 large egg
- flatbread , to serve (optional)

Method

STEP 1

Heat a small non-stick frying pan over a medium heat, add the asparagus and chorizo and fry for 8 mins. Stir through the paprika, cooking for a further 1 min.

STEP 2

Stir the spinach into the pan and cook for 5 mins until wilted before stirring through the crème fraîche. Season, then make a well in the middle of the mixture and crack the egg into it. Cover the pan and cook for 5-6 mins or until the egg is just set. Serve with a flatbread, if you like.

Winter berry & white chocolate pots

Prep:40 mins **Cook:**30 mins

plus 8 hrs chilling

Serves 6

Ingredients

- pomegranate seeds , to serve

For the white chocolate layer

- 100ml double cream
- 200g white chocolate , chopped
- 2 large lemons , zested

For the berry layer

- 300g mixed frozen berries , defrosted
- 150g frozen raspberries
- 2 tbsp lemon juice
- 600ml double cream
- 160g golden caster sugar

For the pistachio shortbread

- 100g unsalted butter , softened
- 50g golden caster sugar
- 135g plain flour
- 50g pistachios , finely chopped, plus extra to serve

Method

STEP 1

For the white chocolate layer, heat the cream in a saucepan until steaming and bubbles appear around the edge. Add the chocolate and lemon zest and stir until melted. Set six short tumblers tilted on their sides in a muffin tin (this is how you get a slanted layer). Pour the mixture into the glasses, then chill for 4 hrs, or until set.

STEP 2

For the berry layer, put all the frozen berries in a food processor and whizz until puréed. Push through a sieve using a wooden spoon directly into a jug, then stir through the lemon juice. Put the cream and sugar in a saucepan and warm gently until the sugar melts. Increase the heat and boil for 3 mins, stirring continuously. Remove from the heat and stir through the purée. Cool for 15 mins before sitting the glasses upright and pouring over the white chocolate layer. Chill for 4 hrs or until set.

STEP 3

Heat the oven to 170C/150C fan/gas 3. Line a baking sheet with non-stick parchment. To make the shortbread, put the butter and sugar in a bowl and beat with an electric whisk until pale and fluffy. Mix in ¼ tsp fine sea salt, the flour and pistachios to get a stiff dough, then bring together with your hands into a smooth ball. Put between two sheets of baking parchment and roll out to around ½cm. Chill for 20 mins. Cut into 20 rounds about 4cm and place on the baking sheet. Bake for 20-25 mins, then slide off the sheet onto a wire rack and leave to cool. *Can be made two days ahead and kept in an airtight container.*

STEP 4

When ready to serve, top the possets with the chopped pistachios and pomegranate seeds, and serve with the pistachio biscuits.

Jambalaya

Prep:20 mins **Cook:**50 mins

Serves 4 - 6

Ingredients

- 2 tbsp olive oil
- 6 skinless boneless chicken thighs fillets, chopped
- 200g cooking chorizo , sliced

- 2 onions , finely sliced
- 4 garlic cloves , crushed
- 2 red peppers , sliced
- 2 celery sticks , chopped

- 1 tsp fresh thyme leaves
- 1 tsp dried oregano
- ½ tsp garlic salt
- 1 tsp smoked paprika
- 1 tsp cayenne pepper
- ½ tsp mustard powder
- pinch of white pepper
- 300g long-grain rice
- 400g can cherry tomatoes
- 300ml chicken stock
- 12 large raw tiger prawns (whole in their shells)
- 12 mussels , cleaned and de-bearded
- 24 clams
- ½ small pack parsley , chopped
- 4 spring onions , sliced on a diagonal

Method

STEP 1

Heat oven to 200C/180C fan/ gas 6. Heat the oil in a heavy-based flameproof casserole dish on a medium-high heat. Season the chicken thighs, add to the dish and cook for 4 mins until they start to brown, stirring occasionally so they don't stick. Add the chorizo and cook for a further 4 mins until it releases its oils and has started to crisp. Remove the meat with a slotted spoon and set aside on a plate.

STEP 2

Add the onions to the chorizo oils, lower the heat and soften for 8 mins. Stir through the garlic, peppers, celery, thyme and oregano , and cook for 2 mins more.

STEP 3

Return the meat to the dish, add the garlic salt, paprika, cayenne, mustard powder and white pepper, and cook for 2 mins until fragrant. Stir in the rice, then the tomatoes. Add the stock and give it all a really good stir. Bring to the boil , then cover with a well-fitting lid and put in the oven for 20 mins.

STEP 4

Take from the oven and fluff up the rice with a big fork. Fold through the prawns, then put the mussels and clams on top. Put the lid on ,return to the oven for 10 mins, then take the dish out and give everything a good stir. Sprinkle with the parsley and spring onions to serve.

Tuna Niçoise protein pot

Prep: 10 mins **Cook:** 10 mins

Serves 1

Ingredients

- 1 large egg
- 80g green beans
- 1 tomato , amber or red, quartered

- 120g can tuna in spring water
- 1½ -2 tbsp French dressing

Method

STEP 1

Boil the egg for 8-10 mins depending on if you want a soft or hard yolk, then at the same time steam the green beans for 6 mins above the pan until tender. Cool the egg and beans under running water then carefully shell and quarter the egg. Leave to cool.

STEP 2

Tip the beans into a large packed lunch pot. Top with the tomato, tuna and quartered egg and spoon on the French dressing. Seal until ready to eat (see tip below).

Pesto chicken stew with cheesy dumplings

Prep: 50 mins **Cook:** 2 hrs and 20 mins

Serves 8

Ingredients

- 2 tbsp olive oil
- 12-15 chicken thighs , skin removed, bone in
- 200g smoked bacon lardon or chopped bacon
- 1 large onion , chopped
- 4 celery sticks, chopped

- 3 leeks , chopped
- 4 tbsp plain flour
- 200ml white wine
- 1l chicken stock
- 2 bay leaves
- 200g frozen pea
- 140g sundried tomato

- 140g fresh pesto

For the dumplings

- 140g butter
- 250g self-raising flour

- small bunch basil , chopped

- 100g parmesan , grated
- 50g pine nut

Method

STEP 1

Heat the oil in a large casserole dish. Brown the chicken until golden on all sides – you might have to do this in batches – remove the chicken from the pan as you go and set aside.

STEP 2

Add the lardons to the pan and sizzle for a few mins, then add the onion, celery and leeks, and cook over a medium heat for 8-10 mins until the vegetables have softened. Stir in the flour, season and cook for a further 2 mins.

STEP 3

Gradually stir in the wine and allow it to bubble away, then stir in the stock. Return the chicken to the pan with the bay leaves and cover with a lid. Reduce the heat and simmer gently for 1½ hrs or until the chicken is tender. The stew can now be cooled and frozen if you're making ahead. Just defrost thoroughly, then gently warm through back in the pan before continuing.

STEP 4

Heat oven to 200C/180C fan/gas 6. Add the peas, sundried tomatoes, pesto and basil to the stew. To make the dumplings, rub the butter into the flour until it resembles fine breadcrumbs. Mix in the grated cheese and add 150ml water, mixing with a cutlery knife to bring the crumbs together to form a light and sticky dough. Break off walnut-sized lumps and shape into small balls. Roll the tops of the dumplings in the pine nuts so a few stick to the outside, then place the dumplings on top of the stew and scatter with any remaining nuts. Put the dish in the oven and bake for 25 mins until the dumplings are golden brown and cooked through. Serve with mashed potato and extra veg if you like.

Pesto chicken stew with cheesy dumplings

Prep: 50 mins **Cook:** 2 hrs and 20 mins

Serves 8

Ingredients

- 2 tbsp olive oil
- 12-15 chicken thighs , skin removed, bone in
- 200g smoked bacon lardon or chopped bacon
- 1 large onion , chopped
- 4 celery sticks, chopped
- 3 leeks , chopped

- 4 tbsp plain flour
- 200ml white wine
- 1l chicken stock
- 2 bay leaves
- 200g frozen pea
- 140g sundried tomato
- 140g fresh pesto
- small bunch basil , chopped

For the dumplings

- 140g butter
- 250g self-raising flour

- 100g parmesan , grated
- 50g pine nut

Method

STEP 1

Heat the oil in a large casserole dish. Brown the chicken until golden on all sides – you might have to do this in batches – remove the chicken from the pan as you go and set aside.

STEP 2

Add the lardons to the pan and sizzle for a few mins, then add the onion, celery and leeks, and cook over a medium heat for 8-10 mins until the vegetables have softened. Stir in the flour, season and cook for a further 2 mins.

STEP 3

Gradually stir in the wine and allow it to bubble away, then stir in the stock. Return the chicken to the pan with the bay leaves and cover with a lid. Reduce the heat and simmer gently for 1½ hrs or until the chicken is tender. The stew can now be cooled and frozen if you're making ahead. Just defrost thoroughly, then gently warm through back in the pan before continuing.

STEP 4

Heat oven to 200C/180C fan/gas 6. Add the peas, sundried tomatoes, pesto and basil to the stew. To make the dumplings, rub the butter into the flour until it resembles fine breadcrumbs. Mix in the grated cheese and add 150ml water, mixing with a cutlery knife to bring the crumbs together to form a light and sticky dough. Break off walnut-sized lumps and shape into small balls. Roll the tops of the dumplings in the pine nuts so a few stick to the outside, then place the dumplings on top of the stew and scatter with any remaining nuts. Put the dish in the oven and bake for 25 mins until the dumplings are golden brown and cooked through. Serve with mashed potato and extra veg if you like.

Salted caramel popcorn pots

Prep: 10 mins **Cook:** 15 mins

plus at least 8 hrs chilling

Serves 2

Ingredients

- 400ml double cream
- 200ml milk
- 140g toffee popcorn , plus a little to serve

- 2 gelatine leaves
- 4 tbsp caramel from a can (we used Carnation)
- ¼-½ tsp flaky sea salt

Method

STEP 1

Pour the cream and milk into a large pan, add the popcorn and bring to a gentle simmer, pushing the popcorn under the liquid and squashing gently on the bottom of the pan. Bubble for 1 min, then remove from the heat, transfer to a jug and chill for at least 6 hrs, or preferably overnight.

STEP 2

Strain the popcorn cream back into a clean pan and gently reheat, discarding the remaining bits of popcorn. Meanwhile, place the gelatine leaves in cold water to soften for 3-5 mins. When the popcorn cream is steaming and the gelatine is soft, remove it from the water and squeeze out any excess drops. Place in the hot popcorn cream and stir until dissolved. Set aside to cool a little.

STEP 3

Mix the caramel with the sea salt – start with 1/4 tsp, taste, then add more if you think it needs it. Divide the salted caramel between 2 glasses or pots. Pour the popcorn cream on top and chill for at least 2 hrs, or overnight.

STEP 4

Serve each pot topped with a few pieces of toffee popcorn and dive in!

Sticky orange chicken with parsnips, maple & pecans

Prep: 25 mins **Cook:** 1 hr and 5 mins

Serves 2

Ingredients

- 2 blood oranges , 1 juiced, 1 thickly sliced
- 3 tbsp maple syrup
- 2 tbsp olive oil
- 2 tbsp sherry vinegar
- 1 tbsp wholegrain mustard
- 1 tbsp cranberry or redcurrant jelly , melted
- 2 parsnips , quartered, peeled and the core cut out and discarded
- 4 chicken thighs , skin on
- 140g small shallots , left whole but peeled
- 2 thyme sprigs , broken up a bit
- 25g pecans , barely chopped
- mixed leaf salad or wilted spinach, to serve (optional)
- cooked rice , to serve (optional)

Method

STEP 1

Heat oven to 180C/160C fan/gas 4. Juice 1 of the oranges and whisk together with the maple syrup, olive oil, vinegar, mustard and cranberry jelly. Cut the parsnips into chunky lengths. Put the parnips, chicken thighs and shallots in a roasting tin – make sure everything can sit in a single layer but quite snug. Drizzle over half the orange sauce with some seasoning and toss to coat everything. Roast for 35 mins.

STEP 2

Remove the tin from the oven and poke the orange slices in among everything. Scatter over the thyme and drizzle over the rest of the orange sauce. Roast for another 15 mins until the chicken is tender and cooked through, and everything is sticky and golden. Mix in the pecans and cook for another 5 mins. Serve straight away, remembering to scrape out all the sticky juices from the tin, and eat with a mixed leaf salad or some wilted spinach, plus a little rice to soak up the sauce, if you like.

Chorizo & cabbage stew

Prep: 10 mins **Cook:** 20 mins

Serves 2

Ingredients

- 100g piece of spicy chorizo sausage (not cooking chorizo), halved lengthways and shredded
- 1 onion , halved and thinly sliced

- 100g baby Charlotte potatoes , thinly sliced
- 400g can chopped tomatoes
- 1 chicken stock cube
- 100g Savoy cabbage , shredded

Method

STEP 1

Put the chorizo, onion and potatoes in a large non-stick pan. Leave to fry in the oil that comes from the chorizo, stirring occasionally for about 5 mins.

STEP 2

Tip in the tomatoes with 2 cans of water, add the stock cube, then bring to the boil. Cover and simmer for 10 mins. Add the cabbage, then cover and cook 3-5 mins more until it is just tender. Ladle into bowls and serve.

Chicken casserole with herby dumplings

Prep: 30 mins **Cook:** 1 hr and 10 mins

Serves 6

Ingredients

- 12 skinless chicken pieces - a mixture of thighs and drumsticks on the bone, and halved chicken breasts
- 3 tbsp plain flour
- 2 tbsp sunflower oil
- 2 onions, sliced
- 2 carrots, diced

For the herby dumplings

- 140g cold butter, diced
- 250g self-raising flour

- 200g bacon lardons, smoked or unsmoked, or streaky rashers, snipped
- 3 bay leaves
- 3 sprigs thyme
- 250ml red wine
- 3 tbsp tomato paste
- 1 chicken stock cube

- 2 tbsp chopped mixed herb - try parsley, thyme and sage or chives

Method

STEP 1

Heat oven to 180C/160C fan/gas 4. Toss the chicken pieces with the flour and some salt and pepper, to coat them – it's easy to do this in a plastic food bag.

STEP 2

Heat the oil in a casserole with a lid. Brown the chicken pieces well on all sides – you'll need to do this in batches. Remove all the pieces to a plate, and tip the onions, carrot, lardons, bay and thyme into the pan. Cook gently for 10 mins until the onion is softened.

STEP 3

Return the chicken pieces, with any juices that have collected on the plate. Then pour in the red wine, 250ml water and tomato paste and crumble in the stock cube. Add a splash more of water if you need, until the chicken is almost covered. Bring to the boil, then cover with a lid and bake in the oven for 20 mins. Remove the lid and bake for another 10 mins while you make the dumplings.

STEP 4

Rub the butter into the flour with your fingertips until it feels like fine breadcrumbs. Stir in the herbs with ½ tsp salt and some pepper. Drizzle over 150ml water, and stir in quickly with a cutlery knife to form a light dough. Use floured hands to shape into ping pong sized balls.

STEP 5

Place the dumplings on top of the stew and bake for 20 mins more until the dumplings are cooked through.

One-pan lentil dhal with curried fish & crispy skin

Prep: 20 mins **Cook:** 1 hr

Serves 2

Ingredients

- 2 onions , chopped
- 1 tbsp grated ginger
- 1 tbsp sunflower oil , plus a splash
- 2 tbsp mild curry powder , plus 1/2 tsp
- 1 tsp brown mustard seeds
- 1 ½ tsp onion or nigella seeds
- 85g red lentils
- 85g split peas or chana dhal lentils
- 1 ¼ tsp ground turmeric
- 400g can coconut milk
- 3 tbsp natural yogurt , plus extra for serving
- 2 firm white fish fillets with skin - we used sustainably sourced cod
- 2 plum tomatoes , diced
- juice 1 lime , plus 1 cut into wedges, to serve
- handful coriander leaves
- 2 tbsp crispy onions from a tub
- warm naan , to serve
- mango chutney , to serve

Method

STEP 1

Heat oven to 200C/180C fan/gas 6. Mix the onions, ginger, oil, 2 tbsp curry powder, the mustard seeds and 1 tsp of the onion or nigella seeds with 5 tbsp water in a baking dish roughly 25 x 18cm. Roast in the oven for 10-15 mins until the onions are softened.

STEP 2

Stir in the lentils, split peas or chana dhal lentils, 1 tsp of the turmeric, the coconut milk and half a can of water,   and return to the oven for 30 mins. Meanwhile, mix together the remaining turmeric, onion seeds and curry powder and the yogurt. Carefully slice the skin off the fish fillets and place on kitchen paper to dry, then rub the yogurt all over the fish fillets and leave to marinate in the fridge while you cook the lentils.

STEP 3

Give the dhal a good stir, mix in the tomatoes and juice from 1 lime, plus1 tsp salt. Sit the fish fillets on top witha sprinkling of extra seasoning. Return to the oven and cook for a further 15 mins until the fish is done. Removethe dish from the oven and turnon the grill. Place the fish skin ona baking tray, sprinkle with some salt and grill, turning, until crispy. Snap into pieces and scatter over the fish with some coriander and the crispy onions. Serve with more yogurt, lime wedges, naan bread and mango chutney.

Muffin tin chilli pots

Prep:15 mins **Cook:**5 mins

Serves 2

Ingredients

- 400g can kidney beans in spicy sauce
- 4 medium tortilla wraps
- 400g can chopped tomatoes with herbs
- 230g green salad

Method

STEP 1

Heat oven to 200C/180C fan/gas 6. Simmer the beans and tomatoes in a pan for 15 mins, then season.

STEP 2

Meanwhile, grease four holes of a muffin tin with oil. Line each with a tortilla, making a cup, and fill with a ball of foil. Bake for 5 mins until lightly crisped. Remove the foil, divide the bean mix between the tortilla cups and serve with the green salad.

5-minute mocha pots

Prep:5 mins **Cook:**2 mins

Serves 4

Ingredients

- 200g milk or dark chocolate with coffee, broken into chunks
- 300ml pot double cream

- 1 tsp vanilla extract
- 2 tbsp crème fraîche

Method

STEP 1

Melt the chocolate in the microwave for 2 mins, stirring halfway through, or over a pan of gently simmering water. Leave to cool a little.

STEP 2

Using an electric whisk, whip the double cream with the vanilla in a bowl until lightly whipped. Fold in the cooled, melted chocolate until fully combined.

STEP 3

Split the mixture between four small bowls or ramekins and serve topped with a dollop of crème fraîche. If you aren't serving straight away, chill in the fridge and then add the crème fraîche just before bringing to the table.

One-pan pigeon breast with spinach & bacon

Prep:5 mins **Cook:**15 mins

Serves 2

Ingredients

- 50g butter
- 100g smoked bacon lardons or chopped smoked bacon
- 2 slices white sourdough
- 2 pigeon breasts

- 50g chestnut or wild mushrooms , sliced
- 200g spinach
- 1 tbsp red wine or sherry vinegar

Method

STEP 1

Heat half the butter in a large frying pan, then fry the bacon for 5 mins until starting to crisp. Transfer to a plate using a slotted spoon. Fry the bread in any leftover bacon fat for 1 min on each side until crisp and golden, then transfer to a plate and set aside.

STEP 2

Season the pigeon generously with salt and pepper, and heat the remaining butter in the pan until sizzling. Sear the pigeon for 2-3 mins on each side until golden, then transfer to a chopping board and leave to rest.

STEP 3

Return the fried bacon to the pan and turn up the heat. Scatter over the mushrooms and fry for 3-4 mins until softened, then add the spinach, season and splash in the vinegar. Turn the heat up to high and stir-fry until the spinach is wilted. Divide the spinach mixture between the fried bread slices. Finely slice the pigeon breasts, arrange over the spinach and serve.

Moroccan fish stew

Prep: 15 mins **Cook:** 35 mins

Serves 4

Ingredients

- 1 tbsp cold-pressed rapeseed oil
- 1 medium onion , thinly sliced
- 2 thin leeks , trimmed and sliced
- 1/2 small fennel bulb , quartered and very thinly sliced
- 2 large garlic cloves , finely sliced
- 2 tsp ground coriander
- 1 tsp ground cumin
- 1/2 tsp chilli flakes
- 1/4 tsp ground cinnamon
- 400g can chopped tomatoes
- 375g sweet potatoes , peeled and cut into chunks
- 1 yellow pepper , deseeded and cut into chunks
- 1 red pepper , deseeded and cut into chunks
- 400g can chickpeas , drained and rinsed
- juice 1 large orange , the peel thickly sliced with a vegetable peeler
- 200g skinless line-caught cod , haddock or pollock fillet, cut into chunks
- 200g skinless wild salmon , cut into chunks
- 1/2 small pack flat-leaf parsley , roughly chopped

Method

STEP 1

Heat the oil in a large flameproof casserole dish or saucepan and gently fry the onion, leeks and fennel for 10 mins, stirring occasionally, or until the veg is well softened and lightly browned. Add the garlic and spices, and cook for 30 secs more. Season well with ground black pepper.

STEP 2

Tip in the chopped tomatoes, sweet potatoes, peppers, chickpeas, orange juice and peel with 300ml water and bring to a gentle simmer. Cover loosely and cook for 20 mins, stirring occasionally, until the potatoes are softened but not breaking apart.

STEP 3

Add the fish pieces on top of the bubbling liquid and cover. Poach over a medium heat for 3-4 mins or until the fish is just cooked. Adjust the seasoning and serve scattered with parsley.

Mexican beef chilli

Prep: 15 mins **Cook:** 2 hrs and 15 mins

Serves 15

Ingredients

- up to 6 tbsp sunflower oil
- 4kg stewing beef
- 4 white onions , sliced
- 4 tbsp chipotle paste
- 8 garlic cloves , crushed
- 50g ginger , grated
- 1 tbsp ground cumin
- 2 tsp ground cinnamon
- 1 tbsp plain flour
- 2l beef stock
- 3 x 400g cans chopped tomatoes
- 1 tbsp dried oregano
- 5 x 400g cans pinto or kidney beans , drained

Method

STEP 1

Heat a small drizzle of the oil in an extra-large flameproof dish. Brown the meat in batches, adding a drop more oil, remove from the dish and set aside. Add 1 tbsp oil to the dish, then the onions, and cook for 7-10 mins or until caramelised.

STEP 2

Stir the chipotle paste, garlic, ginger, cumin, cinnamon and flour in with the onions and cook for a couple of mins. Gradually add the stock, stirring all the time, so it's fully mixed in with the other ingredients. Add the tomatoes and oregano, season and simmer for 10 mins.

STEP 3

Now tip in the beef, cover and simmer very gently for about 1 hr 45 mins until tender, removing the lid and adding the beans for the final 15 mins. If the sauce is thin, let it boil down for a further 5-10 mins with the lid off. Before serving, adjust the seasoning. Serve with the garlic bread and salsa.

Bean & barley soup

Prep:5 mins **Cook:**1 hr

Serves 4

Ingredients

- 2 tbsp vegetable oil
- 1 large onion , finely chopped
- 1 fennel bulb , quartered, cored and sliced
- 5 garlic cloves , crushed
- 400g can chickpea , drained and rinsed
- 2 x 400g cans chopped tomatoes

- 600ml vegetable stock
- 250g pearl barley
- 215g can butter beans , drained and rinsed
- 100g pack baby spinach leaves
- grated parmesan , to serve

Method

STEP 1

Heat the oil in a saucepan over a medium heat, add the onion, fennel and garlic, and cook until softened and just beginning to brown, about 10-12 mins.

STEP 2

Mash half the chickpeas and add to the pan with the tomatoes, stock and barley. Top up with a can of water and bring to the boil, then reduce the heat and simmer, covered, for 45 mins or until the barley is tender. Add another can of water if the liquid has significantly reduced.

STEP 3

Add the remaining chickpeas and the butter beans to the soup. After a few mins, stir in the spinach and cook until wilted, about 1 min. Season and serve scattered with Parmesan.

Beef in red wine with melting onions

Prep: 20 mins **Cook:** 2 hrs and 10 mins

Serves 4 - 6

Ingredients

- 25g butter
- 2 large onions, sliced into rings
- 6 garlic cloves, halved
- 3 tbsp plain flour
- 600g piece beef skirt or slices of shin, cut into large chunks
- 2 tbsp olive or rapeseed oil

- 3 bay leaves
- 400ml red wine
- 1 tbsp tomato purée
- 300ml strong beef stock
- 250g mushrooms, halved (we used small Portobello mushrooms)
- chopped parsley, to serve (optional)

Method

STEP 1

Heat oven to 150C/130C fan/gas 2. In a large, heavy-based flameproof casserole dish with a lid, melt the butter over a medium heat. Add the onions and garlic, cook for 10 mins until starting to brown, then transfer to a small plate.

STEP 2

Put the flour in a large plastic food bag with plenty of black pepper. Add half the beef, shake to coat, then remove, leaving some flour in the bag. Add the rest of the beef and shake to coat in the remaining flour.

STEP 3

Heat the oil in the same casserole dish you cooked the onions in (there's no need to clean it first). Add the beef and bay leaves, and fry until the meat is browned all over. Pour in the wine and return the onions to the dish. Add the tomato purée and stock, stir and return to a simmer. Cover with the lid and put in the oven to stew for 1 hr.

STEP 4

After 1 hr, add the mushrooms and return to the oven for another hour. Taste the meat – if it's tender, remove from the oven. If it's still a little firm, cook for 30 mins more and test again. Serve scattered with parsley, if you like.

Chilli Marrakech

Prep: 30 mins Cook 1 hr (plus heating from frozen)

Serves 10

Ingredients

- 1 ½ tbsp cumin seed
- 1 tbsp olive oil
- 3 onions , halved and thinly sliced
- 3 x 400g packs lean lamb mince
- 2 tbsp finely chopped ginger
- 4 garlic cloves , finely chopped
- 2 x 400g cans chopped tomatoes
- 1 tbsp paprika
- 1 tbsp ground cinnamon
- 1 ½ tbsp ground coriander

- 3 tbsp harissa
- 3 red peppers , deseeded and cut into large chunks
- 2 x 400g cans chickpeas , drained
- 2 x 20g packs coriander , most chopped, a few leaves left whole to serve
- 500ml beef or lamb stock , made with 2 cubes

Method

STEP 1

Heat your largest non-stick wok or pan, tip in the cumin seeds and toast for a few secs. Remove. Add the oil to the pan and fry the onions for 5 mins until starting to colour. Add the mince, ginger and garlic, and cook, breaking up the mince with your wooden spoon, until no longer pink. Drain any excess liquid or fat from the pan.

STEP 2

Stir in the tomatoes, toasted cumin, remaining spices and harissa – add more spice if you like an extra kick. Add the peppers, chickpeas, three-quarters of the chopped coriander and the stock. Cover and cook for 40 mins, stirring occasionally, until the sauce is slightly thickened. Remove from the heat. Cool, then stir in the remaining chopped coriander. Can be served or frozen at this point.

STEP 3

Pack into freezer bags and smooth the mince through the bag to flatten. Use within 3 months. To serve, remove from the bags and heat from frozen in a pan on the hob with a little water until bubbling hot, then scatter with coriander.

Lamb & aubergine pastitsio

Prep: 20 mins **Cook:** 1 hr and 50 mins

Serves 6

Ingredients

- 1 tbsp olive oil
- 2 onions , chopped
- 3 garlic cloves
- 300g frozen lamb mince
- 2 tsp cinnamon
- ½ tsp ground allspice
- 1 tbsp dried oregano or mixed herbs
- 1 large aubergine , cut into small cubes
- 1 lamb or beef stock cube
- 2 x 400g cans chopped tomatoes
- 400g macaroni
- For the bechamel sauce
- 1l semi-skimmed milk
- 2 bay leaves
- 85g butter
- 85g plain flour
- 75g parmesan , plus extra for the top

Method

STEP 1

Heat the oil in a large pan. Add the onions and cook until softened, then add the garlic and stir around the pan for 1 min more. Scoop the onions to one side of the pan, add the lamb and cook until browned. Pour off any excess oil from the pan.

STEP 2

Add the spices and oregano, then tip in the aubergine. Fry for another 5 mins until the aubergine has softened a little, then crumble in the stock cube and add the tomatoes, along with half a can of water. Season, cover the pan and simmer for 30 mins.

STEP 3

Uncover the lamb mince and continue to simmer until the sauce is thick and clinging to the meat – about 15 mins. Meanwhile, make the béchamel sauce. Warm the milk in a large pan with the bay leaves. Melt the butter in another large pan, stir in the flour to make a paste, then add the warm milk, ladle by ladle, stirring well between each addition, until you have a thick, smooth sauce. Season well and add the Parmesan. Meanwhile, cook the pasta following pack instructions, then drain.

STEP 4

Heat oven to 200C/180C fan/gas 6. Tip the mince into a large baking dish. Mix the macaroni into the cheesy sauce and pour this over the lamb. Sprinkle with the remaining cheese. Can now be frozen, defrost before cooking. Bake for 35-40 mins until golden brown and crispy on top. Leave to cool for 5 mins before serving.

Keralan chicken coconut ishtu

Prep: 20 mins **Cook:** 1 hr and 20 mins

Serves 4

Ingredients

- 5 tbsp coconut oil or vegetable oil
- 5cm/2in cinnamon stick
- 6 green cardamom pods
- 4 cloves
- 10 black peppercorns , lightly crushed
- 1 star anise
- 15 curry leaves
- 1 medium onion , finely sliced
- thumb-sized piece of ginger , peeled and finely chopped
- 6 garlic cloves , finely chopped
- 2-3 green chillies
- 2 tsp fennel seeds
- ½ tsp ground turmeric
- 1 tbsp ground coriander
- 600g chicken thighs , skinned
- handful green beans , ends trimmed, halved if very long
- 400ml can coconut milk
- 2 tbsp coconut cream

- 1 tsp vinegar (or to taste)
- large handful baby spinach , blanched and water squeezed out
- small handful fresh coriander , to garnish

Method

STEP 1

Heat the oil in a wide pan (a karahi or wok is ideal), then add the cinnamon stick, cardamom pods, cloves, peppercorns and star anise. Once the seeds have stopped popping, add the curry leaves and the onion and cook over a medium heat until translucent. Add the ginger, garlic and green chillies, and sauté gently for 1-2 mins or until the garlic is cooked.

STEP 2

Grind the fennel seeds to a fine powder in a spice grinder or with a pestle and mortar, then add to the pan with the turmeric, ground coriander and a pinch of salt. Add a splash of water and cook for 2 mins. Put the chicken in the pan and cook in the spice paste for 2 mins. Add water to come a third of the way up the chicken, bring to a boil, then reduce the heat and cook, covered, for 1 hr, stirring occasionally.

STEP 3

Once the liquid has reduced, add the green beans and coconut milk (including the thin milk that collects at the bottom of the can), cover and cook for another 10 mins. Uncover and cook off most of the excess liquid, stirring occasionally. Check the chicken is cooked all the way through. Stir in the coconut cream, vinegar and spinach, and bring to a simmer. Taste and adjust the seasoning, and serve topped with the coriander.

Spiced lamb pilaf

Prep: 10 mins **Cook:** 40 mins

Serves 6

Ingredients

- 2 tbsp vegetable oil
- 1 large onion , finely chopped
- 3 garlic cloves , finely chopped
- 4 cloves
- 8 cardamom pods , crushed
- 2 tsp turmeric
- 1 large cinnamon stick
- 2 lamb stock cubes
- 450g basmati rice
- 500g lamb leftovers, shredded

- 100g raisins
- 5 spring onions , finely sliced
- 3 tomatoes , deseeded and roughly chopped
- small bunch parsley , roughly chopped, plus a few leaves picked, to serve
- small bunch coriander , roughly chopped, plus a few leaves picked, to serve
- 50g flaked almonds , toasted
- 200ml natural yogurt , to serve

Method

STEP 1

Put the oil in a large pan over a medium heat. Add the onion to the pan and cook until soft and translucent, about 15 mins. Add the garlic and spices, and stir in for 2 mins.

STEP 2

Crumble the stock cubes into 1.2 litres of just-boiled water. Add the rice and shredded lamb to the pan. Stir well to coat the grains in the oil and spices, then pour over the stock. Bring to the boil, then cover with a lid and lower the heat. Cook for 12 mins or until the rice is tender and the stock absorbed.

STEP 3

Once the rice is ready, remove from the heat and add the raisins, spring onions, tomatoes and herbs, mixing well. Season to taste and serve topped with more herbs, almonds and a drizzle of natural yogurt.

Steak & broccoli protein pots

Prep: 10 mins **Cook:** 9 mins

Serves 2

Ingredients

- 250g pack wholegrain rice mix with seaweed (Merchant Gourmet)
- 2 tbsp chopped sushi ginger
- 4 spring onions , the green part finely chopped, the white halved lengthways and cut into lengths
- 160g broccoli florets, cut into bite-sized pieces
- 225g lean fat-trimmed fillet steak

Method

STEP 1

Tip the rice mix into a bowl and stir in the ginger, chopped onion greens and 4 tbsp water. Add the broccoli and the spring onion whites, but keep the onions together, on top, as you will need them in the next step. Cover with cling film, pierce with the tip of a knife and microwave for 5 mins.

STEP 2

Meanwhile heat a non-stick frying pan and sear the steak for 2 mins each side, then set aside. Take the onion whites from the bowl and add to the pan so they char a little in the meat juices while the steak rests.

STEP 3

Tip the rice mixture into 2 large packed lunch pots. Slice the steak, pile the charred onions on top and seal until you're ready to eat (see tip below).

Lemon drizzle cake

Prep: 15 mins **Cook:** 45 mins

Cuts into 10 slices

Ingredients

- 225g unsalted butter, softened
- 225g caster sugar
- 4 eggs
- 225g self-raising flour
- 1 lemon, zested
- For the drizzle topping
- 1½ lemons, juiced
- 85g caster sugar

Method

STEP 1

Heat the oven to 180C/160C fan/gas 4.

STEP 2

Beat together the butter and caster sugar until pale and creamy, then add the eggs, one at a time, slowly mixing through.

STEP 3

Sift in the self-raising flour, then add the lemon zest and mix until well combined.

STEP 4

Line a loaf tin (8 x 21cm) with greaseproof paper, then spoon in the mixture and level the top with a spoon.

STEP 5

Bake for 45-50 mins until a thin skewer inserted into the centre of the cake comes out clean.

STEP 6

While the cake is cooling in its tin, mix together the lemons juice and caster sugar to make the drizzle.

STEP 7

Prick the warm cake all over with a skewer or fork, then pour over the drizzle – the juice will sink in and the sugar will form a lovely, crisp topping.

STEP 8

Leave in the tin until completely cool, then remove and serve. *Will keep in an airtight container for 3-4 days, or freeze for up to 1 month.*

Roast dinner for one

Prep:10 mins **Cook:**35 mins

Serves 1

Ingredients

- 2 tbsp olive oil
- 1 large chicken breast , skin on
- 6 small new potatoes (about 200g/7oz), halved

- 2 carrots , cut into rounds
- 1 small onion , cut into wedges
- 3 broccoli spears or florets
- 3 thyme sprigs

- 1 bay leaf
- 150ml chicken stock , warmed
- ½ tbsp plain flour

Method

STEP 1

Heat oven to 200C/180C fan/gas 6. Rub 1 tbsp of the oil over the chicken skin,then season. Put the potatoes, carrots, onion and broccoli in a small roasting tin with the thyme and bay leaf. Drizzle over the remaining oil, season well and toss together to coat everything. Sit the chicken breast on top and roast in the oven for 25-30 mins until it is cooked and the veg are tender.

STEP 2

Remove the chicken, potatoes and broccoli from the roasting tin and set aside while you make the gravy. Set the tin on the hob over a high heat and add the stock. Bring to the boil, then simmer for a few mins. Add the plain flour and stir constantly to remove any lumps. Once the sauce has thickened, take off the heat.

STEP 3

Slice the chicken breast into 3-4 pieces at an angle. Serve with the potatoes, broccoli, carrots and onion gravy.

Spaghetti puttanesca

Prep:15 mins **Cook:**20 mins

Serves 4

Ingredients

- 3 tbsp olive oil
- 1 onion, finely chopped
- 2 large garlic cloves, crushed
- ½ tsp chilli flakes (optional)
- 400g can chopped tomatoes
- 5 anchovy fillets, finely chopped
- 120g pitted black olives
- 2 tbsp capers, drained
- 300g dried spaghetti
- ½ small bunch of parsley, finely chopped

Method

STEP 1

Heat the oil in a non-stick pan over a medium-low heat. Add the onion along with a generous pinch of salt and fry for 10 mins, or until soft. Add the garlic and chilli, if using, and cook for a further minute.

STEP 2

Stir the tomatoes, anchovies, olives and capers into the onion, bring to a gentle simmer and cook, uncovered, for 15 mins. Season to taste.

STEP 3

Meanwhile, bring a large pan of salted water to the boil. Cook the spaghetti following pack instructions, then drain and toss with the sauce and parsley.

Slow-braised pork shoulder with cider & parsnips

Prep:20 mins **Cook:**2 hrs and 30 mins

Serves 5

Ingredients

- 2 tbsp olive oil
- 1kg/2lb 4oz pork shoulder , diced
- 2 onions , sliced
- 2 celery sticks, roughly chopped
- 3 parsnips , cut into chunks
- 2 bay leaves
- 1 tbsp plain flour
- 330ml bottle cider
- 850ml chicken stock
- handful parsley , chopped
- mashed potato and greens , to serve (optional)

Method

STEP 1

Heat oven to 180C/160C fan/gas 4. Heat the oil in a large lidded flameproof casserole and brown the meat in batches, then set aside. Fry the onions, celery and parsnips with the bay leaves for 10 mins until golden brown. Sprinkle in the flour and give a good stir, then add the pork and any juices back to the dish.

STEP 2

Add the cider and stock so that the meat and vegetables are covered. Season and bring to a simmer, then cover and put in the oven for 2 hrs. Serve sprinkled with parsley, with mashed potato and greens, if you like.

Thai shellfish pot

Prep: 30 mins **Cook:** 20 mins

Serves 4

Ingredients

- 1 tbsp sunflower oil
- 4 lime leaves
- 200g prepared squid , cut into rings
- 400ml coconut milk

For the curry paste

- 1 large shallot , sliced
- 1 lemongrass stalk , shredded
- 2 red chillies , sliced
- 5 garlic cloves
- thumb-sized piece of galangal or ginger, peeled and sliced

To serve

- chopped coriander
- sliced chillies

- 300g boneless firm white fish like monkfish or hake, cut into chunks
- 500g mussels , cleaned

- 1 tsp ground coriander
- 1 tsp ground cumin
- 2 tbsp fish sauce
- 4 tbsp roasted peanuts
- 1 tsp soft brown sugar

- lime wedges

Method

STEP 1

For the curry paste, put all the ingredients in a spice grinder or blender and blitz to a fine paste. Will keep in the fridge for a few days.

STEP 2

Heat the oil in a wok or casserole dish. Add the curry paste and lime leaves, and fry for a minute or so. Stir in the squid so it's coated all over in the paste, then pour over the coconut milk. Bring to a simmer, then submerge the white fish in the sauce and scatter over the mussels. Cover the wok with a lid and cook for 5-8 mins or until the mussel shells are fully open and the fish is just cooked. Sprinkle with the coriander and chilli, then put in the middle of the table, along with the lime wedges. Let everyone help themselves.

Steak & broccoli protein pots

Prep: 10 mins **Cook:** 9 mins

Serves 2

Ingredients

- 250g pack wholegrain rice mix with seaweed (Merchant Gourmet)
- 2 tbsp chopped sushi ginger
- 4 spring onions , the green part finely chopped, the white halved lengthways and cut into lengths
- 160g broccoli florets, cut into bite-sized pieces
- 225g lean fat-trimmed fillet steak

Method

STEP 1

Tip the rice mix into a bowl and stir in the ginger, chopped onion greens and 4 tbsp water. Add the broccoli and the spring onion whites, but keep the onions together, on top, as you will need them in the next step. Cover with cling film, pierce with the tip of a knife and microwave for 5 mins.

STEP 2

Meanwhile heat a non-stick frying pan and sear the steak for 2 mins each side, then set aside. Take the onion whites from the bowl and add to the pan so they char a little in the meat juices while the steak rests.

STEP 3

Tip the rice mixture into 2 large packed lunch pots. Slice the steak, pile the charred onions on top and seal until you're ready to eat (see tip below).

Roast dinner for one

Prep:10 mins **Cook:**35 mins

Serves 1

Ingredients

- 2 tbsp olive oil
- 1 large chicken breast , skin on
- 6 small new potatoes (about 200g/7oz), halved
- 2 carrots , cut into rounds
- 1 small onion , cut into wedges

- 3 broccoli spears or florets
- 3 thyme sprigs
- 1 bay leaf
- 150ml chicken stock , warmed
- ½ tbsp plain flour

Method

STEP 1

Heat oven to 200C/180C fan/gas 6. Rub 1 tbsp of the oil over the chicken skin,then season. Put the potatoes, carrots, onion and broccoli in a small roasting tin with the thyme and bay leaf. Drizzle over the remaining oil, season well and toss together to coat everything. Sit the chicken breast on top and roast in the oven for 25-30 mins until it is cooked and the veg are tender.

STEP 2

Remove the chicken, potatoes and broccoli from the roasting tin and set aside while you make the gravy. Set the tin on the hob over a high heat and add the stock. Bring to the boil, then simmer for a few mins. Add the plain flour and stir constantly to remove any lumps. Once the sauce has thickened, take off the heat.

STEP 3

Slice the chicken breast into 3-4 pieces at an angle. Serve with the potatoes, broccoli, carrots and onion gravy.

Rosemary chicken with oven-roasted ratatouille

Prep:15 mins **Cook:**40 mins

Serves 4

Ingredients

- 1 aubergine , cut into chunky pieces
- 2 courgettes , sliced into half-moons
- 3 mixed peppers , deseeded and roughly chopped
- 2 tsp finely chopped rosemary , plus 4 small sprigs
- 2 large garlic cloves , crushed
- 3 tbsp olive oil
- 4 skinless, boneless chicken breasts
- 250g cherry or baby plum tomato , halved

Method

STEP 1

Heat oven to 200C/180C fan/gas 6. In a large roasting tin, toss together the aubergine, courgettes and peppers with half the chopped rosemary, half the garlic, 2 tbsp oil and some seasoning. Spread out the vegetables in an even layer, then roast in the oven for 20 mins.

STEP 2

Meanwhile, mix remaining rosemary, garlic and oil together. Slash each of the chicken breasts 4-5 times with a sharp knife, brush over the flavoured oil, season and chill for 15 mins.

STEP 3

After veg have cooked for 20 mins, stir in the tomatoes. Make spaces in the roasting tin and nestle the chicken breasts amongst the vegetables. Place a rosemary sprig on top of each chicken breast. Return the tin to the oven for 18-20 mins, until the chicken is cooked through and the vegetables are lightly caramelised. Serve with some new potatoes, if you like.

Honey, mustard & crème fraîche baked chicken

Prep: 10 mins **Cook:** 45 mins

Serves 4

Ingredients

- 4 tbsp crème fraîche
- 2 tbsp grainy mustard
- 2 garlic cloves , crushed
- 150ml chicken stock
- 8 skin-on chicken drumsticks and thighs
- 500g baby potatoes
- 200g green beans

310

- 2 tbsp clear honey

- ½ small bunch tarragon , roughly chopped

Method

STEP 1

Heat oven to 200C/180C fan/gas 6. Mix together the crème fraîche, mustard, garlic and stock with some seasoning. Arrange the chicken, skin-side up, in a roasting tray just large enough for the chicken and vegetables.

STEP 2

Tuck the potatoes and beans in between the chicken pieces. Pour over the stock mixture then season the chicken and drizzle with honey. Cook for 40-45 mins until the chicken is cooked through and the potatoes tender. Scatter over the tarragon before serving

Pork & chorizo enchiladas

Prep:30 mins **Cook:**1 hr and 10 mins

Serves 8

Ingredients

- 1 tbsp olive oil
- 2 large onions , halved and thinly sliced
- 3 garlic cloves , chopped
- 1 tbsp ground cumin
- 2 heaped tbsp smoked paprika
- 2 tsp cinnamon
- 2 red chillies , halved, deseeded and sliced
- 500g pack pork mince
- 2 x 200g packs cooking chorizo sausages, removed from their skins

- 680g bottle passata
- 1 pork or chicken stock cube
- 2 red and 2 green peppers , deseeded, quartered and sliced
- 2 x 400g cans borlotti beans , drained
- 30g pack coriander , chopped
- 500g tub fromage frais (not fat-free)
- 1 large egg
- 2 packs of 8 soft corn tortillas
- 140g mature cheddar , grated
- green salad , to serve

Method

STEP 1

Heat the oil in a large, deep pan and fry the onions and garlic for about 10 mins. Add the spices and half the chilli, and cook for 1 min more. Tip in the pork and chorizo, turn up the heat and fry the meat, stirring and breaking it down until it changes colour. Pour in the passata and 300ml water, then crumble in the stock cube. Pile in the peppers, stir, cover and simmer over a low heat for 30 mins until the meat and peppers are tender. Stir in the beans and two-thirds of the coriander.

STEP 2

Meanwhile, tip the fromage frais (with any liquid in the tub) into a bowl, and beat in the egg, remaining coriander and seasoning. Get out 2 ovenproof and freezer-proof dishes.

STEP 3

Spoon the meat onto the centre of the tortillas, roll up and arrange 8 in each dish. Spoon half of the fromage frais mixture on top and smooth it to cover the tortillas. Scatter each with half the cheese and remaining chillies. If eating now, heat oven to 190C/170C fan/gas 5 and bake for 25 mins until golden, then serve. If freezing, when cold cover with cling film and foil. Will keep for 3 months. To serve, thaw in the fridge and reheat uncovered as above, adding an extra 15 mins to the time, checking that it is hot all the way through. You can also bake from frozen. Put the dish (covered with fresh foil) on a baking tray in the oven, then heat oven to 180C/160C fan/gas 4 and bake for 2 hrs. Don't put the frozen dish in a preheated oven as it might crack – it's better to let it heat slowly. Remove the foil and bake for 20 mins more. Serve with a green salad.

Chicken & egg-fried rice

Prep: 5 mins **Cook:** 10 mins

Serves 4

Ingredients

- 1 tbsp sunflower oil
- 3 eggs, beaten with some seasoning
- 320g pack mixed stir-fry vegetable
- 1 tbsp mild curry powder
- 140g frozen sweetcorn
- 600g cooked rice see tip, below

- 1 roasted chicken breast, finely shredded
- 2 tbsp low-salt soy sauce
- 2 tbsp sweet chilli sauce
- 2 tbsp ketchup

Method

STEP 1

Heat a splash of oil in a large frying pan and tip in the beaten eggs. Swirl the pan to coat in a thin layer of egg and cook for a few mins until set. Tip onto a chopping board, roll up, slice thinly and set aside.

STEP 2

Heat a little more oil, add the stir-fry veg, curry powder and sweetcorn with a splash of water. Cook for 1-2 mins until the veg starts to wilt, then tip into a bowl. Add the last of the oil to the pan, tip in the rice and chicken, mix well, then add the soy sauce, sweet chilli, ketchup, a splash of water and some black pepper.

STEP 3

Finally, add the eggs and the veg, toss together and heat through until hot. Tip into bowls and serve immediately.

Sausages with oregano, mushrooms & olives

Prep: 10 mins **Cook:** 20 mins

Serves 4

Ingredients

- 450g pack reduced-fat sausage
- 1 tsp sunflower oil
- 2 tsp dried oregano
- 2 garlic cloves , sliced

- 400g can chopped or cherry tomato
- 200ml beef stock
- 100g pitted black olives in brine
- 500g pack mushroom , thickly sliced

Method

STEP 1

Using kitchen scissors, snip the sausages into meatball-size pieces. Heat a large pan and fry the pieces in the oil for about 5 mins until golden all over.

STEP 2

Add the oregano and garlic, fry for 1 min more, then tip in the tomatoes, stock, olives and mushrooms.

STEP 3

Simmer for 15 mins until the sausages are cooked through and the sauce has reduced a little. Serve with mashed potato or pasta.

Vegetarian casserole

Prep:10 mins **Cook:**40 mins

Serves 4

Ingredients

- 1 tbsp olive or rapeseed oil
- 1 onion, finely chopped
- 3 garlic cloves, sliced
- 1 tsp smoked paprika
- ½ tsp ground cumin
- 1 tbsp dried thyme
- 3 medium carrots, sliced (about 200g)
- 2 medium sticks celery, finely sliced (about 120g)
- 1 red pepper, chopped
- 1 yellow pepper, chopped

- 2 x 400g cans tomatoes or peeled cherry tomatoes
- 1 vegetable stock cube made up to 250ml (we used 1 Knorr vegetable stock pot)
- 2 courgettes, sliced thickly (about 300g)
- 2 sprigs fresh thyme
- 250g cooked lentils (we used Merchant Gourmet ready-to-eat Puy lentils)

Method

STEP 1

Heat 1 tbsp olive or rapeseed oil in a large, heavy-based pan. Add 1 finely chopped onion and cook gently for 5 – 10 mins until softened.

STEP 2

Add 3 sliced garlic cloves, 1 tsp smoked paprika, ½ tsp ground cumin, 1 tbsp dried thyme, 3 sliced carrots, 2 finely sliced celery sticks, 1 chopped red pepper and 1 chopped yellow pepper and cook for 5 minutes.

STEP 3

Add two 400g cans tomatoes, 250ml vegetable stock (made with 1 stock pot), 2 thickly sliced courgettes and 2 sprigs fresh thyme and cook for 20 - 25 minutes.

STEP 4

Take out the thyme sprigs. Stir in 250g cooked lentils and bring back to a simmer. Serve with wild and white basmati rice, mash or quinoa.

Thai shellfish pot

Prep: 30 mins **Cook:** 20 mins

Serves 4

Ingredients

- 1 tbsp sunflower oil
- 4 lime leaves
- 200g prepared squid , cut into rings
- 400ml coconut milk

- 300g boneless firm white fish like monkfish or hake, cut into chunks
- 500g mussels , cleaned

For the curry paste

- 1 large shallot , sliced
- 1 lemongrass stalk , shredded
- 2 red chillies , sliced
- 5 garlic cloves
- thumb-sized piece of galangal or ginger, peeled and sliced

- 1 tsp ground coriander
- 1 tsp ground cumin
- 2 tbsp fish sauce
- 4 tbsp roasted peanuts
- 1 tsp soft brown sugar

To serve

- chopped coriander
- sliced chillies

- lime wedges

Method

STEP 1

For the curry paste, put all the ingredients in a spice grinder or blender and blitz to a fine paste. Will keep in the fridge for a few days.

STEP 2

Heat the oil in a wok or casserole dish. Add the curry paste and lime leaves, and fry for a minute or so. Stir in the squid so it's coated all over in the paste, then pour over the coconut milk. Bring to a simmer, then submerge the white fish in the sauce and scatter over the mussels. Cover the wok with a lid and cook for
5-8 mins or until the mussel shells are fully open and the fish is just cooked. Sprinkle with the coriander and chilli, then put in the middle of the table, along with the lime wedges. Let everyone help themselves.

Seafood paella

Prep:40 mins **Cook:**1 hr and 10 mins

Serves 8

Ingredients

- 20-24 raw shell-on king prawns
- 2 tbsp olive oil
- 500g monkfish, cut into chunks
- 1 large onion, finely chopped
- 500g paella rice
- 4 garlic cloves, sliced
- 2 tsp smoked paprika
- 1 tsp cayenne pepper (optional)

For the stock

- 1 tbsp olive oil
- 1 onion, roughly chopped
- ½ x 400g can chopped tomatoes

- pinch of saffron
- ½ x 400g can chopped tomatoes (save the rest for the stock, below)
- 500g mussels, cleaned
- 100g frozen peas
- 100g frozen baby broad beans
- handful parsley leaves, roughly chopped

- 6 garlic cloves, roughly chopped
- 1 chicken stock cube
- 1 star anise

Method

STEP 1

Peel and de-vein the prawns, reserving the heads and shells. Return the prawns to the fridge.

STEP 2

To make the stock, heat the oil in a large pan over a medium-high heat and add the onion, tomatoes, garlic, and reserved prawn shells and heads. Cook for 3-4 mins, then pour in 2 litres of water and add the stock cube and star anise. Bring to a boil, then simmer for 30 mins. Leave to cool slightly, then whizz in batches in a blender or food processor. Strain through a fine sieve.

STEP 3

Heat the oil in a large paella pan or an extra-large frying pan. Brown the monkfish for a few mins each side, then remove and set aside. Add the onion and fry for 4-5 mins until softened.

STEP 4

Stir in the rice and cook for 30 secs to toast. Add the garlic, paprika, cayenne (if using) and saffron, cook for another 30 secs, then stir in the tomatoes and 1.5 litres of the fish stock. Bring to the boil, then turn down to a simmer and cook, stirring, for about 10 mins (the rice should still be al dente). Return the monkfish to the pan with the prawns, mussels, peas and broad beans.

STEP 5

Cover the pan with a large baking tray, or foil, and cook on a low heat for another 10-15 mins until the mussels are open and the prawns are cooked through. Scatter over the parsley before serving.

Oven-baked leek & bacon risotto

Prep:10 mins **Cook:**30 mins

Serves 4

Ingredients

- 1 tbsp olive oil
- 6 rashers smoked back bacon, roughly chopped
- 2 leeks, halved lengthways and finely sliced
- 250g risotto rice
- 700ml hot chicken or vegetable stock
- 175g frozen peas
- 3 tbsp soft cheese
- zest 1 lemon

Method

STEP 1

Heat oven to 200C/180C fan/ gas 6. Tip the oil into an ovenproof casserole dish. Add bacon and fry for 2 mins. Add the leeks and cook until soft, but not coloured, for about 4-5 mins. Tip in rice and cook for 1 min more. Pour over stock. Cover and place in the oven for 20 mins, stirring halfway.

STEP 2

When rice is just tender and all liquid is absorbed, remove from oven and stir in peas. Place back in oven for 2 mins more. Remove and stir in cheese. Add zest and season.

Chicken, ginger & green bean hotpot

Prep: 10 mins **Cook:** 25 mins

Serves 2

Ingredients

- ½ tbsp vegetable oil
- 2cm piece ginger , cut into matchsticks
- 1 garlic clove , chopped
- ½ onion , thinly sliced into half moons
- 1 tbsp fish sauce
- ½ tbsp soft brown sugar
- 250g skinless chicken thigh fillets, trimmed of all fat and cut in half
- 125ml chicken stock
- 50g green bean , trimmed and cut into 2.5cm lengths
- 1 tbsp chopped coriander
- steamed rice , to serve

Method

STEP 1

Heat the oil in a saucepan over a medium-high heat. Add the ginger, garlic and onion, and stir-fry for about 5 mins or until lightly golden. Add the fish sauce, sugar, chicken and stock. Cover and cook over a medium heat for 15 mins.

STEP 2

For the final 3 mins of cooking, add the green beans. Remove from the heat and stir through half of the coriander. Serve with steamed rice and the remaining coriander scattered over.

Baked eggs with potatoes, mushrooms & cheese

Prep: 10 mins **Cook:** 25 mins

Serves 4

Ingredients

- 3 baking potatoes , peeled and cubed
- 1 tbsp sunflower oil
- 600g mushrooms , quartered
- 2 garlic cloves , sliced

- 2 tbsp thyme leaves
- 140g cheddar , grated
- 4 eggs

Method

STEP 1

Heat oven to 200C/180C fan/gas 6. Put the potatoes in a pan of water, bring to the boil, cook for 5 mins, then drain. Heat the oil in a large frying pan. Cook the potatoes, mushrooms and garlic for 5-8 mins to soften the mushrooms and brown the edges of the potatoes. Stir in half the thyme and cook for 1 min more.

STEP 2

Spoon the potato mixture into a baking dish and sprinkle with the cheese and the remaining thyme. Make holes in the mixture and break in 4 eggs. Bake in the oven for 12-15 mins until the eggs are set and the cheese has melted.

One-pan summer eggs

Prep: 5 mins **Cook:** 12 mins

Serves 2

Ingredients

- 1 tbsp olive oil
- 400g courgettes (about 2 large ones), chopped into small chunks
- 200g/7oz pack cherry tomatoes , halved

- 1 garlic clove , crushed
- 2 eggs
- few basil leaves , to serve

Method

STEP 1

Heat the oil in a non-stick frying pan, then add the courgettes. Fry for 5 mins, stirring every so often until they start to soften, add the tomatoes and garlic, then cook for a few mins more. Stir in a little seasoning, then make two gaps in the mix and crack in the eggs. Cover the pan with a lid or a sheet of foil, then cook for 2-3 mins until the eggs are done to your liking. Scatter over a few basil leaves and serve with crusty bread.

Pot-roast beef with French onion gravy

Prep: 15 mins **Cook:** 2 hrs and 15 mins

Serves 4

Ingredients

- 1kg silverside or topside of beef with no added fat
- 2 tbsp olive oil
- 8 young carrots, tops trimmed (but leave a little, if you like)
- 1 celery stick, finely chopped
- 200ml white wine
- 600ml rich beef stock
- 2 bay leaves
- 500g onion
- a few thyme sprigs
- 1 tsp butter
- 1 tsp light brown or light muscovado sugar
- 2 tsp plain flour

Method

STEP 1

Heat oven to 160C/140C fan/gas 3. Rub the meat with 1 tsp of the oil and plenty of seasoning. Heat a large flameproof casserole dish and brown the meat all over for about 10 mins. Meanwhile, add 2 tsp oil to a frying pan and fry the carrots and celery for 10 mins until turning golden.

STEP 2

Lift the beef onto a plate, splash the wine into the hot casserole and boil for 2 mins. Pour in the stock, return the beef, then tuck in the carrots, celery and bay leaves, trying not to submerge the carrots too much. Cover and cook in the oven for 2 hrs. (I like to turn the beef halfway through cooking.)

STEP 3

Meanwhile, thinly slice the onions. Heat 1 tbsp oil in a pan and stir in the onions, thyme and some seasoning. Cover and cook gently for 20 mins until the onions are softened but not coloured. Remove the lid, turn up the heat, add the butter and sugar, then let the onions caramelise to a dark golden brown, stirring often. Remove the thyme sprigs, then set aside.

STEP 4

When the beef is ready, it will be tender and easy to pull apart at the edges. Remove it from the casserole and snip off the strings. Reheat the onion pan, stir in the flour and cook for 1 min. Whisk the floury onions into the beefy juices in the casserole, to make a thick onion gravy. Taste for seasoning. Add the beef and carrots back to the casserole, or slice the beef and bring to the table on a platter, with the carrots to the side and the gravy spooned over.

Korean rice pot

Prep: 15 mins **Cook:** 20 mins

Serves 4

Ingredients

- 500ml/ 18 fl oz hot chicken stock
- 250g/ 9oz long grain rice
- 300g/ 11oz cooked turkey , diced
- 250g/ 9oz baby spinach
- 2 carrots , shredded

- 1 tsp toasted sesame oil
- 1 tsp toasted sesame seed
- 2 tbsp vegetable oil
- 4 eggs
- 2 tbsp thick chilli sauce

Method

STEP 1

Pour the chicken stock into a large pan and bring to the boil. Add the rice and turkey, bring back to the boil and simmer for 12-15 mins until the stock has been absorbed and rice is tender.

STEP 2

Meanwhile, put the spinach in a colander and pour over a kettle of hot water to lightly wilt. Keep the spinach and carrots separate, but dress both with the sesame oil and seeds.

STEP 3

Cover the cooked rice with a lid and leave to sit for a couple of mins. Meanwhile, heat vegetable oil in a non-stick pan set over a high heat. Fry eggs so the white crisps up nicely round the edges.

STEP 4

Spoon the rice into large bowls and arrange the spinach and carrots on top. Finish each with a fried egg and a dollop of chilli sauce. Serve immediately.

Greek lamb with orzo

Prep:20 mins **Cook:**2 hrs and 35 mins

Serves 6

Ingredients

- 1kg shoulder of lamb
- 2 onions, sliced
- 1 tbsp chopped oregano, or 1 tsp dried
- ½ tsp ground cinnamon
- 2 cinnamon sticks, broken in half
- 2 tbsp olive oil

- 400g can chopped tomato
- 1.2l hot low-sodium chicken or vegetable stock
- 400g orzo (see know-how below)
- freshly grated parmesan, to serve

Method

STEP 1

Heat oven to 180C/fan 160C/gas 4. Cut the lamb into 4cm chunks, then spread over the base of a large, wide casserole dish. Add the onions, oregano, cinnamon sticks, ground cinnamon and olive oil, then stir well. Bake, uncovered, for 45 mins, stirring halfway.

STEP 2

Pour over the chopped tomatoes and stock, cover tightly, then return to the oven for 1½ hrs, until the lamb is very tender.

STEP 3

Remove the cinnamon sticks, then stir in the orzo. Cover again, then cook for a further 20 mins, stirring halfway through. The orzo should be cooked and the sauce thickened. Sprinkle with grated Parmesan and serve with crusty bread.

Poached salt beef & root veg

Prep: 20 mins **Cook:** 3 hrs

Serves 8

Ingredients

- 1 ½l chicken stock
- 4 tbsp English mustard
- 8 baby heritage carrots , peeled
- 8 baby turnips , peeled and halved
- 16 medium salad potatoes , scrubbed

- 1 ½kg piece salt beef
- 16 French Breakfast radishes , tops left on
- 16 cocktail or small pickled onions
- small handful picked dill fronds

Method

STEP 1

Heat oven to 160C/140C fan/gas 3. Pour the stock into a flameproof roasting tin or shallow casserole dish, add 3 tbsp mustard and bring to the boil. Turn off the heat, then scatter in all of the vegetables except the radishes and onions. Nestle the beef in the middle, fat-side up. Brush the top of the beef with the remaining mustard, scatter over 1 tsp cracked black pepper, cover with a lid or foil and put in the oven for to braise for 3 hrs, or until the beef is tender.

STEP 2

Leave everything to cool a little, then lift the meat from the dish, transfer to a board and carve into thin slices. Stir the onions through the broth with the other vegetables, then divide the braised vegetables between bowls and pour in the mustardy cooking juices. Drape the slices of beef over the top, then poke in some radishes so they're in amongst it all. Scatter the dill over just before serving.

Turkish one-pan eggs & peppers (Menemen)

Prep: 10 mins **Cook:** 25 mins

Serves 4

Ingredients

- 2 tbsp olive oil
- 2 onions , sliced
- 1 red or green pepper , halved deseeded and sliced
- 1-2 red chillies , deseeded and sliced
- 400g can chopped tomatoes
- 1-2 tsp caster sugar
- 4 eggs
- small bunch parsley , roughly chopped
- 6 tbsp thick, creamy yogurt
- 2 garlic cloves , crushed

Method

STEP 1

Heat the oil in a heavy-based frying pan. Stir in the onions, pepper and chillies. Cook until they begin to soften. Add the tomatoes and sugar, mixing well. Cook until the liquid has reduced, season.

STEP 2

Using a wooden spoon, create 4 pockets in the tomato mixture and crack the eggs into them. Cover the pan and cook the eggs over a low heat until just set.

STEP 3

Beat the yogurt with the garlic and season. Sprinkle the menemen with parsley and serve from the frying pan with a dollop of the garlic-flavoured yogurt.

Chipotle bean chilli with baked eggs

Prep:5 mins **Cook:**30 mins

Serves 4

Ingredients

- 1 tbsp sunflower oil
- 1 onion , chopped
- 1-2 tbsp chipotle paste (depending on how hot you like it)
- 2 x 400g cans black beans , drained and rinsed
- 400g can mixed bean , drained and rinsed
- 2 x 400g cans chopped tomatoes with garlic & herbs
- 1 heaped tbsp brown sugar
- 4 eggs
- small handful coriander leaves
- soured cream , to serve
- warm flour tortillas , to serve

Method

STEP 1

Heat the oil in a deep frying pan and cook the onion for about 5 mins until soft. Add the chipotle paste, beans, tomatoes and sugar, and simmer for about 15-20 mins until thickened. Season to taste.

STEP 2

Make 4 holes and crack an egg into each one. Cover and simmer over a low heat for 8-10 mins until the eggs are cooked to your liking. Sprinkle with coriander leaves and serve with a bowl of soured cream and some warm flour tortillas.

Spinach & chickpea curry

Prep:5 mins **Cook:**15 mins

Serves 4

Ingredients

- 2 tbsp mild curry paste
- 1 onion, chopped
- 400g can cherry tomatoes
- 2 x 400g cans chickpeas, drained and rinsed
- 250g bag baby leaf spinach
- squeeze lemon juice
- basmati rice, to serve

Method

STEP 1

Heat the curry paste in a large non-stick frying pan. Once it starts to split, add the onion and cook for 2 mins to soften. Tip in the tomatoes and bubble for 5 mins or until the sauce has reduced.

STEP 2

Add the chickpeas and some seasoning, then cook for 1 min more. Take off the heat, then tip in the spinach and allow the heat of the pan to wilt the leaves. Season, add the lemon juice, and serve with basmati rice.

Piri-piri chicken with smashed sweet potatoes & broccoli

Prep:20 mins **Cook:**55 mins

Ingredients

- 3 large sweet potatoes (about 900g), peeled and cut into large chunks
- oil , for drizzling
- 6-8 chicken thighs, skin left on
- 2 red onions , cut into wedges
- 25g sachet piri-piri spice mix (or a mild version, if you like)
- 300g long-stem broccoli

Method

STEP 1

Heat the oven to 180C/160C fan/gas 4. Toss the sweet potatoes with a generous drizzle of oil and some seasoning, and tip into a very large roasting tin. Push the potatoes to one end of the tin, then, in the other end, toss the chicken with the onions, spice mix, a drizzle of oil and some seasoning. Roast for 40 mins, stirring everything halfway through. Add the broccoli to the tin, drizzle with a little oil and season, then roast for 10-15 mins more.

STEP 2

Remove the chicken, onions and broccoli from the tin. Roughly mash the potatoes using a fork, making sure you incorporate all the chicken juices and spices from the pan. Spread the mash over the base of the tin, then top with the broccoli, chicken and onions and serve from the tin in the middle of the table.

Sausage, kale & gnocchi one-pot

Prep:5 mins **Cook:**15 mins

Serves 4

Ingredients

- 1 tbsp olive oil
- 6 pork sausages
- 1 tsp chilli flakes
- 1 tsp fennel seeds (optional)
- 500g fresh gnocchi

- 500ml chicken stock (fresh if you can get it)
- 100g chopped kale
- 40g parmesan, finely grated

Method

STEP 1

Heat the oil in a large high-sided frying pan over a medium heat. Squeeze the sausages straight from their skins into the pan, then use the back of a wooden spoon to break the meat up. Sprinkle in the chilli flakes and fennel seeds, if using, then fry until the sausagemeat is crisp around the edges. Remove from the pan with a slotted spoon.

STEP 2

Tip the gnocchi into the pan, fry for a minute or so, then pour in the chicken stock. Once bubbling, cover the pan with a lid and cook for 3 mins, then stir in the kale. Cook for 2 mins more or until the gnocchi is tender and the kale has wilted. Stir in the parmesan, then season with black pepper and scatter the crisp sausagemeat over the top.

Chicken cacciatore one-pot with orzo

Prep:5 mins **Cook:**55 mins

Serves 4

Ingredients

- 2 tbsp olive oil
- 4-6 skin-on, bone-in chicken thighs
- 1 onion , finely sliced
- 2 garlic cloves , sliced
- 250ml red wine
- 2 bay leaves
- 4 thyme sprigs
- 2 rosemary sprigs
- small bunch of parsley , stalks and leaves separated, finely chopped
- 2 x 400g cans cherry tomatoes
- 1 chicken stock cube
- 1 tbsp balsamic vinegar
- 2 tbsp capers (optional)
- handful of pitted green olives
- 300g orzo , rinsed (to keep it from getting too sticky when baked)

Method

STEP 1

Heat the oven to 220C/200C fan/gas 7. Rub 1 tbsp oil over the chicken and season well, then put skin-side up in an ovenproof casserole dish or roasting tin and bake for 20-25 mins until crisp and golden, but not cooked all the way though. Remove from the dish and put on a plate.

STEP 2

Add the remaining oil to the dish, mixing it with the chicken fat. Tip in the onion and garlic, then bake for 5-8 mins until the onion is tender.

STEP 3

Pour in the wine, stirring it with the onions, then leave to evaporate slightly in the residual heat before adding the bay, thyme, rosemary, parsley stalks and tomatoes. Dissolve the stock cube in 300ml boiling water and pour this in, then add the vinegar, capers, if using, olives and orzo. Stir well and season.

STEP 4

Nestle the chicken back in the pan, skin-side up, and roast for 20 mins until the sauce is thickened, the orzo is tender and the meat is cooked through. Give it a stir, then leave for 10 mins for the orzo to absorb the excess liquid. Scatter over the parsley leaves to serve.

One-pot paneer curry pie

Prep:25 mins **Cook:**1 hr and 30 mins

Serves 6

Ingredients

- 2 tbsp vegetable oil
- 440g paneer , cut into 2cm cubes
- 4 tbsp ghee or butter
- 2 large onions , finely sliced
- 2 large garlic cloves , crushed
- thumb-sized piece of ginger , finely grated
- ½ tsp hot chilli powder
- 2 tsp ground cumin
- 2 tsp fenugreek seeds
- 1½ tbsp garam masala
- 2 x 400g cans chopped tomatoes
- 1 tbsp caster sugar
- 300g potato , peeled and cut into 2cm cubes
- 150g spinach
- 150g frozen peas
- 100ml double cream

- 2 tbsp cashew nut butter
- plain flour , for dusting
- 320g sheet all-butter puff pastry
- 2 large eggs , 1 whole, 1 yolk only, lightly beaten together (freeze the leftover egg white for another recipe)
- 2 tsp nigella seeds
- pilau rice or green veg, to serve

Method

STEP 1

Heat the oil over a medium heat in a shallow flameproof casserole dish roughly 30cm wide. Add the paneer and fry for 5 mins, turning with tongs until each side is golden. Remove from the pan and set aside on a plate lined with kitchen paper.

STEP 2

Heat the ghee or butter in the same dish over a medium-low heat, then add the onions and a big pinch of salt. Fry for 15 mins, or until softened and caramelised. Stir in the garlic and ginger, cook for 1 min, then tip in the spices and fry for a further 2 mins. Scrape the spiced onions into a food processor or blender along with the tomatoes and blitz until smooth. Pour back into the pan with 1½ cans of water, then stir through the sugar and potatoes. Bring to the boil, lower to a simmer, then cover and cook, stirring occasionally, for 20-25 mins or until the potato is just tender.

STEP 3

Add the spinach and peas, and cook for 5 mins. Stir in the cream and cashew butter, then return the paneer to the pan and season to taste. Remove from the heat and set aside to cool completely.

STEP 4

Heat the oven to 220C/200C fan/gas 8. On a lightly floured surface, roll the pastry out to just bigger than your casserole dish. Cut a thin strip off each side and fix these around the edge of the casserole. Roll the pastry sheet over the top and press the edges with a fork to seal, and tuck in any overhang. Brush with the egg, sprinkle with the nigella seeds and bake for 30-35 mins or until deep golden brown. Leave to rest for 15 mins before serving with pilau rice or green veg.

Hearty lentil one pot

Prep: 10 mins **Cook:** 1 hr

Serves 4

Ingredients

- 40g dried porcini mushrooms , roughly chopped
- 200g dried brown lentils
- 1 ½ tbsp chopped rosemary
- 3 tbsp rapeseed oil
- 2 large onions , roughly chopped
- 150g chestnut baby button mushrooms

- 4 garlic cloves , finely grated
- 2 tbsp vegetable bouillon powder
- 2 large carrots (350g), cut into chunks
- 3 celery sticks (165g), chopped
- 500g potatoes , cut into chunks
- 200g cavolo nero , shredded

Method

STEP 1

Cover the mushrooms in boiling water and leave to soak for 10 mins. Boil the lentils in a pan with plenty of water for 10 mins. Drain and rinse, then tip into a pan with the dried mushrooms and soaking water (don't add the last bit of the liquid as it can contain some grit), rosemary and 2 litres water. Season, cover and simmer for 20 mins.

STEP 2

Meanwhile, heat the oil in a large pan and fry the onions for 5 mins. Stir in the fresh mushrooms and garlic and fry for 5 mins more. Stir in the lentil mixture and bouillon powder, then add the carrots, celery and potatoes. Cover and cook for 20 mins, stirring often, until the veg and lentils are tender, topping up the water level if needed.

STEP 3

Remove any tough stalks from the cavolo nero, then add to the pan and cover and cook for 5 mins more. If you're following our Healthy Diet Plan, serve half in bowls, then chill the rest to eat another day. *Will keep in the fridge for two to three days.* Reheat in a pan until hot.

Lemony tuna, tomato & caper one-pot pasta

Prep: 5 mins **Cook:** 30 mins

Serves 4

Ingredients

- 2 tbsp olive oil
- 1 red onion , finely chopped
- 500g cherry tomatoes , halved
- 400g dried pasta (we used rigatoni)
- 1l hot vegetable stock
- 2 x 110g cans tuna in olive oil, drained

- 3 tbsp mascarpone
- 30g parmesan , grated
- 2 heaped tbsp capers
- ½ lemon , zested
- small bunch parsley , finely chopped

Method

STEP 1

Heat the oil in a saucepan over a medium-low heat. Add the onion and a pinch of salt and fry gently for 7 mins or until softened and turning translucent. Add 350g of the tomatoes, the pasta and veg stock to the pan and bring to the boil, then reduce to a simmer and cook for 15 mins, uncovered, stirring occasionally. The tomatoes should have broken down and the pasta will be just cooked.

STEP 2

Add the remaining tomatoes and bubble uncovered on a medium-high heat for 5 mins or until the liquid has reduced. Gently fold through large flakes of tuna, the mascarpone, parmesan, capers, lemon zest and parsley as well as salt and a generous grind of black pepper. Place a lid on the pan and leave to sit for 5 mins before serving in deep bowls.

Tomato, pepper & bean one pot

Prep:15 mins **Cook:**45 mins

Makes 6 portions

Ingredients

- 1 tbsp olive oil
- 1 large onion , finely chopped
- 2 celery sticks , finely chopped
- 3 carrots , finely chopped
- 3 red peppers , sliced
- 2 garlic cloves , crushed

- 2 tbsp tomato purée
- 400g can cannellini beans , rinsed and drained
- 400g pinto beans , rinsed and drained
- 400g borlotti beans , rinsed and drained
- 2 x 400g cans chopped tomatoes

- 1 vegetable stock cube (check the label if you're vegan)
- 2 bay leaves
- 1 tbsp brown sugar
- ½ tbsp red wine vinegar

Method

STEP 1

Heat the oil in a large pan or casserole on a medium heat. Fry the onion, celery and carrots for 10 mins until soft and golden, then add the peppers and fry for another 5 mins.

STEP 2

Stir in the garlic for a minute, then add the tomato purée, all the beans and chopped tomatoes, then swirl out the tomato cans with a splash of water and add to the pan with the stock cube, bay leaves, sugar and vinegar. Season and simmer, uncovered, for 25 mins until the sauce reduces to coat the beans and the peppers are soft. Leave to cool before storing in transportable containers. *Will keep in the fridge for 3 - 4 days or freeze in portions and defrost in the fridge overnight.*

Choose your toppings

Sweet & spicy
Add diced dried apricots and 1 tbsp harissa. Top with yogurt swirled with more harissa, and toasted flaked almonds.

Tex-Mex
Stir in ½ - 1 tbsp chipotle paste, shredded leftover roast chicken if you have any, and top with diced avocado, grated cheddar and coriander.

Smoky BBQ beans
Stir in 1 tbsp smoky BBQ sauce and crumble over shop-bought crispy bacon, a dollop of soured cream or yogurt, and some chopped herbs.

Added greens
Stir in some spinach and top with a sliced boiled egg.

Beans on toast
Serve the beans on toast or bread, add a dash of Tabasco or chilli flakes, crumble over feta and drizzle with olive oil.

Italian-inspired
Top with toasted croutons, chopped rosemary, lemon zest and parmesan.

One-pot coconut fish curry

Prep:5 mins **Cook:**25 mins

Serves 4

Ingredients

- 1 tbsp sunflower oil , vegetable oil or coconut oil
- 1 onion , chopped
- 1 large garlic clove , crushed
- 1 tsp turmeric
- 1 tsp garam masala

- 1 tsp chilli flakes
- 400ml can coconut milk
- 390g pack fish pie mix
- 200g frozen peas
- 1 lime , cut into wedges
- yogurt and rice, to serve

Method

STEP 1

Heat the oil in a large saucepan over a medium heat, add the onion and a big pinch of salt. Gently fry until the onion is translucent, so around 10 mins, then add the garlic and spices. Stir and cook for another minute, adding a splash of water to prevent them sticking. Tip in the coconut milk and stir well, then simmer for 10 mins.

STEP 2

Tip the fish pie mix and the frozen peas into the pan and cook until the peas are bright green and the fish is starting the flake, so around 3 mins. Season and add lime juice to taste. Ladle into bowls and serve with yogurt and rice.

One-pot chicken & mushroom risotto

Prep:15 mins **Cook:**35 mins

Serves 4

Ingredients

- 60g butter
- 1 large onion, finely chopped

- 2 thyme sprigs, leaves picked
- 250g pack chestnut mushrooms, sliced

- 300g risotto rice
- 1½l hot chicken stock
- 200g cooked chicken, chopped into chunks
- 50g grated parmesan, plus extra to serve (optional)
- small pack parsley, finely chopped

Method

STEP 1

Heat the butter in a large pan over a gentle heat and add the onion. Cook for 10 mins until softened, then stir in the thyme leaves and mushrooms. Cook for 5 mins, sprinkle in the rice and stir to coat in the mixture.

STEP 2

Ladle in a quarter of the stock and continue cooking, stirring occasionally and topping up with more stock as it absorbs (you may not need all the stock).

STEP 3

When most of the stock has been absorbed and the rice is nearly cooked, add the chicken and stir to warm through. Season well and stir in the parmesan and parsley. Serve scattered with extra parmesan, if you like.

Sausage, roasted veg & Puy lentil one-pot

Prep:5 mins **Cook:**45 mins

Serves 4

Ingredients

- 8 sausages
- 2 x 400g packs ready-to-roast vegetables
- 3 garlic cloves , bashed in their skins
- 2 tbsp olive oil
- 1 tsp smoked paprika
- 2 x 250g pouches puy lentils
- 1 ½ tbsp sherry or red wine vinegar
- 1 small pack parsley , roughly chopped

Method

STEP 1

Heat grill to high. Put the sausages in a large roasting tin and grill for 8-10 mins until browning, then switch the oven on to 200C/180C fan/gas 6. Remove the tin from the oven and add the vegetables and garlic, then drizzle over the oil and toss in the paprika and some seasoning.

STEP 2

Roast for 30-35 mins more until the sausages and veg are mostly tender, then stir through the lentils and vinegar. Return to the oven for 5 mins until everything is heated through. Squeeze the garlic cloves out of their skins and stir the garlic into the lentils, then season to taste, stir through the parsley and serve.

Moroccan chicken one-pot

Prep: 20 mins **Cook:** 50 mins

Serves 6

Ingredients

- 4 boneless, skinless chicken breasts
- 3 tbsp olive oil
- 2 onions, 1 roughly chopped, 1 sliced
- 100g tomatoes
- 100g ginger, roughly chopped
- 3 garlic cloves
- 1 tsp turmeric

- 1 tbsp each ground cumin, coriander and cinnamon
- 1 large butternut squash, deseeded and cut into big chunks
- 600ml chicken stock
- 2 tbsp brown sugar
- 2 tbsp red wine vinegar
- 100g dried cherries

To serve

- 1 small red onion, finely chopped
- zest 1 lemon
- handful mint leaves

- 100g feta cheese, crumbled
- couscous and natural yogurt

Method

STEP 1

Season 4 boneless, skinless chicken breasts. Heat 2 tbsp olive oil in a flameproof dish, then brown the chicken on all sides. Remove the chicken to a plate.

335

STEP 2

Whizz 1 chopped onion, 100g tomatoes, 100g chopped ginger and 3 garlic cloves into a rough paste.

STEP 3

Fry 1 sliced onion in 1 tbsp olive oil in the dish until softened, then add 1 tsp turmeric, 1 tbsp cumin, 1 tbsp coriander and 1 tbsp cinnamon and fry for 1 min more until fragrant. Add the paste and fry for another few mins to soften.

STEP 4

Return the chicken to the dish with 1 large butternut squash, cut into big chunks, 600ml chicken stock, 2 tbsp brown sugar and 2 tbsp red wine vinegar.

STEP 5

Bring to a simmer, then cook for 30 mins until the chicken is cooked through.

STEP 6

Lift the chicken out and stir in 100g dried cherries, then continue simmering the sauce to thicken while you shred the chicken into bite-sized chunks. Stir the chicken back into the sauce and season.

STEP 7

Mix 1 finely chopped small red onion, the zest of 1 lemon, a handful of mint leaves and 100g crumbled feta cheese. Scatter over the dish, then serve with couscous and natural yogurt.

One-pot Chinese chicken noodle soup

Prep: 10 mins **Cook:** 15 mins

Serves 4

Ingredients

- 1 tbsp honey
- 3 tbsp dark soy
- 1 red chilli , sliced
- 1l chicken stock

- 80g leftover roast chicken (optional)
- 20g pickled pink ginger or normal ginger, peeled and finely sliced
- ½ Chinese cabbage , shredded

- 300g pouch straight-to-wok thick noodles
- 4 spring onions , sliced

Method

STEP 1

Drizzle the honey over the base of a large saucepan and bubble briefly to a caramel, then splash in the soy, bubble, add half the chilli and the chicken stock and simmer for 5 mins.

STEP 2

Add the chicken, if using, and ginger, and simmer for another 5 mins. Stir in the cabbage and noodles and cook until just wilted and the noodles have heated through. Ladle into bowls and sprinkle over the remaining chilli and the spring onions.

Spring one-pot roast chicken

Prep: 20 mins **Cook:** 1 hr and 20 mins

Serves 4

Ingredients

- 1 ½kg whole chicken
- 250g mascarpone
- ½ small lemon , zested and juiced
- small bunch of tarragon , finely chopped
- 3 tbsp olive oil
- 800g new potatoes , halved if large
- 1 garlic bulb , halved
- 200g radishes , halved if large
- ½ bunch of spring onions , trimmed
- 150ml chicken stock
- 200g frozen peas , defrosted
- 100g spring greens , shredded

Method

STEP 1

Heat the oven to 200C/180C fan/gas 6. Remove any string from the chicken and sit in a large roasting tin or a baking dish, with plenty of space around it.

STEP 2

Mash 2 tbsp of the mascarpone with the lemon zest, 1 tbsp of the tarragon and some seasoning. Slip your hand beneath the chicken skin to pull it away from the meat, then spread the mixture beneath the skin in a thin layer. Spoon another 3 tbsp mascarpone into the cavity of the chicken, to melt in with the roasting juices and enrich the sauce later on. Rub 2 tbsp olive oil into the skin, season well with sea salt, then loosely tie the legs together with butcher's string. Roast for 20 mins.

STEP 3

Aarrange the potatoes and the garlic around the chicken, drizzle over another 1 tbsp oil and cook for another 30 mins.

STEP 4

Toss the radishes and whole spring onions into the dish, in and around the potatoes, coating everything in the fat, then roast for another 25 mins. The potatoes and radishes will be golden and tender, and the chicken should be cooked through. Remove the chicken from the tin, cover loosely with foil and leave to rest.

STEP 5

Pour off or spoon away the excess oil from the tin. Stir the remaining mascarpone (about 150g) with the stock in a jug until lump-free, then pour into the tin and bubble on the hob for few minutes, stirring to coat the potatoes and veg. Squeeze over some lemon juice and season.

STEP 6

Stir in the peas, spring greens and most of the remaining tarragon, and bubble for a few more minutes until bright green. Sit the chicken back in the middle of the tin to serve and scatter over the reserved tarragon.

Chicken nacho one-pot

Prep: 5 mins **Cook:** 20 mins

Serves 4

Ingredients

- 2 tbsp olive oil
- 100g chorizo or pepperoni, skin removed, cut into chunks
- 1 tsp paprika
- 20 cherry tomatoes , cut in half

- 4 skinless chicken breasts , each cut lengthways into 4 (or buy chicken fillets)
- 200g bag corn chips (spicy if you like a bit of heat)
- 200ml tub crème fraîche

To serve

- jar of jalapeño peppers
- extra crème fraîche or soured cream

- smashed avocado

Method

STEP 1

Heat oven to 180C/160C fan/gas 4. Put the oil and chorizo in an ovenproof frying pan over a high heat and cook for 3 mins until the chorizo has released its oils and is starting to crisp. Stir in the paprika and tomatoes, and cook for 1 min.

STEP 2

Season the chicken, add to the pan and cook for 5 mins, keeping the heat high. Add 2 tbsp water so there is a little sauce and the tomatoes cook down a little. Tip into a bowl.

STEP 3

Put the corn chips in the pan and pour the chicken mix on top. Spoon over the crème fraîche and cook in the oven for 10 mins. Serve with the jalapeños, extra crème fraîche or soured cream, and smashed avocado.

Chicken & couscous one-pot

Prep: 10 mins **Cook:** 1 hr

Serves 4

Ingredients

- 8 skin on, bone-in chicken thighs
- 2 tsp turmeric
- 1 tbsp garam masala

- 2 tbsp sunflower oil
- 2 onions, finely sliced
- 3 garlic cloves, sliced

- 500ml chicken stock (from a cube is fine)
- large handful whole green olives
- zest and juice 1 lemon
- 250g couscous
- small bunch flat-leaf parsley, chopped

Method

STEP 1

Toss the chicken thighs in half the spices and a pinch of salt until completely coated. Heat 1 tbsp oil in a large sauté pan with a lid. Fry chicken, skin-side down, for 10 mins until golden brown, turn over, then cook for 2 mins before removing from the pan. Pour the rest of the oil into the pan, then fry the onions and garlic for 8 mins until golden. Stir in the rest of the spices, then cook for 1 min longer. Pour over the chicken stock and scatter in the olives. Bring everything to the boil, turn down the heat, then sit the chicken, skinside up, in the stock.

STEP 2

Cover the pan with a lid, then simmer gently for 35-40 mins until the chicken is tender. Put the kettle on, then lift the chicken onto a plate and keep warm. Take the pan off the heat. Stir the lemon juice and couscous into the saucy onions in the pan and top up with enough boiling water just to cover the couscous if you need to. Place the lid back on the pan, then leave to stand for 5 mins until the couscous is cooked through. Fluff through half the parsley and the lemon zest, then sit the chicken on top. Scatter with the rest of the parsley and zest before serving.

One-pot chicken chasseur

Prep:20 mins **Cook:**1 hr and 30 mins

Serves 4

Ingredients

- 1 tsp olive oil
- 25g butter
- 4 chicken legs
- 1 onion, chopped
- 2 garlic cloves, crushed
- 200g pack small button or chestnut mushrooms
- 225ml red wine
- 2 tbsp tomato purée
- 2 thyme sprigs
- 500ml chicken stock

Method

STEP 1

Heat 1 tsp olive oil and half of the 25g butter in a large lidded casserole.

STEP 2

Season 4 chicken legs, then fry for about 5 mins on each side until golden brown. Remove and set aside.

STEP 3

Melt the remaining butter in the pan. Add 1 chopped onion, then fry for about 5 mins until soft.

STEP 4

Add 2 crushed garlic cloves, cook for about 1 min, add 200g small button or chestnut mushrooms, cook for 2 mins, then add 225ml red wine.

STEP 5

Stir in 2 tbsp tomato purée, let the liquid bubble and reduce for about 5 mins, then stir in 2 thyme sprigs and pour over 500ml chicken stock.

STEP 6

Slip the chicken legs back into the pan, then cover and simmer on a low heat for about 1 hr until the chicken is very tender.

STEP 7

Remove the chicken legs from the pan and keep warm. Rapidly boil down the sauce for 10 mins or so until it is syrupy and the flavour has concentrated.

STEP 8

Put the chicken legs back into the sauce and serve.

One-pot poached spring chicken

Prep:25 mins **Cook:**2 hrs and 10 mins

Serves 5 - 6

Ingredients

- 100g butter
- 1 large chicken , about 2kg
- 15 Jersey Royal potatoes , scrubbed and halved
- 100g smoked bacon or pancetta lardons
- 1 thyme sprig
- 6 white peppercorns
- 3 bay leaves
- 250g carrots , tops cut off, halved lengthways
- 200g bunch small turnips , peeled and halved
- 150g podded peas
- 150g podded and peeled broad beans
- 8 spring onions , topped and tailed, then cut into 2cm lengths
- 8 asparagus spears , trimmed
- small handful parsley leaves, chopped
- 1 small tarragon sprig, leaves picked
- 1 lemon , cut in to wedges, to serve

Method

STEP 1

Melt the butter in a small pan, discard the milky liquid, then pour the golden fat into a bowl and set aside – this is clarified butter. Heat oven to 150C/130C fan/gas 2. Sit the chicken in a large flameproof casserole dish, breast-side up, and arrange the potatoes and bacon around it. Pour over 1 litre of water. Add the thyme, pepper and bay, drizzle over the clarified butter and season everything with sea salt. Transfer the dish to the hob and heat until the liquid is starting to simmer. Cover the dish, cook in the oven for 1 hr 15 mins, then add the carrots and turnips. Pop the lid back on and put it back in the oven for another 35 mins.

STEP 2

Scatter the peas, broad beans, onions and asparagus around the chicken, submerging them in the liquid, then cover and return to the oven for a further 10-15 mins or until the vegetables are just cooked.

STEP 3

Remove from the oven, leave to stand for 5 mins, then carefully lift the chicken from the broth onto a board. If you want to crisp up the skin, blast it with a blowtorch. Stir the parsley and tarragon through the broth. Serve in the middle of the table with the vegetables and broth, and offer lemon wedges for squeezing over.

One-pot crystal chicken

Prep: 15 mins **Cook:** 20 mins

plus 1 hr cooling

Serves 6

Ingredients

- 1 chicken , about 1.5kg (the best quality you can get)
- bunch spring onions , green and white parts separated (keep the whites for ginger & chilli oil, see goes well with)
- 2 thumb-sized pieces ginger , sliced
- small pack coriander , leaves and stalks separated

- 3 garlic cloves , peeled and left whole
- 1 star anise
- 500ml chicken stock , or a chicken stock cube
- 200ml Chinese rice wine or dry sherry
- 4 tbsp soy sauce
- cooked rice and Sichuan pepper, to serve

Method

STEP 1

Put the chicken in a saucepan or stock pot large enough to fit it comfortably. Add the green spring onion parts, ginger, coriander stalks, garlic and star anise. Pour over the stock (or crumble in the stock cube), rice wine and 3 tbsp of the soy sauce, then top up with water to just cover.

STEP 2

Bring everything to the boil and skim once. Turn down to a gentle simmer and poach for 20 mins, then turn off the heat and leave the chicken to cool in the broth for at least 1 hr. This can be done a day ahead but musn't be chilled, otherwise the chicken will be too cold. Remove the chicken from the broth and leave to cool completely, then strain the broth, ready to pour some over the rice later.

STEP 3

To serve, carve the chicken as if you were jointing it. Arrange on a platter, drizzle over the remaining soy and scatter over the coriander leaves and Sichuan pepper. Serve with rice, ginger and chilli oil, and some of the heated broth to moisten the rice. Any leftover broth can be frozen.

One-pot chicken with chorizo & new potatoes

Prep: 15 mins **Cook:** 1 hr and 40 mins

Serves 4

Ingredients

- 1 whole chicken (about 1.5kg), the best quality you can afford
- small knob of butter
- 1 tbsp olive oil
- ½ lemon
- 1 bay leaf
- 1 thyme sprig
- 300g chorizo ring, thickly sliced
- 700g new potatoes , halved (or quartered if really large)
- 12 garlic cloves , left whole and unpeeled
- large splash of dry sherry
- 150ml chicken stock
- handful parsley leaves, roughly chopped

Method

STEP 1

Heat oven to 180C/160C fan/gas 4 and season the chicken all over. In a large flameproof casserole dish with a lid, heat the butter and oil until sizzling, then spend a good 15 mins slowly browning the chicken well all over. Remove from the dish and pop the lemon, bay and thyme in the cavity. Set aside.

STEP 2

Pour most of the oil out of the dish, place back on the heat and sizzle the chorizo for 5 mins until it starts to release its red oil. Throw in the potatoes, sizzle them until they start to colour, then add the garlic. Splash in the sherry, let it bubble down a little, then pour in the stock.

STEP 3

Nestle the chicken, breast-side up, among the potatoes, place the lid on the dish and cook in the oven for 1 hr 15 mins or until the legs easily come away from the body. Leave the chicken to rest for 10 mins, then scatter with parsley and serve straight from the dish.

Easy one-pot chicken casserole

Prep:5 mins **Cook:**50 mins

Serves 4

Ingredients

- 8 bone-in chicken thighs, skin pulled off and discarded
- 1 tbsp oil
- 5 spring onions, sliced
- 2 tbsp plain flour
- 2 chicken stock cubes
- 2 large carrots, cut into batons (no need to peel)
- 400g new potato, halved if large
- 200g frozen peas
- 1 tbsp grainy mustard
- small handful fresh soft herbs, like parsley, chives, dill or tarragon, chopped

Method

STEP 1

Put the kettle on. Fry 8 bone-in chicken thighs in 1 tbsp oil in a casserole dish or wide pan with a lid to quickly brown.

STEP 2

Stir in the whites of 5 spring onions with 2 tbsp plain flour and 2 chicken stock cubes until the flour disappears, then gradually stir in 750ml hot water from the kettle.

STEP 3

Throw in 2 large carrots, in batons and 400g new potatoes, bring to a simmer. Cover and cook for 20 mins.

STEP 4

Take off the lid and simmer for 15 mins more, then throw in 200g peas for another 5 mins.

STEP 5

Season, stir in 1 tbsp grainy mustard, the green spring onion bits, a small handful of fresh soft herbs and some seasoning.

One-pot chicken with quinoa

Prep:5 mins **Cook:**30 mins

Serves 2

Ingredients

- 1 tbsp cold-pressed rapeseed oil
- 2 skinless chicken breasts (about 300g/11oz)
- 1 medium onion , sliced into 12 wedges
- 1 red pepper , deseeded and sliced
- 2 garlic cloves , finely chopped
- 100g green beans , trimmed and cut in half

- 1/4-1/2 tsp chilli flakes , according to taste
- 2 tsp ground cumin
- 2 tsp ground coriander
- 100g uncooked quinoa
- 85g frozen sweetcorn
- 75g kale , thickly shredded

Method

STEP 1

Heat the oil in a large, deep frying pan or sauté pan. Season the chicken and fry over a medium-high heat for 2-3 mins each side or until golden. Transfer to a plate. Add the onion and pepper to the pan and cook for 3 mins, stirring, until softened and lightly browned.

STEP 2

Tip in the garlic and beans, and stir-fry for 2 mins. Add the chilli and spices, then stir in the quinoa and sweetcorn. Pour in 700ml just-boiled water with 1/2 tsp flaked sea salt and bring to the boil.

STEP 3

Return the chicken to the pan, reduce the heat to a simmer and cook for 12 mins, stirring regularly and turning the chicken occasionally. Add the kale and cook for a further 3 mins or until the quinoa and chicken are cooked through.

Spicy sausage & bean one-pot

Prep: 5 mins **Cook:** 20 mins

Serves 4

Ingredients

- 1 tbsp vegetable oil
- 1 onion , thickly sliced
- 8 Cumberland sausages
- 1 fat garlic clove , crushed

- 2 x 400g cans kidney beans in chilli sauce
- 2-3 sprigs curly parsley , chopped

Method

STEP 1

Heat the oil in a large frying pan. Cook the onion and sausages over a fairly high heat for 8-10 mins, turning the sausages often so they brown all over.

STEP 2

Add the garlic to the pan with the kidney beans and their sauce. Half-fill one of the cans with water, swirl and then add this to the pan. Stir everything together and bring to the boil. Turn down to simmer and cook for 10 mins, or until the sausages are cooked through. Season and sprinkle with the parsley.

Spring chicken one-pot

Prep: 10 mins **Cook:** 55 mins

Serves 4

Ingredients

- 1 tbsp olive oil
- 8 chicken thighs , skin on and bone in
- 1 onion , sliced
- 200g streaky bacon , chopped
- 1 carrot , chopped
- 2 large spring greens , shredded

- 600ml chicken stock
- 300g baby new potato
- 2 tbsp crème fraîche
- 2 tbsp basil pesto
- crusty bread , to serve (optional)

347

Method

STEP 1

Heat the oil in a large, heavy-based pan with a lid. Season the chicken and brown all over. Remove the chicken to a plate and cook the onion and bacon for 5 mins until softened and lightly coloured.

STEP 2

Return the chicken to the pan, and add the remaining ingredients, except the crème fraîche and pesto, along with plenty of freshly ground black pepper. Bring to the boil, then cover and gently simmer for 30-40 mins until the potatoes are tender and chicken cooked through.

STEP 3

Stir in the crème fraîche and pesto. Serve with some crusty bread for mopping up the sauce, if you like.

One-pot mushroom & potato curry

Prep:10 mins **Cook:**20 mins

Serves 4

Ingredients

1 tbsp oil

1 onion, roughly chopped

1 large potato, chopped into small chunks

1 aubergine, trimmed and chopped into chunks

250g button mushrooms

2-4 tbsp curry paste (depending on how hot you like it)

150ml vegetable stock

400ml can reduced-fat coconut milk

chopped coriander, to serve

Method

STEP 1

Heat the oil in a large saucepan, add the onion and potato. Cover, then cook over a low heat for 5 mins until the potatoes start to soften. Throw in the aubergine and mushrooms, then cook for a few more mins.

STEP 2

Stir in the curry paste, pour over the stock and coconut milk. Bring to the boil, then simmer for 10 mins or until the potato is tender. Stir through the coriander and serve with rice or naan bread.

Smoky pork & Boston beans one-pot

Prep: 15 mins **Cook:** 40 mins

Serves 4

Ingredients

- 2 tbsp olive oil
- 2 garlic cloves , crushed
- 2 tbsp smoked paprika
- 500g pork loin steaks , quartered
- 2 x 400g cans cannellini beans , drained and rinsed
- 400g passata
- 2 tsp chipotle paste
- 1 tbsp dark soft brown sugar
- 100g ham hock , in large shreds
- 4 slices crusty white bread
- small handful flat-leaf parsley , roughly chopped

Method

STEP 1

Heat oven to 180C/160C fan/gas 4. Mix the oil, garlic and paprika together and rub into the pork. In a large, shallow ovenproof dish, mix the cannellini beans, passata, chipotle, sugar and ham hock. Nestle the pork into the beans. Bake in the oven for 40 mins until the pork is cooked through.

STEP 2

Toast the bread and serve on the side. Sprinkle the parsley over the pork and beans to serve.

Chilli chicken one-pot

Prep: 20 mins **Cook:** 1 hr and 5 mins

Serves 8

Ingredients

- 2 large onions, halved and sliced
- 2 tbsp olive oil
- 265g chorizo ring, peeled and thickly sliced
- 4 red peppers, deseeded and cut into large chunks
- 2 x 400g/14oz can chopped tomato

- 2 chicken stock cubes
- ½-1 tsp dried chilli flakes
- 2 tsp dried oregano
- 16 boneless skinless chicken thighs
- 3 x 410g/14oz cans red kidney beans, drained

To serve

- 15g pack coriander, chopped
- 2-3 avocado, skinned and sliced

- good squeeze lime juice

Method

STEP 1

Heat oven to 180C/fan 160C/gas 4. Fry the onions in the oil for 5 mins until they become soft and start to colour. Add the chorizo and fry for a few mins more. Stir in the peppers, then pour in the tomatoes, followed by a can of water, the stock cubes, chilli and oregano.

STEP 2

Arrange the chicken thighs on top of the sauce, pushing them under the liquid. Bring to a simmer, cover, then cook in the oven for 40 mins. Add the beans, stir, then cook for 20 mins more. You can make this up to 2 days ahead and keep chilled.

STEP 3

To serve, reheat on the top of the stove or in the oven at 190C/fan 170C/gas 5 for 1 hr 10 mins until piping hot. Stir in most of the coriander, toss the rest with the avocado, lime and a little salt, then pile this on top. Serve with Garlic & oregano bread (below) and a bag of green salad tossed with olives, cherry tomatoes and finely sliced red onion.

Chinese-style braised beef one-pot

Prep: 10 mins **Cook:** 2 hrs - 2 hrs and 30 mins

Serves 6

Ingredients

- 3-4 tbsp olive oil
- 6 garlic cloves, thinly sliced
- good thumb-size piece fresh root ginger, peeled and shredded
- 1 bunch spring onions, sliced
- 1 red chilli, deseeded and thinly sliced
- 1 ½kg braising beef, cut into large pieces (we used ox cheek)
- 2 tbsp plain flour, well seasoned
- 1 tsp Chinese five-spice powder

steamed bok choi and steamed basmati rice, to serve

- 2 star anise (optional)
- 2 tsp light muscovado sugar (or use whatever you've got)
- 3 tbsp Chinese cooking wine or dry sherry
- 3 tbsp dark soy sauce, plus more to serve
- 500ml beef stock (we used Knorr Touch of Taste)

Method

STEP 1

Heat 2 tbsp of the oil in a large, shallow casserole. Fry the garlic, ginger, onions and chilli for 3 mins until soft and fragrant. Tip onto a plate. Toss the beef in the flour, add 1 tbsp more oil to the pan, then brown the meat in batches, adding the final tbsp oil if you need to. It should take about 5 mins to brown each batch properly.

STEP 2

Add the five-spice and star anise (if using) to the pan, tip in the gingery mix, then fry for 1 min until the spices are fragrant. Add the sugar, then the beef and stir until combined. Keep the heat high, then splash in the wine or sherry, scraping up any meaty bits. Heat oven to 150C/fan 130C/gas 2.

STEP 3

Pour in the soy and stock (it won't cover the meat completely), bring to a simmer, then tightly cover, transfer to the oven and cook for 1½-2 hrs, stirring the meat halfway through.

The meat should be very soft, and any sinewy bits should have melted away. Season with more soy. This can now be chilled and frozen for up to 1 month.

STEP 4

Nestle the cooked bok choi into the pan, then bring to the table with the basmati rice straight away and tuck in.

Spanish rice & prawn one-pot

Prep:4 mins **Cook:**16 mins

Serves 4

Ingredients

- 1 onion, sliced
- 1 red and 1 green pepper, deseeded and sliced
- 50g chorizo, sliced
- 2 garlic cloves, crushed
- 1 tbsp olive oil

- 250g easy cook basmati rice (we used Tilda)
- 400g can chopped tomato
- 200g raw, peeled prawns, defrosted if frozen

Method

STEP 1

Boil the kettle. In a non-stick frying or shallow pan with a lid, fry the onion, peppers, chorizo and garlic in the oil over a high heat for 3 mins. Stir in the rice and chopped tomatoes with 500ml boiling water, cover, then cook over a high heat for 12 mins.

STEP 2

Uncover, then stir – the rice should be almost tender. Stir in the prawns, with a splash more water if the rice is looking dry, then cook for another min until the prawns are just pink and rice tender.

Sausage & lentil one-pot

Prep: 5 mins **Cook:** 40 mins

Serves 4

Ingredients

- 1 tbsp olive oil
- 400g pack sausage
- 1 onion, finely chopped
- 1 garlic clove, crushed

- 1 red pepper, sliced
- 250g lentil (we used puy lentils)
- 150ml vegetable stock
- 125ml red wine or extra stock

Method

STEP 1

Heat oil in a pan, cook the sausages until browned, then remove. Tip in remaining oil, onion, garlic and pepper, then cook, about 5 mins more until softened. Add lentils and sausages to the pan with the stock and wine, if using.

STEP 2

Bring up to the boil, then simmer for 20 mins until lentils have softened and sausages are cooked through. Serve with plenty of crusty bread.

Sausage & veg one-pot

Prep: 10 mins **Cook:** 55 mins

Serves 4

Ingredients

- 1 tbsp olive oil
- 12 good-quality sausages
- 1 small onion , chopped
- 1 fennel bulb , quartered, then sliced
- 2 garlic cloves , crushed
- ½ red chilli , finely chopped
- 2 tsp fennel seed

- 2 tbsp plain flour
- 150ml white wine
- 500ml chicken stock
- 200g pack green bean , halved
- 300g broad bean , double podded (unpodded weight)
- 300g pea

- 200g pot half-fat crème fraîche
- zest 1 lemon , juice of ½
- handful parsley , chopped
- handful basil , chopped
- ½ red chilli , finely chopped, to serve
- crusty bread , to serve

Method

STEP 1

Heat the oil in a large pan. Add the sausages, cook for a few mins until browned all over, then transfer to a plate. Tip the onion and fennel into the pan and cook for 10-15 mins until nice and soft, then add the garlic, half the chilli and the fennel seeds. Cook for a few mins more, moving everything around the pan now and then, to prevent the garlic from burning.

STEP 2

Stir the flour into the vegetables, and cook for 1 min. Pour in the wine, let it bubble for 1 min, give everything a good stir, then add the stock and return the sausages to the pan, seasoning well. Cover, then gently simmer for 30 mins.

STEP 3

Add the green beans, broad beans and peas, then cook, uncovered, for 2 mins more. Stir in the crème fraîche, lemon zest and juice, and herbs. Add a little more salt and pepper if it needs it, sprinkle with the chilli, then serve with plenty of bread for soaking up the juices.

One-pot Moroccan chicken

Prep: 5 mins **Cook:** 25 mins

Serves 4

Ingredients

- 4 skinless chicken breasts
- 1 tsp ground cumin
- 1 tbsp olive oil
- 1 onion , finely sliced
- 400g can cherry tomato
- 2 tbsp harissa paste (we used Belazu Rose Harissa)
- 1 tbsp clear honey
- 2 medium courgettes , thickly sliced
- 400g can chickpea , drained and rinsed

Method

STEP 1

Season the chicken breasts all over with the cumin and lots of ground black pepper. Heat the oil in a large non-stick frying pan and cook the chicken with the onion for 4 mins. Turn the chicken over and cook for a further 3 mins. Stir the onions around the chicken regularly as they cook.

STEP 2

Tip the tomatoes and 250ml water into the pan and stir in the harissa, honey, courgettes and chickpeas. Bring to a gentle simmer and cook for 15 mins until the chicken is tender and the sauce has thickened slightly.

Fragrant pork & rice one-pot

Prep: 15 mins **Cook:** 30 mins

Serves 4

Ingredients

- 4-6 good-quality sausages
- 1 tbsp olive oil
- ½ onion , finely chopped
- 2 garlic cloves , crushed
- 2 tsp each ground cumin and coriander
- 140g long grain rice
- 850ml vegetable stock
- 400g can chopped tomato
- ½ small bunch coriander , leaves picked

Method

STEP 1

Split the sausage skins, squeeze out the meat, then roll it into small meatballs about the size of a large olive. Heat the oil in a large non-stick saucepan, then brown the meatballs well on all sides until cooked – you might need to do this in batches. Set the meatballs aside.

STEP 2

Add the onion and garlic to the pan. Soften for 5 mins, stir in the spices and rice, then cook for another min. Pour in the stock and tomatoes. Bring to a simmer, scraping up any sausagey bits from the bottom of the pan. Simmer for 10 mins until the rice is just cooked, then stir in the meatballs with some seasoning. Ladle into bowls, scatter with coriander and serve with crusty bread.

One-pot partridge with drunken potatoes

Prep:30 mins **Cook:**40 mins

Serves 2

Ingredients

- 2 partridge
- 2 juniper berries , crushed
- 2 thyme sprigs
- 2 bay leaves
- 2 garlic cloves , skin on, bashed
- 4 thin slices smoked streaky bacon
- chopped parsley , to serve
- buttered cavolo nero or shredded sprout tops, to serve

- 2 tbsp duck fat or butter
- 1 large Maris Piper potato (about 300g)
- glass of full-bodied red wine (about 100ml)
- 150ml chicken stock

Method

STEP 1

Season the partridges (including the cavity) generously. Put a juniper berry, a thyme sprig, a bay leaf and a garlic clove in each cavity. Chop the bacon into chunky pieces and slice the potato lengthways into six thick slices, discarding the ends.

STEP 2

Heat oven to 180C/160C fan/gas 4. Heat half the duck fat or butter in a flameproof casserole dish until just sizzling, then brown the birds on all sides for 10 mins. Remove them from the dish and set aside. Add the rest of the fat to the dish and gently fry the potato slices until very brown and crisp on each side. Add the bacon and sizzle with the potatoes until starting to brown. Sit the birds on top of the potatoes and pour over the wine and stock. Put in the oven, uncovered, for 15 mins.

STEP 3

Remove the birds from the dish and leave somewhere warm to rest for 10 mins. Baste the potatoes, return to the oven until cooked through, then scatter over the parsley.

STEP 4

To serve, sit the birds back in the pan and bring to the table or plate up with the potatoes. Serve with cavolo nero or sprout tops.

Chorizo, new potato & haddock one-pot

Prep: 10 mins **Cook:** 20 mins

Serves 2

Ingredients

- 1 tbsp extra-virgin olive oil , plus extra to serve
- 50g chorizo , peeled and thinly sliced
- 450g salad or new potatoes , sliced (I used Charlotte)

- crusty bread , to serve

- 4 tbsp dry sherry , or more if you need it (or use white wine)
- 2 skinless thick fillets white fish (I used sustainably caught haddock)
- good handful cherry tomatoes , halved
- 20g bunch parsley , chopped

Method

STEP 1

Heat a large lidded frying pan, then add the oil. Tip in the chorizo, fry for 2 mins until it starts to release its oils, then tip in the potatoes and some seasoning. Splash over 3 tbsp sherry, cover the pan tightly, then leave to cook for 10-15 mins until the potatoes are just tender. Move them around the pan a bit halfway through.

STEP 2

Season the fish well. Give the potatoes another stir, add the cherry tomatoes and most of the chopped parsley to the pan, then lay the fish on top. Splash over 1 tbsp sherry, put the lid on again, then leave to cook for 5 mins, or until the fish has turned white and is flaky when prodded in the middle. Scatter the whole dish with a little more parsley and drizzle with more extra virgin oil. Serve straight away with crusty bread.

Summer chicken one-pot

Prep: 10 mins **Cook:** 40 mins

Serves 4

Ingredients

- 8 chicken thighs
- 2 tbsp plain flour
- 1 tbsp olive oil
- 8 rashers streaky bacon , chopped
- 400ml stock
- 500g bag baby new potatoes , halved

- 200g pack full fat soft cheese
- 200g broad beans , podded
- 200g sweetcorn (frozen, fresh or from a can)
- 200g cherry tomatoes , halved

Method

STEP 1

Dust the chicken in the flour and some seasoning. Heat the oil in a lidded pan and brown the chicken, in batches if needed, then transfer to a plate. Throw in the bacon and fry for 5 mins, until crisp.

STEP 2

Return the chicken to the pan. Add the stock, cover and simmer for 30 mins, adding the potatoes after 10 mins.

STEP 3

Make sure the chicken is cooked and the potatoes are tender, then stir in the cheese, the rest of the vegetables and some seasoning. Simmer for 5 mins more, uncovered, then serve.

One-pot chicken pilaf

Prep: 5 mins **Cook:** 20 mins

Serves 1

Ingredients

- 1 tsp sunflower oil

- 1 small onion , chopped

- 1 large or 2 small boneless, skinless chicken thigh fillets, cut into chunks
- 2 tsp curry paste (choose your favourite)

- a third of a mug basmati rice
- two-thirds of a mug chicken stock
- 1 mug frozen mixed vegetables
- half a mug frozen leaf spinach

Method

STEP 1

Heat the oil in a frying pan, then fry the onion for 5-6 mins until softened. Add the chicken pieces, fry for a further couple of mins just to colour the outside, then stir in curry paste and rice. Cook for another min.

STEP 2

Pour in the chicken stock and throw in any larger bits of frozen veg. Bring to the boil, lower the heat, then cover the pan with a lid. Cook for 10 mins, then stir in the remaining veg. Scatter over the spinach, cover, then cook for 10 mins more until all the stock is absorbed and the rice is tender. Give everything a good stir, season to taste, then tuck in.

One-pot chicken & bacon stew

Prep: 20 mins **Cook:** 1 hr and 30 mins

Serves 8

Ingredients

- 3 tbsp olive oil
- 16 chicken pieces on the bone (about 3kg/6lb 8oz in total)
- 140g smoked bacon, chopped or lardons or cubetti di pancetta
- 4 medium carrots, thickly sliced
- 2 onions, roughly chopped
- 2 tbsp plain flour
- 1 tbsp tomato purée

- 75ml white wine or cider vinegar
- 1l chicken stock
- 2 bay leaves
- 4 tbsp double cream or crème fraîche
- 600g small new potatoes, halved
- 12 large white mushrooms, quartered
- chopped herbs, such as parsley, tarragon or chives

Method

STEP 1

Heat oven to 200C/180C fan/gas 6. Heat the oil in a large flameproof casserole with a lid. Fry the chicken pieces in batches for 5 mins on each side until well browned, then transfer to a plate. Sizzle the bacon in the casserole for a few mins until beginning to crisp. Stir in the carrots and onions, then cook for 5 mins until starting to soften. Stir in the flour and tomato purée and cook for 1 min more. Finally, splash in the vinegar and stir well.

STEP 2

Pour in the stock and bring to a simmer. Add the bay, cream and seasoning. Slide in the chicken pieces and scatter over the potatoes, turning everything over a few times so that the potatoes are immersed in the sauce. Put the lid on and place in the oven. After 40 mins, remove from the oven and stir in the mushrooms. Cover again and cook in the oven for 10 mins more until the chicken is cooked through and tender but not completely falling off the bone. You can now turn off the heat, and chill and freeze some or all of it (see freezing tips, below). If eating straight away, cook for 10 mins more, then sprinkle over the herbs and serve.

Squash, chicken & couscous one-pot

Prep:15 mins **Cook:**45 mins

Serves 4

Ingredients

- 2 tbsp harissa paste
- 1 tsp each ground cumin and ground coriander
- 2 red onions , halved and cut into thin wedges
- 2 skinless chicken breasts , cut into bite-sized chunks

- 1 small butternut squash , cut into 1cm chunks (no need to peel)
- x cans tomatoes
- zest and juice 2 lemons
- 200g cherry tomato , halved
- 140g couscous
- small bunch coriander , roughly chopped

Method

STEP 1

Heat a large non-stick casserole dish or pan on the hob. Add the harissa, spices and onions, stir and cook gently for 10 mins until soft. Add chicken and brown for 5-10 mins. Add squash, stirring to combine, and a splash of water if it starts to stick. Cook for 5 mins more.

STEP 2

Tip canned tomatoes into the pan with ½ can of water, cover and simmer for 20-30 mins. Add the lemon zest and juice, cherry tomatoes, couscous and seasoning. Cover and turn off the heat. Leave on the hob for 10 mins, then stir through the coriander and serve.

Mushroom & rice one-pot

Prep:20 mins **Cook:**30 mins

Serves 4

Ingredients

- 200g basmati rice
- 1 tbsp olive oil
- 1 large onion , chopped
- 2 tsp chopped rosemary or 1 tsp dried
- 250g chestnut mushroom , quartered

- 2 red peppers , sliced
- 400g can chopped tomato
- 425ml vegetable stock
- handful parsley , chopped

Method

STEP 1

Heat oven to 190C/fan 170C/gas 5. Tip the rice into a sieve, rinse under cold running water, then leave to drain. Heat the oil in a flameproof casserole, add the onion, then fry until softened, about 5 mins. Stir in the rosemary and mushrooms, then fry briefly. Add the rice, stir to coat in the oil, then add the peppers, tomatoes, stock and some freshly ground pepper. Bring to the boil, give it a stir, cover tightly with a lid, then bake for 20-25 mins until the rice is tender. Scatter over the parsley and serve.

One-pot pork with orange, olives & bay

Prep:35 mins **Cook:**2 hrs and 40 mins

Serves 6

Ingredients

- 85g sundried tomato in oil, roughly chopped, plus 2-3 tbsp oil from the jar
- 1kg pork shoulder , cut into chunky cubes
- 2 tbsp plain flour , seasoned
- 400g shallot (see tip, below)
- 1 onion , thinly sliced
- 3 bay leaves
- few thyme sprigs
- 5 garlic cloves , thinly sliced
- 400ml red wine
- strip of zest and juice from 1 orange
- 350ml chicken stock
- 400g can chopped plum tomato
- 800g large new potato , peeled & halved or cut into fat slices, depending on size
- 70g pack dry black olive

Method

STEP 1

Heat 1 tbsp of the sundried tomato oil in a large, flameproof casserole dish. Toss the pork in the flour, tap off any excess, then brown it in 2 batches, transferring to a large bowl once golden and crusted. Use a splash more oil for the second batch if needed.

STEP 2

Tip 1 tbsp oil, shallots, onion, bay leaves and thyme into the pan and fry for 5 mins until golden here and there. Stir in the garlic and sundried tomatoes, cook for 1 min more, then tip onto the pork.

STEP 3

Splash the wine and orange juice into the dish, add the orange zest and boil hard for 5 mins. Add the meat and onions back in.

STEP 4

When ready to cook, heat oven to 160C/140C fan/gas 3. Stir the stock, canned tomatoes, potatoes and olives into the casserole, then bring to a simmer. Prod the potatoes as far under the surface of the liquid as you can. Cover, leaving a slight gap to one side, then cook in the oven for 2½ hrs, or until the meat is tender enough to cut with a spoon. Spoon away any excess fat and let the stew rest for a few mins before ladling into shallow bowls.

Squash, lentil & bean one-pot with fig raita

Prep: 30 mins **Cook:** 15 mins

Serves 2

Ingredients

- 400g piece butternut squash , peeled, deseeded and chunkily diced
- 1 onion , sliced
- 1 tbsp olive oil
- 2 tsp ground cumin
- ½ tsp chilli flakes
- 400g can chopped tomato
- 100g dried red lentil

- 2 tsp agave syrup or brown sugar
- 2 tsp red or white wine vinegar
- 400g can kidney bean , drained and rinsed
- 2 dried figs , finely chopped
- 150ml pot fat-free natural yogurt
- ½ small bunch parsley , chopped

Method

STEP 1

Fry the squash and onion in the oil for 5-8 mins until the onion is softened. Stir in the cumin and chilli for 1 min. Add the tomatoes plus a canful of water from the tomato can, the lentils, agave or sugar and vinegar. Bring to a simmer and cook for 10 mins, then stir in the beans and cook for a further few mins until the lentils are tender and the beans heated through.

STEP 2

Meanwhile, mix the figs, yogurt and parsley together. Season the stew, then serve in bowls with fig raita on the side.

One-pot beef brisket & braised celery

Prep: 30 mins **Cook:** 5 hrs

Serves 8

Ingredients

- 2.2kg piece of rolled beef brisket
- 1 bottle full-bodied red wine

- 3 tbsp olive oil

- 8 celery sticks , cut into little-finger-length pieces
- 2 carrots , roughly chopped
- 1 onion , sliced
- 3 garlic cloves , roughly chopped
- 4 thyme sprigs
- 4 bay leaves
- small pack parsley , roughly chopped

Method

STEP 1

If you have time, up to 24 hrs before, sit the beef in a snug plastic container and pour over the wine. Cover and leave to marinate in the fridge, turning the beef as and when you can.

STEP 2

Heat oven to 170C/150C fan/gas 3½. Drain the wine from the beef (if you've marinated), but keep the wine. Heat the oil in a flameproof casserole dish that will fit the beef and all the vegetables – don't worry if the beef is too tall for the dish. Season the beef and spend a good 15 mins browning it on all sides, then remove from the dish. Add the celery, carrots and onion to the dish, sizzle in the beef fat for 5 mins, then add the garlic and herbs. Nestle the beef among the vegetables, pour over the wine and bring to a simmer. Cover the dish with its lid (or foil if the beef is too tall) and braise in the oven for 4-4½ hrs until very tender, turning the beef once.

STEP 3

Once cooked, leave to rest for 10 mins, then lift the beef onto a carving board. Drain the vegetables (reserving the braising juices), toss with the parsley and tip into a dish. Spoon the fat off the braising juices and pour into a bowl for spooning over. *The sauce can be chilled in the fridge – the fat will solidify and can be lifted off the sauce before it's reheated.*

Speedy salmon and leek one-pot

Cook:25 mins

Serves 4

Ingredients

- 700g leeks , finely sliced
- 3 tbsp olive oil
- 2 tbsp wholegrain mustard
- 2 tbsp clear honey
- juice of half a lemon
- 250g pack cherry tomatoes , halved

- 4 skinless salmon fillets , about 175g/6oz each

Method

STEP 1

Cook the leeks: Put the leeks into a large microwave dish and sprinkle over 2 tablespoons water. Cover the dish with cling film and pierce a couple of times with a fork. Cook on 850W for 3 minutes, then leave to stand for 1 minute.

STEP 2

Make the sauce: Whisk the olive oil, mustard, honey and lemon juice together and season with a little salt and pepper. Scatter the tomatoes on top of the leeks and spoon over half the sauce.

STEP 3

Cook the salmon: Lay the salmon fillets side by side on top of the vegetables and spoon the remaining sauce over them. Replace the cling film and continue cooking on 850W for 9 minutes. Leave to stand for a couple of minutes before serving.

One-pot chicken with braised vegetables

Prep:20 mins **Cook:**1 hr and 30 mins

Serves 4

Ingredients

- 1 ½kg chicken
- 25g butter
- 200g smoked back bacon , preferably from a whole piece, cut into small chunks
- 1kg new potato , peeled

- 16-20 shallot or small onions
- ½ bottle white wine
- 250g pea , frozen are fine
- bunch soft green herbs such as tarragon , chives or parsley, chopped

Method

STEP 1

Heat oven to 220C/fan 200C/gas 7. Season the chicken inside and out with salt and pepper. Heat the butter in a casserole dish until sizzling, then take 10 mins to brown the chicken on all sides. Remove the chicken from the dish, then fry the bacon until crisp. Add the potatoes and shallots, then cook until just starting to brown. Nestle the chicken among the veg, pour over the wine, then pot-roast, undisturbed, for 1 hr or until the chicken is cooked.

STEP 2

After 1 hr, remove the chicken and place the pan back on the heat. Stir the peas into the buttery juices, adding a splash of water if the pan is dry, then simmer until the peas are cooked through. Finally, add any juices from the rested chicken, then stir through the herbs and serve with the chicken.

Sea bass & seafood Italian one-pot

Prep: 15 mins **Cook:** 45 mins

Serves 4

Ingredients

- 2 tbsp olive oil
- 1 fennel bulb , halved and sliced, fronds kept separate to garnish
- 2 garlic cloves , sliced
- ½ red chilli , chopped
- 250g cleaned squid , sliced into rings

- bunch basil , leaves and stalks separated, stalks tied together, leaves roughly chopped
- 400g can chopped tomato
- 150ml white wine
- 2 large handfuls of mussels or clams
- 8 large raw prawns (whole look nicest)
- 4 sea bass fillets (about 140g/5oz each)

- crusty bread , to serve

Method

STEP 1

Heat the oil in a large saucepan with a tight-fitting lid, then add the fennel, garlic and chilli. Fry until softened, then add the squid, basil stalks, tomatoes and wine. Simmer over a low heat for 35 mins until the squid is tender and the sauce has thickened slightly, then season.

STEP 2

Scatter the mussels and prawns over the sauce, lay the sea bass fillets on top, cover, turn up the heat and cook hard for 5 mins. Serve scattered with the basil leaves and fennel fronds, with crusty bread.

Bean & bangers one-pot

Prep: 10 mins **Cook:** 30 mins

Serves 4

Ingredients

- 1 tbsp olive oil
- 8 good-quality pork sausages (Toulouse or Sicilian varieties work well)
- 2 carrots , halved lengthways and sliced
- 2 onions , finely chopped
- 2 tbsp red wine vinegar

- 2 x 410g cans mixed beans in water, rinsed and drained
- 400ml chicken stock
- 100g frozen pea
- 2 tbsp Dijon mustard

Method

STEP 1

Heat the oil in a large pan. Sizzle the sausages for about 6 mins, turning occasionally, until brown on all sides, then remove to a plate. Tip the carrots and onions into the pan, then cook for 8 mins, stirring occasionally, until the onions are soft. Add the vinegar to the pan, then stir in the drained beans. Pour over the stock, nestle the sausages in with the beans, then simmer everything for 10 mins.

STEP 2

Scatter in the frozen peas, cook for 2 mins more until heated through, then take off the heat and stir in the mustard. Season to taste. Serve scooped straight from the pan.

Printed in Great Britain
by Amazon